ABOUT THE AUTHOR

Susan Kessler Barnard is a native Atlantan and long-time resident of Buckhead whose involvement in social, cultural, and civic projects in the community led to her interest in its history and this book. Her interest was heightened when she worked at the Atlanta History Center. She has a degree in journalism and public relations and is the co-author of a history of Atlanta's First Presbyterian Church. Barnard has contributed articles to the *Georgia Historical Quarterly*, the *Atlanta Journal-Constitution*, and other publications.

BUCKHEAD

Buckhead

A PLACE FOR ALL TIME

■

Susan Kessler Barnard

ɗ

HILL STREET PRESS
ATHENS, GEORGIA

Published by Hill Street Press, LLC
191 East Broad Street
Suite 209
Athens, Georgia 30601-2848
www.hillstreetpress.com

First printing

1 2 3 4 5 6 7 8 9 10

ISBN # 1-892514-02-8

Library of Congress Card Catalog Number: 98-87990

Printed in the United States of America by Maple-Vail.

The paper in this book contains a significant amount of post-consumer recycled fiber.

Text design by Penstroke Graphics, Atlanta, Georgia
Cover design by Anne Richmond Boston
Cover photograph of the Swan House in Atlanta, Georgia, courtesy of Van Jones Martin.
Copyright © 1998 Van Jones Martin.

I dedicate this book to the memory of my parents, Walter H. and Cecilia T. Kessler, who brought our family to Buckhead in 1949.

TABLE OF CONTENTS

Photographs appear after page 138

FOREWORD

*T*he area of Atlanta and Fulton County called Buckhead, a unique name slightly antedating *Terminus, Marthasville* and *Atlanta*, has been referred to in more recent years as "Cross Roads of the North Side" and "Destination of Distinction."

Buckhead: A Place for All Time, the interesting and informative history of Buckhead from prehistoric times to 1960, copiously footnoted and fully indexed, is the result of several years of research and writing by Susan K. Barnard, a long-time and devoted resident of the area. Indeed, she not only made liberal use of basic historical sources, but also conducted personal interviews with more than 120 local citizens—young, old and in between — of the Buckhead area.

The result is both informative and highly readable. Indeed, it is a welcome addition to the literature of an important and colorful part of Georgia.

Franklin M. Garrett, Historian
Atlanta Historical Society

INTRODUCTION

*W*ow! Before you is a treatise that's certain to impress even Buckhead's oldest native residents. This is not just a recitation of the standard 'buck's head at Irbyville' story, but an extremely well-documented, detailed recording of the facts and figures in Buckhead's history.

It's our good fortune that the author is schooled in archaeology, which has allowed her to set the stage for this work at over eight thousand years ago! She tells us of the Indian cultures that likely existed, and how the lands were used. She takes us through the Civil War period and the important battles fought in Buckhead. She gives us a glimpse of modern commerce and hints at the prosperity the place later came to enjoy.

Old-timers like to recall what they've been told about how the community of Buckhead got its name 148 years ago. Firsthand they can tell you Lenox Square wasn't even considered part of Buckhead when it was opened in 1959. This book tells us of all their memories, and practically everything ever reduced to writing about the area.

This study gives us places, names, and dates. It reminds the reader that the area was once in Henry County and later DeKalb County, before it became part of Fulton County (and was subsequently incorporated into the City of Atlanta). There are references to politics, transportation, religion, farming, business, education, and recreation, imaging the lifestyles over the decades.

The reader senses the thirst for data pursued throughout, resulting in a codification of all available information in one document. It's like a family tree of a community. Names of streets and neighborhoods we frequently travel come alive in the roles our ancestors played.

There's also fun in anecdotes with which many would not be familiar. Like gold being discovered...and you'll have to read the book to learn just where. Or land being sold at five cents per acre...for which the price has since escalated as much as fifty million times!

We must appreciate this meticulous labor of love in methodically collecting information that otherwise might later be lost forever. Here is a clear drawing of a community's foundation, from wild and primitive wooded settlements, to an urbanization that sets Buckhead aside as an "Edge City" envied by others around the country. With its 1996 statistics at 61,000 residents; 12,000,000 square feet of office space; 4,000 hotel rooms; 1,300 retail outlets; 16,500 multi-family units; two of the largest church congregations in America and much, much more, it has certainly earned a place in history.

One might say…"and on the eighth day He created Buckhead."

Sam Massell
President, Buckhead Coalition Inc.
Mayor, City of Atlanta 1970-1974

ACKNOWLEDGEMENTS

*W*riting *Buckhead: A Place for All Time* was a group effort made possible through many hours of personal interviews with 120 people who either live or have lived in Buckhead, or are descendants of families whose roots are buried deep in the community's soil. They opened their homes and offices to me, pulled pictures off their walls and out of their photo albums for use in the book. Some drove around the neighborhood with me, reminiscing about what used to be. I attended church services, roamed around cemeteries, and broke bread with interviewees.

I know that there are hundreds of neighbors who have worthwhile information and wonderful stories, but, unfortunately, I could not interview everyone. There is no sin of omission, only of time and space.

My friend and mentor, Franklin M. Garrett, cannot be thanked enough for all that he did. Not only was he interviewed, but he also checked the manuscript for accuracy and wrote the foreword.

A special thanks goes to Samuel A. Massell Jr., president of the Buckhead Coalition. He was an early believer and supporter of my history of Buckhead and gave the Buckhead Coalition's endorsement of the project. He, too, took time to be interviewed and to write the Introduction.

Without the help of Anne Salter, Kate Denison, Helen Matthews, Priscilla Pomazal, Sara Saunders, Carlisle Young, Jennie Williams, Michael Rose and Donald Rooney at the Atlanta History Center Library/Archives, writing this book would have been an impossible task.

The Reference Departments of the Atlanta/Fulton County Library in Buckhead and downtown were also tremendously helpful with my research.

My thanks to the late Councilwoman Barbara Miller Asher, City of Atlanta Associate Attorney Corlis Cummings, and City of Atlanta Department of Water and Pollution Control's Joseph Studgeon for granting a Writ of Entry allowing me and my fellow members of the Greater Atlanta Archaeological Society (GAAS) to do an archaeological dig at Standing Peachtree in 1993-1994. Those members who have worked with me on the dig are David Chase, Glen Armstrong, David Smith, Faye Burrell, and Terri Hynes. GAAS member Mary Job deserves special mention for acting as my secretary during a photographic shoot throughout Buckhead. Her note-taking freed me up to be *artistic*.

An eagle feather to Grace Morris (Mrs. Robert) Schwartzman and Royce Bemis, who helped with the editing of the manuscript.

Sadly, some of those who were interviewed or helped me have passed away. I would like to think of this book as a tribute to the memories of Dr. F. Phinizy Calhoun Jr., Mary Daniel, Herbert Elsas, Dorothy Dean (Mrs. Joel Chandler Jr.) Harris, Jane (Mrs. George Jr.) Murray, Ellie Patterson, Lil (Mrs. M. T. Jr.) Salter, Mrs. Hilton Stanaland and Ruth Carter Vanneman.

My sincere thanks go to all the people I interviewed and who supplied me with material. Listed in alphabetical order are: Ruth Cox Adams; Cecil Alexander; Louise (Richardson) and Ivan E. Allen Jr.; Tate Anderson; Florence Bryan (Mrs. Bonneau) Ansley; John Bair; Polly Orr Bates; Irwin G. Baumer; Mary Margaret Beecy, Elissa Jones Bridgen and Mildred Petty of Trinity School; Luther Bootle and Clair (Mrs. Walker) Willingham of Second Ponce de Leon Baptist Church; William Brand Jr.; Mary Ann and Lon Bridges Jr.; Weyman Brown; Ellen Newell (Mrs. Wright) Bryan; William Wright Bryan Jr.; James Bryant, president of the Cherokee Town and Country Club; Ruby Chapman; Annye Mae Cobb; Aline (Cocke) and Eugene Cofield; Merrell H. Collier; Anne Comer; Marcus Cook III; Jacque Coxe and Marylynn Lavender of the Fulton County Teaching Museum; Judy Beers (Mrs. Rufus) Darby; Margaret Cheshire (Mrs. Hilton) Dickerson; Sam Dorsey; William T. Dreger III; Roberta Eberhart; Edith (Mrs. Herbert) Elsas; William E. Erquitt; Patricia G. Evans of Peachtree Road United Methodist Church; Elizabeth Campbell (Mrs. Moses) Few, Helen Few, and Milton Few; Reuben A. Garland Jr.; Harriet Grant; Louise (Arnold) and John W. Grant III; Kitty Graves; Rev. Jai S. Haithco Sr. of New Hope A.M.E. Church; Berneda Johnson Haney; Dr. Judson Hawk Jr.; Joseph K. Heyman; Emily and George B. Hightower; Virginia D. Hobbs of The Atlanta Speech School; Rev. Kay Horres-Durst of Sardis Methodist Church; Barrett Howell Sr.; Henry Howell; Johnny Hutchins; Florence and Sam Inman; Martha and John Edward Irby Jr.; T. Sinclair Jacobs; Parthenia Jetter; Columbus Johnson; Janie Johnson; Nick Jones, Program Editor of the Atlanta Symphony Orchestra; Sue (Mrs. Hayden) Jones of the Peachtree Presbyterian Church; Sara Hammett (Mrs. Binion N.) Jordan; Mary Tesler (Mrs. Ike) Kadis; Francis Yudelson (Mrs. Harry) Kuniansky; Carolyn Patterson Laudermilk; Mildred (Rand) and Alva Lines; William and Susie Lowenstein; Charlotte (Mrs. Sidney) Marcus; Sharon (Mrs. James H.) Matthews; Rose Tesler (Mrs. Herman) Mechlowitz; Stanley P. Meyerson; Helen Bagley McDuffie; Nancy Kamper (Mrs. Henry) Miller; Roy Milling; Edith Adams (Mrs. George) Minhinnett; Janet Knox (Mrs. Thomas) Moore; Virlyn Moore Jr.; Ken Moss; George Murray III; Thomas M. Murray; Carol Meadows (Mrs. Mike) Murphy; Darlene Neyrey; Maybelle "Snookie" Tatum (Mrs.

Daniel) Osburn; John K. Ottley Jr.; Mr. and Mrs. Guy Patterson; Richard Pattillo; Richard P. Perry; Nancy (Mrs. John) Pritchett of Morris Brandon School; Luther H. Randall Sr.; Sandy Redella of The Lovett School; Agnes Dorsey Roberts; Donald W. "Pete" Rolader; Elizabeth Cassells (Mrs. Richard) Rubenoff; William E. Rudolph; Cornelius Sawyer; Lillian Pace (Mrs. Paul) Scoville; Rev. Michael A. Shinn of Piney Grove Baptist Church; Marcelle and Lonnie Simpson; Elizabeth (Mrs. Vernon) Skiles; Laura Maddox (Mrs. Edward D.) Smith; Mrs. Hal Smith; Patricia Smith of Pace Academy; Jack J. Spalding; Taylor & Mathis Co.; Sue (Mrs. Charles E.) Stephens; J. T. Tharpe; Evelyn (Mrs. J. W.) Thomas; Kenneth H. Thomas, Jr.; J. T. Tolbert; Margaret (Chapman) and Leon Townsend; Newell Bryan Tozzer; Willard Tumlin; Phylis Wigton of The Cathedral of Christ The King; Leonard Walker Jr.; Betty Slaton (Mrs. John) Wallace; Gloria Donaldson Wells; William Wender; Anita Willard of The Heiskell School; Charles Wilson; Bruce F. Woodruff Jr.; and Rita (Mrs. Landis) Worthy.

PREFACE

$\mathcal{B}$uckhead is a community in northwest Atlanta that has been described as "the Beverly Hills of Georgia," "a state of mind" and "a place to aspire to." And some just call it "richnorthwestAtlanta."

Over the years the boundaries of the Buckhead community have changed. In 1838, when the area became known as Buck's Head, the parameters were placed around the present Peachtree, Roswell, and West Paces Ferry roads. At times even Sandy Springs was considered part of Buckhead. Today Buckhead encompasses 28 square miles, bounded above Lenox Square and Phipps Plaza on the north by the DeKalb County line; to the south by the junction of Interstates 75 and 85; on the east by DeKalb County, and on the west by the Chattahoochee River. (1)

The history of Buckhead began thousands of years ago when Paleo-Indians lived and hunted in the virgin forest along the Chattahoochee River. In the 1770s the Muscogee Indians (whom the English called Creek) inhabited the village of Standing Peach Tree along the river at Peachtree Creek. They and their Cherokee neighbors were there when the War of 1812 came to "Buckhead." In 1821, the Muscogee Indians ceded this portion of their land to the state, and pioneers moved in to make claim. These early settlers began operating farms, taverns, mills, and ferries. It wasn't long before others followed.

In 1864 Buckhead stood in the path of war. Federal troops skirmished throughout her forests and bivouacked during the night, preparing for the eventual Battle of Peachtree Creek and the Battle of Atlanta.

Following the war, Buckhead's population increased and the community became a marketplace for people living in the northern part of Fulton County. New residents established gristmills and sawmills and pottery factories. As the twentieth century unfolded, Atlanta residents began building summer cottages in the area to escape the heat of downtown. When Atlanta became too crowded, many of her citizens escaped to the country and became permanent Buckhead residents. The streetcar followed.

The Buckhead community felt the effects of World War I, The Depression, and World War II. However, one of the most important things that happened to the area was the annexation of Buckhead to the city of Atlanta in 1952. From that date on, it was on a collision course with progress.

Within a few short years, the small country town exploded into the Buckhead of today, which is unrecognizable from the pristine, game-rich forest that once existed, with its clear river and creeks. The advancing civilization has replaced the beautiful trees with homes, schools, churches, concrete and steel buildings, and sprawling shopping centers. The once-quiet, meandering trails traveled by moccasined feet and horse's hooves have become busy roads, which bear the names of the earliest settlers: Moore, Howell, Randall, Irby, and Pace.

Buckhead: A Place for All Time is the history and heritage of the area as told by the residents who lived there and whose ancestors were the early settlers who established the community. Interviews with these gracious people have enabled me to paint a picture of the Buckhead community through their eyes and memories. Their photographs enrich the story and make it come alive. In order, however, to tell the fascinating tale, literary license has been taken, and the parameters of the community have been stretched and gerrymandered. Interspersed throughout this history is part of the story of Atlanta. For without Atlanta, Buckhead would not have grown and developed as it did.

Buckhead is more than a name...it *is* a place for all time.

CHAPTER ONE
Prehistoric Buckhead

*T*he first residents of Buckhead were the Paleo-Indians of the Archaic Period (8000 B.C.-1000 B.C.), who lived and hunted along the Chattahoochee River near Peachtree Creek. Their village was known as Standing Peach Tree. The waterways in this area of the Georgia Piedmont, (which encompasses eighty thousand square miles of beautiful rolling terrain between the Appalachian Mountain range and the Atlantic Coastal Plain) (1) provided fresh water for drinking and bathing. The virginal forest of oaks, pines, and chestnut trees was home to an abundance of bear, deer, wildcat, fox, raccoon, squirrel, beaver, and rabbit that provided food for the inhabitants.

Quartz and chert flakes have been discovered at the site of Standing Peach Tree, which intimates that this area was a settlement and a workshop for making tools. The people of this early period chipped at quartz, flint, bone, and stone to make knives, scrapers, points, mortars, and pestles. The discovery of a plano-convex type scraper and a large, quartz, bifaced blade "suggests an Archaic activity—probably early 7,000 to 8,000 years ago. It is a good probability that this site was used by prehistoric hunters over thousands of years and that several cultural periods may be involved." (2)

A "very small fragment of what appeared to be fiber-tempered pottery" was unearthed at this site, and if it's an accurate identification, "it represents the earliest pottery known in Georgia and may date to 2000 B.C." (3)

The most exciting discovery to date has been a hearth of granite rocks. Scattered nearby are pieces of plain, sand-tempered potsherds, quartz flakes, and a small projectile point which "suggests an as yet unidentified Woodland manifestation." (4)

The people of the Woodland Period (1000 B.C.-A.D. 500) developed agricultural cultivation to supplement their hunting and fishing. This produced a more sedentary life, resulting in permanent homes, with some seasonal moving. They made luxury items such as gorget and freshwater jewelry, and carved stone effigies to decorate their pipes.

An archaeological survey of the area in 1971 dated their finds to the Mississippian Period (A.D.500-1200), and pottery found at that time was classified as Etowah I, which dates back "to the ancestors of people who later built such ceremonial centers as the Etowah mounds near Cartersville, Georgia." (5) These people lived in villages, planted extensive crops and had intricate social relationships. Religious centers with large earth lodges and temples were a part of their culture.

Therefore, building on the evidence of artifacts uncovered from different archaeological periods, it can be said that the first residents of Buckhead began to appear between 8000 B.C and 1000 B.C. And they continue to come.

CHAPTER TWO
1770
Standing Peach Tree

A 1770 document mentions a Muscogee Indian village at Standing Peach Tree, located at the junction of the Chattahoochee River and Peachtree Creek (present site of the City of Atlanta pumping station), approximately eight miles north of the villages of Sand Town and Buzzard's Roost. (1) The river served as an approximate boundary line between the Muscogees on the eastern side and the Cherokee Indians on the western side, and was used by both for fishing and transportation. The village also served as a place for meetings and trade.

The origin of the name *Standing Peach Tree* is not known. One story contends that the name came from peach trees growing in the area (2); another suggests that a pine tree was struck by lightning, or that Indians set fire to the pines in order to harvest the pitch or resin. The "pitch tree" may have later been called "peach tree." (3) The village was also known as Pakana Huilli, the Muscogee names for standing peach tree. (4) Whatever the derivation, Peachtree has become one of the most familiar names in Atlanta.

Major trails led in and out of the Standing Peach Tree village. The Peach Tree Trail, which began in the northern part of the state near Toccoa, ran down the Peach Tree ridge (along the current Peachtree Road) to the center of today's Buckhead. There it split. One part of the trail turned right (onto today's West Paces Ferry Road) and continued through the woods until it reached the village of Standing Peach Tree. The southern extension of the trail went down to an artesian well at present-day Atlanta's Five Points, where it joined the Sandtown Trail. The area around the well was a major watering source for game in the area and was a favorite hunting ground for Indians. The Stone Mountain Trail led from Standing Peach Tree eastward to the mountain.

The Muscogee Indians of Standing Peach Tree lived and hunted peacefully in the unsullied forests in the late 1700s and early 1800s. They built log cabins and farmed a community field along with their individual gardens. Their town square, comprised of four arbors which served as the summer council house, was situated along compass points around a Sacred Fire, which was the heart and soul of the community. Nearby stood a round, enclosed, winter council house used by the Council of Elders during inclement weather. The chunkey field, a ball ground which was the site for games and celebrations, was nearby. The Council of Elders, headed by a micco (chief), was responsible for the everyday management of the community. The major governing body for the Nation was the National Council, which met at Tuckabatchee (in present-day Alabama) and Coweta (now the Fort Benning area in Columbus, Georgia).

The Muscogees were a matrilineal society that lived on the land given to them by the Great Spirit. This all-powerful one empowered the Indians to protect the land, the two-leggeds, the four-leggeds, the birds that flew in the sky and the fish that swam in the waters.

***

Following America's War for Independence, settlers began demanding more land. Consequently, the newly-established federal government asked each state to define its boundaries and relinquish its unneeded land in order to create new territories for the expanding nation. Each state in the new Republic complied with the request, except Georgia, who was determined to hold onto her lands, which began at the Atlantic Ocean and stretched to the Mississippi River. In fact, most of what Georgia claimed belonged to the Muscogee and Cherokee Indians. (5)

Using the excuse that Georgia needed money to retire debts incurred during the war, the Georgia Legislature met on January 7, 1795, and passed the Yazoo Land Act, which granted 35 million acres of the state's western land to four development companies. When these companies, with the blessing of the state, attempted to illegally sell the lands belonging to the Indians, a hue and cry erupted from the Indians. The Georgia Legislature was forced to rescind the act on January 14, 1796. This debacle became known as the Yazoo Land Fraud. (6)

The federal government continued to press Georgia for a cession of land. Finally, under an agreement called the "Compact of 1802," the United States government was given title to land Georgia claimed, from her present border with Alabama, to the Mississippi River. In return, the government agreed to remove all Indians from Georgia at federal expense. In compliance with the Compact of 1802, the federal government began negotiations with the Muscogee Nation. Over the next twenty-four years, a series of treaties were signed with the Nation, and by 1826 the Muscogee Indians had ceded all of their Georgia lands. Twelve years later, following the expulsion of the Cherokees from Georgia along the "Trail of Tears," Georgia was free of all Indians and their rich culture. (7)

But as the nineteenth century opened, the Muscogees at Standing Peach Tree lived in relative harmony.

CHAPTER THREE
1812-1814
Standing Peach Tree

*D*uring the War of 1812, the Hostile Red Sticks of the Upper Muscogee Indians were led by Shawnee chief Tecumseh, who sided with the British against the United States. Tecumseh, the son of a Muscogee mother, attempted to unite all the Indians east of the Mississippi River to expunge their land of the white man. They planned to assist the British in overthrowing the Americans, afterwards driving the English from the land. The Lower Muscogees, who had adopted many of the settlers' ways, sided with the Americans against Tecumseh and the British. This alliance led to a major rift within the Muscogee Nation, resulting in the Creek Indian War (1813-1814). (1)

Georgia settlers, ignoring Indian protests, continued to encroach upon Indian land and were robbed and murdered in 1813 by a group of Hostile Red Sticks. Georgia governor David B. Mitchell (1809-1813, 1815-1817), concerned about protecting the frontier from the Indians, mobilized 1,500 Georgia Militiamen, under the command of Brigadier General John Floyd. (2)

Due to mounting hostilities between the Indians and the settlers, the federal government concluded that a line of communication was needed along the Georgia frontier. Consequently, a series of forts was constructed from Fort Strother, on the Alabama River, to the town of Etowah, on the Etowah River in present-day Cartersville, Georgia. A chain of mounted couriers delivered and exchanged vital messages among these fortifications. (3)

In November of 1813 a company of Georgia militia, under the command of Captain Nehemiah Garrison, was sent to Hog Mountain in Jackson (now Gwinnett) County (4) to build a fort and stockade as part of this communications link. The fort was completed in December of 1813 and was named Fort Daniel in honor of General Allen Daniel. (5)

In March of 1814 U.S. Army lieutenant George Rockingham Gilmer (later a Georgia congressman and governor), led a contingent of twenty-two men to Standing Peach Tree to construct Fort Peachtree, also called

Fort Gilmer. From Hog Mountain, Gilmer's men traveled thirty miles south-west along an Indian trail that had been improved by local men. (6) The soldiers followed the Peach Tree ridge down the Peach Tree Trail (present-day Peachtree Road south, past Lenox Square and Phipps Plaza), continued along the path as it went west (at the present Buckhead five points onto West Paces Ferry Road) for a mile and a half before it veered left (onto current Moores Mill Road) and continued to Standing Peach Tree.

Along the journey, Gilmer's men were joined by Wagon Master and Special Commissary James McConnell Montgomery and his boatmen. They were ordered to build ten boats for a supply line 150 miles south on the Chattahoochee River for Gen. Floyd's troops at Fort Mitchell in Coweta (Columbus, Georgia). (7) The road Gilmer and Montgomery traveled, now known as Peachtree Road, is the oldest road in Atlanta.

At Standing Peach Tree, Gilmer's men built the fortress with accompanying buildings and a palisade atop a prominent hill, allowing the troops an excellent view up and down the Chattahoochee River. Montgomery established the boat yard at the mouth of Peachtree Creek on the river and proceeded to build the boats. For his service, Montgomery "was paid $60 per month and allowed forage for one horse, subsistence, and pay of one private servant." (8)

Montgomery described the activities at Standing Peach Tree in a letter to Gen. Andrew Jackson on July 24, 1814:

> . . . laid off the ground for the Fort and a place for a boatyard adjacent to the mouth of a large creek on the East side of the River and immediately commenc'd building and in two months built two large hew'd logg block houses, six dwelling houses, one fram'd store house, one Bridge half a mile from the Fort across Laurel River, a large branch of the Chatahoochy which heads near the stone mountain, and five boats. (9)

The Creek Indian War ended on March 27, 1814, when Gen. Andrew Jackson's combined forces of Americans, a contingent of Lower Muscogees led by Gen. (Chief) William McIntosh, and Cherokees under the command of Junaluska, defeated the Hostile Red Sticks at Horseshoe Bend along the Alabama River. When the battle was over, the Muscogee Nation was mortally wounded. (10)

Following the battle, the people at Standing Peach Tree were startled by sounds of gunfire emanating from the Cherokee village across the Chattahoochee River. Lt. Gilmer readied his troops for a fight and sent a scout across the river. Shortly, eleven Cherokee warriors and some townspeople met with Gilmer and informed him of the battle and victory at Horseshoe Bend. The jubilant Indians celebrated all night, dancing around poles hung with the eighteen enemy scalps brought home as trophies. (11)

In the wake of the battle lay a crippled nation. The Treaty of Fort Jackson, signed by the defeated Muscogees, gave the United States eight million acres of Indian land west of the Chattahoochee River (Alabama) and punished not only the warring Muscogees, but also those who had sided with the Americans. (12)

With the Creek Indian War over and the war with Britain coming to an end, the U.S. Government had no further use for Fort Peachtree. By the end of May, Montgomery was ordered to Fort Hawkins, while Gilmer stayed on until late summer 1814. Montgomery wondered what was to become of Fort Peachtree. On July 24, 1814, he wrote to Gen. Jackson:

I would just state to you that this is a nice place in the creek country and will no doubt be a convenient place for a public Garsn...[or] a Sub agency or some thing of that kind. It is no doubt a very healthy place and has cost the Government not less than five thousand dollars and it appears like a pity to abandon it...If a public stand was made there such as an Agency, or Factory, I would be glad to have any appointment that you think I merited at that place. I refer you to Colo Milton of the 3rd U. S. Regt, for my character as a soldier and citizen. (13)

No information survives about the Standing Peach Tree area during the next seven years, and one can only speculate that life in the Muscogee village near the fort returned to normal.

Georgia continued to press the federal government for removal of the remaining Indians from the state under the terms of the Compact of 1802. Subsequent treaties were made with the Muscogees in which "the great father in Washington" promised that the remaining land would be theirs as long as the eagle flew and the waters ran. Under pressure, the Muscogees signed the Treaty of Indian Springs on January 8, 1821. Under the terms of the treaty, over four million acres of their land, from the Ocmulgee River to the Flint River, was ceded to the United States and then given to Georgia. Included in this parcel was Standing Peach Tree, and the land that would later be known as Atlanta...and Buckhead. (14)

CHAPTER FOUR
1821-1833
Pioneer Days

*F*ollowing the 1821 Treaty of Indian Springs, the Georgia Legislature created Fayette, Henry, Monroe, Houston, and Dooly counties from the land acquired from that cession. Each of these nine-square-mile tracts was divided into land lots measuring 202 1/2 acres and was distributed by a land lottery, which had been established in 1803. For as little as five dollars, or as much as fifty dollars a ticket, a white man over the age of eighteen, who was a United States citizen and resident of Georgia for at least twelve months, was eligible for a draw. Revolutionary War soldiers, widows, and orphans also qualified to draw for the available parcels of land. (1)

On May 15, 1821, the areas comprising Standing Peach Tree and the future community of Buckhead became part of the county named for Virginia patriot Patrick Henry. On December 24, 1821, the community found itself in the county named for the Marquis de Lafayette. Still not settled, it was placed by the Legislature in DeKalb, named in honor of Johann "Hans" Kalb, on December 9, 1822. There it would remain until December 7, 1853, when this small community finally came to rest in the county of Fulton. (2)

The name *Fulton County* was suggested by Dr. Needom L. Angier, but the question remains, for whom was it named? Does it honor Hamilton Fulton, the chief engineer of Georgia who surveyed part of the state for the possible construction of a railroad or canal from the Chattahoochee River to the Tennessee River? Or was it named for Robert Fulton, because his steamboat, *Savannah,* became the first steam-powered vessel to cross the Atlantic from Savannah, Georgia, to Liverpool, England? (3) No one knows for sure.

***

Quickly moving in behind the retreating Indian moccasins, white settlers came into the greater Standing Peach Tree area. These early pioneers worked to build a community and would leave their mark on present-day Buckhead.

One of the first settlers to return to the area to live was James McConnell Montgomery. Montgomery was born on May 19, 1770, in Lancaster District, South Carolina, and by 1814 he was calling Jackson County, Georgia, home. (4) Between 1821 and 1825 he bought approximately one thousand acres of property in the present Bolton vicinity and built a plantation-style home which stood "right where Moores Mill Road intersects Bolton where the Big B Drug Company is," Virlyn Moore Jr., a descendant of Thomas Moore and Martin DeFoor said. (5) There he settled with his wife, Nancy (Farlow), eight children and eleven slaves. Five more children were born to Montgomery at Standing Peach Tree. (6)

Montgomery was an entrepreneur, involving himself in a variety of enterprises over the next nineteen years. In 1823 he served as a Clerk of the Court of Ordinary of DeKalb County, and the following year he was commissioner of the Poor School, which helped to educate the indigent children in the county. (7)

During this period post offices were conveniently "located at the ferries where people would bring the mail and cross the river," Virlyn Moore Jr. explained. (8) On April 5, 1825, the Standing Peach Tree Post Office, the first post office in DeKalb county, was opened on the site of the old fort and the present City of Atlanta pumping station. Montgomery's son Telemachus F., who graduated from the University of Georgia in 1832, served as its first postmaster. (9) After the first year, James McConnell (McC.) Montgomery and his son James F. alternated as postmaster until 1842, when the post office was moved across the river to Cobb County and renamed Boltonville. (10)

In 1830 James McC. helped take DeKalb County's first census, and between 1831 and 1834, he assessed land in the northern part of the state, which Georgia hoped to claim when the federal government evicted the Cherokee Indians. (11)

On March 6, 1833, James McC. bought Alston H. Green's property at Standing Peach Tree at the site of the old fort. Four years later, on Christmas day, his old War of 1812 colleague Georgia governor George R. Gilmer signed the Legislative Act, allowing him to establish a ferry on the Chattahoochee River at Standing Peach Tree which was "located right where the Seaboard Airline crosses the river." (12) Over the next forty years, his ferry served as a major river crossing for transporting travelers and livestock. Later a road was built that ran from the ferry to Decatur, known as Montgomery's Ferry Road. (13)

"Roads were named for their destination," to mills and ferries or to someone's farm, Eugene Cofield said. He explained that some roads had five or six different names at the same time. (14)

Ferries were considered a public utility and were governed by the Legislature, which also regulated the fees. According to state law, ferry operators had to post a bond and promise to run their business fairly. Ferry operators charged 6¢ per person, from 10¢ to 12¢ to transport a man and horse, 62¢ for a loaded wagon (50¢ if it was empty), and from 2¢ to 4¢ a head for cattle, sheep, and hogs. (15)

James McC. founded Montgomery's Chapel, a Methodist Church, the "first church ever built in Atlanta," Mr. Moore said. It was located in the present Crest Lawn Cemetery. The church was moved after the Civil War by Thomas Moore and Martin DeFoor to Inman Yard, which was then a "growing railroad town," and renamed Mt. Vernon Church, where it remained until 1908. (16)

Some of James McC.'s sons moved to LaGrange and "went into the quarry business. They bought a small college and started LaGrange College, the oldest Methodist chartered women's school in the world," Mr. Moore explained. (17)

James McC.'s wife, Nancy, developed a tumor in her right arm, and in 1832 Dr. N. N. Smith amputated the arm at the shoulder. She lived another ten years and died on July 27, 1842. Her death was a great blow, from which James McC. never recovered; he joined her on October 6 of the same year. (18) Both are buried in one of Atlanta's oldest, private cemeteries, located on the Atlanta-Marietta Highway in Bolton, which is also the final resting place for the DeFoor family. (19)

CHAPTER FIVE
1820s-1830s
A Road By Any Other Name

*D*uring the 1820s more settlers began moving into northwest Georgia, settling in the vicinity of the Chattahoochee River on land that would one day be called Buckhead. Among those early pioneers was the Collier family, whose members have left a legacy of Buckhead street names of Collier Road, and East and West Wesley roads.

The first Collier to arrive was Merrell (1782-1855), who came from Randolph County, North Carolina, around 1820 and settled along the South River. (1) He and his wife raised a large family of daughters and one son, Henry, who became a doctor. (2) Merrell was one of the organizers and a trustee of the DeKalb County Academy in Decatur, which was established in 1823 and opened around 1825. (3)

In 1823 Meredith Collier (1782-1863), Merrell's twin brother, came to the "Buckhead" area of DeKalb County and purchased a large parcel of land in the vicinity of Peachtree Creek. There, he and his wife, Elizabeth (Gray), built a home on the Peach Tree Trail at the present location of Collier Road, and raised their fourteen children. He served as a Representative from DeKalb County in the State Legislature from 1838 to 1839. (4)

In the 1830s Meredith's son Wesley Gray Collier owned land from Peachtree Creek to north of West Wesley Road, which was named for him. He built "the first house north of Peachtree Creek" on (2510) Peachtree Road, (5) across from the present Lindbergh Drive next to the Lucas house. (6) Meredith's son George Washington "Wash" Collier bought property in 1847 near the artisian well in what would later become downtown Atlanta's Five Points. There he operated a grocery store and post office out of his single-story frame building and was the third Postmaster in the town then known as Marthasville. (7) Colonel John Collier, another of Meredith's sons, became a member of the Georgia Legislature in 1853 (8) and voted for the chartering of a medical school in Atlanta in 1853, which became the Atlanta College. (9)

Hardy Pace moved to "Buckhead" from Putnam County, Georgia, in the 1820s. Over the next dozen years or so, the North Carolina native purchased multiple land lots along Peach Tree Road, from the center of present-day Buckhead to the Chattahoochee River (Paces and West Paces Ferry roads), for fifty cents an acre. He built his home on the road approximately where the Reuben Garland home is located today, at the corner of West Paces Ferry and Kingswood roads. (10) Pace and his wife, Lucy (Kirksey, 1786-1842), had five children; Parthena, Karen, Catherine, Solomon, and Bushrod. (11)

In the early 1830's Pace established a ferry across the Chattahoochee River, just north of the present Paces Ferry Road bridge (near the current Lovett School). During this period, the Pace's Ferry Post Office was opened, and Pace served as postmaster. (12)

***

As more people settled in the area, some members of the community joined together and founded Sardis Methodist Church as a place for social gathering and communal prayer. The name *Sardis* was taken from the Bible, where it is referred to as "one of the first seven churches listed in the Old Testament," Margaret (Mrs. Leon) Townsend, granddaughter of Silas H. Donaldson, explained. (13)

The exact date of the founding of the first church in Buckhead, now located at 3725 Powers Ferry Road, N.W., cannot be authenticated, since the church records were destroyed many years ago. Sardis' historians say it is the third oldest church in Georgia, and was founded in 1812 on land "obtained from the Cherokee Indians" and donated by Silas Donaldson that same year. "A log cabin was built in 1812 and housed the church until a frame structure could be completed." (14)

On March 23, 1956, Sardis pastor Edgar A. Padgett wrote to Miss Bess Fouche, Clerk, Superior Court of Henry County:

> The deed to our church site...is dated June 9, 1888, and is from Silas H. Donaldson to James M. Sentell, David H. Martin, James Colley, et. al., Trustees of Sardis Church. The tract conveyed is part of land lot number 97 of originally Henry now Fulton County, the 17th District. A friend who lives nearby, on part of land lot 116, traces the property back to the original grant from the State of Georgia to William Ingram's Orphans, dated January 17, 1825, and recorded Henry County Book. (15)

There is a handwritten note on the page: "Dec. 7, 1825 Land Lot 97 was deeded to Joel Neal after being taken from the Creek Indians. How Silas Donaldson acquired the property is not known." It is signed "M. McGeary 1973." (16)

The most probable date of the founding of Sardis Methodist Church is in 1825, since the Sardis land belonged to the Muscogee Indians before 1821. A check of the Georgia Census Index shows no Silas or S. Donaldson listed until 1860, when an S. H. Donaldson appears in the Fulton County records. Donaldson came to Buckhead from Ireland before the Civil War and married Mary Anne Collier. "I think Meredith Collier was her brother," Margaret Chapman (Mrs. Leon) Townsend said. The couple settled "on the corner of Tuxedo and Roswell Road, near Piedmont" where they reared a large family. (17)

***

James Collie, a Sardis Methodist Church member, reminisced about services before the Civil War in a newspaper article. "We didn't dress up to come to the Saturday meeting, but came right from the field at eleven o'clock. We thought nothing of walking five miles to church. Everybody around here belonged to that church. There wasn't another one in the neighborhood for a long time." (18)

Elizabeth Susan Poss, another Sardis Church member, recalled in a 1926 interview when she was 94 years old:

When I first moved here, there was preaching every two weeks. The first (circuit-riding) preachers I remember were Lane and Owens. One came one week and the other, two weeks later. There weren't any Sunday services, either, they preached Tuesdays or Wednesdays. People rode horseback those days, or walked or hitched up the wagon to get to church. (19)

The burial ground on the present church property was once called Shady Oaks Cemetery, (20) and according to the Sardis Cemetery Records, Abraham N. Clarady is thought to be the first person to have been buried there, though the earliest recorded date of interment in the records is that of Charlie Jett, who died in 1839 at the age of 29. (21)

The Sardis Cemetery serves as the final resting place of many of Buckhead's pioneer families, and field stones mark the sites of fallen Confederate soldiers. Henry Irby, Rial Bailey Hicks and his wife, Sarah Jane (Irby), Seaborn L. and Mary Ophelia Hicks Ivey, Rev. W. J. Rolader, Napoleon Cheshire, Miss Jane Donaldson and James O. Mathieson are buried in the cemetery. Silas Donaldson died in 1892 and was interred in a mausoleum that prominently faces Powers Ferry Road, but his body was later moved to West View Cemetery. (22)

***

On January 24, 1826, the Muscogee Nation signed away their remaining land in Georgia to the federal government. The Nation was to receive like acreage in the west (Oklahoma) and "$217,600 following ratification and $20,000 annually in a perpetual annuity." As in other treaty agreements, they were not properly paid. (23)

Still not satisfied, Georgia continued to pressure the federal government for removal of the Cherokee Indians from Georgia under the Compact of 1802. After lengthy negotiations and legal fights, the Treaty of New Echota became law on May 23, 1836. For all of the Cherokee Indian lands from Georgia to the Mississippi River, the Nation was to receive from the United States $5 million, funds for their homes, and moving expenses. (24)

When the Cherokees refused to leave, General Winfield Scott arrived in Georgia. He rounded up the Georgia Indians in late December of 1838 and forced them to march along the infamous "Trail of Tears" to Ross' Landing in Tennessee, for transport to the Indian Territory in Arkansas. Of the approximately 15,000 Indians evicted from their ancestral homeland, over 4,000 died on the grueling, inhumane journey. (25)

The federal government had finally settled its account with Georgia under the terms of the Compact of 1802.

CHAPTER SIX
1830s
Railroads

"The railroads completely did away with
the canals, and this revolutionized the whole
theory of transportation."
- Virlyn Moore Jr.

*T*he railroad got its start in the mid-1500s in England, when small
wagons were placed on tracks and run down into the mines to haul coal to
the surface. Eventually the idea was refined until a working commercial
railroad system was established, and on October 6, 1829, the first successful steam locomotive run was made by the Liverpool and Manchester Railroad, at the speed of thirty-five miles an hour. (1)

America was also experimenting with the railroad. Prior to the railroad's
emergence, large cities were located along rivers and sea ports, where commercial centers for imports and exports were established. From these commerce centers, canals and roads were used to transport commodities and
people into the interior of the country. (2) In 1825 in Hoboken, New Jersey,
John Stevens "built and operated the first locomotive to run on rails in
America," and in 1830 The Baltimore and Ohio Railroad (B. & O.) "began
carrying revenue traffic…and was the first railway in the U.S. to be chartered as a common carrier of freight and passengers." (3) With the appearance of the railroad, the continent was opened for expansion, which created new markets and new ways to distribute merchandise. (4)

***

In 1826 Wilson Lumpkin and Hamilton Fulton were hired to make a
survey from the Tennessee River to the Georgia coast, to determine whether
to build canals or a railroad in Georgia. They worked under the aegis of the
Board of Public Works, which was created in 1825 by the Georgia Legisla-

ture "to provide a system of Internal Improvement." After careful consideration, Lumpkin and Fulton concluded a railroad could be built successfully from Chattanooga, Tennessee, to Milledgeville, Georgia, and deemed a canal system "impracticable." (5)

In 1833 Governor Wilson Lumpkin, one of the original surveyors, continued to sell the people on the need of a railroad for Georgia. The success of a South Carolina line from Charleston to Hamburg proved the importance of this enterprise in shipping goods. In order not to lose business to other states, the Georgia Legislature "granted three railroad charters" in December of 1833, creating the Central Railroad and Canal Company of Georgia, the Georgia Railroad Company, and the Monroe Railroad Company. (6) In 1836, Governor William Schley "authorized the construction of a railroad" from the Tennessee River "to some point on the southeastern bank of the Chattahoochee River...and for branch railroads...to Athens, Madison, Milledgeville, Forsyth, and Columbus, and to any other points which may be designated." (7) This railroad became the Western and Atlantic Railroad of the State of Georgia.

Engineers were sent to Montgomery's Ferry at Standing Peach Tree to survey the best possible site for the railroad in that area, and Governor George R. Gilmer signed an Act in 1837 that allowed the extension of the railroad "from the southeastern bank of the Chattahoochee river [sic], to some point not exceeding eight miles, as shall be most eligible for running branch roads." (8) In the fall of 1837 the terminal bench mark was selected for several railroads. The town that sprang up around it was named Terminus.

CHAPTER SEVEN
1838
Buck's Head

"*B*uckhead" was born on December 18, 1838, when Henry Irby bought 202½ acres of Land Lot 99, around the present Peachtree, Roswell, and West Paces Ferry roads, from Daniel Johnson for $650. Johnson had moved to the county in 1824 and his legacy is Johnson Road, which runs through the Virginia-Highland area of Atlanta. (1)

Henry Irby, born in South Carolina in 1807, was the son of a harness maker. "When Henry was about ten years old, [his father] loaded his wagon with the harness and left home for Savannah to sell his merchandise," Sara Hammett (Mrs. Binion) Jordan, Irby's great-great-granddaughter said. "He never returned home, and they believed that the Indians killed him to get his harness, wagon, and horses or oxen." (2)

Irby married Sardis Walraven, (whose family came from Germany), on December 26, 1833, in Jackson County, Jefferson, Georgia. They had ten children. Irby's "daughter Agnes was kidnapped by gypsies and given a gypsy name. Henry caught them and brought her back home," Mrs. Jordan explained. (3)

Irby cleared a portion of his land and built a tavern and general store at the present corner of West Paces Ferry and Roswell Road (present-day site of Laura Ashley), and a home nearby. Historian Wilbur Kurtz interviewed Seaborn L. Ivey, Irby's grandson-in-law, in 1935 concerning the buildings, and noted:

> The store was a one story frame building—facing east—had a porch and there was one chimney—which was at the south end of the house. Store was about 20 x 40 feet in size. It sat in the NW angle of Pace's Ferry Rd. and Roswell Rd. Henry sold groceries and liquor. Near by was a fenced in lot where drovers could park their turkeys, hogs or cattle for the night. There seems to have been no 'tavern' here at all, in the usually accepted sense of the word. West of the store, some five or six hundred feet, and N. side of Pace's

Ferry Rd., was Henry Irby's house, which was of logs— faced southward—had a large chimney at each end, and perhaps, not more than three rooms. It was a 1 story house. (4)

"Henry Irby had a home back of his store," Mrs. Jordan said. "It was a low place, and they had a wooden walkway from West Paces back to the house, and then the other side of the house extended to Irby Lane. It's said that was where the hired help lived, maybe his slaves." Irby's sister Agnes Chambers lived nearby on [West] Paces Ferry Road, and his blacksmith shop was located at the present corner of West Paces Ferry Road and Early Street. (5)

Several stories are told, explaining how the area became known as Buckhead, and they all entail someone shooting a buck and hanging the buck's head someplace. One tale goes that "In 1848, a North Carolinian, John Whitely, killed a buck nearby, skinned and dressed it and left the head nailed to a tree. It soon crowned the doorway of Irby's tavern which was then promptly called 'Buck's Head.'" (6) A second story states that an Indian killed the buck and nailed the head to a tree. (7)

The most popular story surrounding the origin of Buckhead is that Irby himself "shot a large buck at a bold spring just south of Pace's Ferry Road and a few hundred feet west of Peachtree Road." Then he mounted the head on a post in front of the tavern or above the door. (8) "When the people from North Georgia started coming down, they remembered the buck's head on the door and they would say, 'I'll see you in Buck's Head,'" Mrs. Jordan explained. (9)

On December 22, 1840, the Georgia Legislature designated Henry Yearby's [Irby] house, in Buckhead, as an election district, and a United States Post Office was opened on October 5, 1841, "at the Irby settlement. The settlement was designated as Irbyville." William W. Sentell served as Postmaster until it was closed on December 8, 1842. (10) The name Irbyville faded into memory.

***

Another early resident of the Buckhead community was Benjamin Plaster Sr., who was born in Rowan County, North Carolina, in 1780 to John and Susanna Plaster. (11) He married his neighbor Sarah Sewell in 1802 and had six children. The family moved to Franklin County, Georgia, where in 1810 he received a commission as a lieutenant of the Franklin County militia; he resigned two years later. During the War of 1812, Plaster served as a private in the Georgia Militia. (12)

In the 1830s the Plasters moved to DeKalb County, where he bought 1,316 acres of prime Buckhead land in the area of Piedmont Road and Lindbergh Drive, and built a home at the "southeast intersection of Lindbergh Drive and the Southern Railway." (13) Some of his land was purchased from Judy Horn, of Washington County, who received a land grant of 202H acres on January 10, 1826, from the state. (14)

When Plaster died in 1836, he was buried in the family cemetery on his property. (15) His land was eventually sold, and the present communities of Peachtree Hills Park, Peachtree Heights, Brookwood Hills, Rock Springs and Lindmont, East Wesley Road, and Piedmont Road sit in all or a part of the Plaster land. At one time, Piedmont Road was called Plaster's Bridge Road. (16)

***

Immigration traffic picked up in the newly-created Cobb County area west of the Chattahoochee River, and to accommodate river crossings, a number of ferries were opened in the 1830s. (17) To get to and from these ferries, roads were constructed and bridges were built to span the creeks.

At the end of the 1830s, Hardy Pace moved his home across the Chattahoochee River to Cobb County and "settled at the foot of Vinings Mountain" in a community that was then named Pace's Settlement, and which is now Vinings. (18) Pace made the move to be near the construction of the Western & Atlantic Railroad and operated a hotel and tavern for the railroad crews. He also relocated his post office to the new community in 1839 and renamed it Cross Roads Post Office. (19)

Work was completed on the W & A rail line through Vinings in 1842, and the name *Vinings* was born. When train loads of supplies were brought onto the construction site, a Mr. Vinings was stationed at a strategic position along the route, and workmen would shout, "Throw the material off at Vinings!" Ruth Carter Vanneman, Hardy Pace's great-granddaughter explained. Soon the name caught on and the area began to be referred to as Vinings. (20)

The inaugural run of the Western & Atlantic was made on Christmas eve of 1842, amid a large crowd of celebrants. Before the train crossed the Chattahoochee River bridge, it stopped to allow skittish passengers to get off and walk across the trestle. (21) This bridge remained in place until after the Civil War, when a new one was built two hundred yards down river. (22)

In later years, as traffic in the area grew, the Pace facilities were used by drovers driving their hogs and cattle from Tennessee and Kentucky, through Marietta to markets in Atlanta. They would buy supplies and replenish their livestock before returning to their homes.

Sometime during this period Pinkney H. Randall (1814-1887) moved to the community from North Carolina and married Pace's daughter Catherine G., "Catron." Randall later established a gristmill along Nancy Creek in 1866 in the vicinity of the present Randall Mill and West Paces Ferry roads. Randall's son Hardy Isaiah (1838-1912) married Laura Chunning and founded the Randall Bros. Lumber Co. in 1885. (23) Another of Pace's daughters, Parthenia, married Thomas M. Kirkpatrick.

***

"On December 30, 1847, William R. Roswell was authorized to build a bridge across Nancy Creek on the Pace's Ferry Road and was to be paid $99.75 for the job, provided he kept the bridge in repair for five years from the time of its completion." (24)

Nancy Creek is one of the most prominent creeks in Buckhead, and the origin of its name is debatable. One suggests that the creek was named for an Indian called Nancy. Another claims that it was named for Nancy Baugh Evins who, as a bride, moved to the area with her husband, John L. Evins, and settled along the waterway around 1818, at the present intersection of Peachtree-Dunwoody and House roads. (25) A third proposes that the creek was named for James McC. Montgomery's wife, Nancy. (26)

CHAPTER EIGHT
1843
Marthasville

"Eureka—Atlanta,"
- J. Edgar Thomson

"*The* new and final location of the southeastern terminus of the Western and Atlantic was placed in the northeast corner of Land Lot 77...between Pryor Street and Central Avenue...It was signed, sealed and delivered on July 11, 1842, by deed from Samuel Mitchell of Pike County, Georgia, owner of the entire land lot since 1822." (1) This new town was called Terminus.

During 1843 the village was renamed Marthasville, in honor of Governor Wilson Lumpkin's daughter Martha. Gov. Lumpkin wrote to Martha in 1853 and described how he and others had laid out the new town and offered lots for sale. He wrote:

> Mr. Mitchell and many others said to me that they wished the town to bear my name—Lumpkin. I promptly and decidedly replied that I would not suffer it to be so. First, because we had already in Georgia a county, as well as a beautiful and flourishing little village, called Lumpkin in honor of myself. And secondly, connected as I was with the whole matter, I considered it indelicate and improper, and suggested to Mr. Mitchell...I thought it would be more proper that the town be called Mitchell than Lumpkin.

Then he wrote that Mr. Mitchell and Colonel Charles Fenton Mercer Garnett suggested the town "be called 'Marthasville,' in honor of my youngest daughter.'" (2)

However, the name *Marthasville* was short-lived after The Hon. John C. Calhoun, on his way to Memphis, Tennessee, came through the town and "prophesied a great city in the future." Richard Peters, the Superintendent of the Georgia Railroad, proposed changing the name of the city, but had no viable suggestions. In 1845 he wrote to J. Edgar Thomson, the Chief Engineer of the Georgia Railroad, and asked if he could suggest a more suitable name for the town. Mr. Thomson wrote back:

> Eureka—Atlanta, the terminus of the Western and Atlanta Railroad—Atlantic masculine, Atlanta, feminine—a coined word, and if you think it will suit, adopt it. (3)

Mr. Peters explained his reaction to the new name in a letter to W. R. Hanleiter in 1871:

> I was delighted with the suggestion, and in a few days issued the circulars adopting the name, and had them very generally distributed throughout Georgia and Tennessee, and at the next session of the Legislature, the act of incorporation was changed by inserting Atlanta in place of Marthasville. (4)

"Sometime between September 15th and October 15, 1845" Marthasville became known as Atlanta. (5) The blossoming of the this new city into a major commercial center contributed to the growth of Buckhead, as the community became a way station for farmers bringing their produce and livestock south from North Carolina, Tennessee, and Kentucky, to the new markets in Atlanta.

CHAPTER NINE
1850s
Where There's a Mill There's a Way

In 1850 the population of the Buckhead District numbered 408 people with 68 "heads of families...Averaging six per family." There were 56 farmers, 8 laborers, a lawyer, a doctor, a blacksmith, and a carpenter. (1) In comparison, Atlanta's population was 2,569. (2) On December 20, 1853, Fulton County became an official part of the state, having been carved out of the western section of DeKalb County. Atlanta was chosen as the county seat. Buckhead now lay in unincorporated Fulton County.

As Buckhead flourished, more ferries became essential to transport people and livestock across the Chattahoochee River. Gristmills, for grinding corn into meal, and sash or sawmills, for cutting lumber, sprang up along creeks which provided water power. Three of the early entrepreneurs of these business enterprises were Clark Howell, Martin DeFoor, and Thomas Moore.

Clark Howell (1811-1882) moved to Buckhead in 1852, after retiring from the Atlanta City Council, and settled on his property at the northwest corner of today's intersection of Collier and Howell Mill roads (now Howell Mill Village shopping center). At one time Howell owned approximately four thousand acres, from that crossroads north to the Chattahoochee River, which was "much of what now would be called greater Buckhead," Henry Howell, his great-great-grandson, explained. (3)

Howell's ancestor, John Howell, arrived in America in 1637 from Wales and settled in Virginia. Around 1822 John's descendant, Evan Howell (1782-1868), moved from Cabarus County, North Carolina, to Georgia with his wife, children, and elderly father, Joseph Howell Jr. The senior Howell, a veteran of the American Revolution who married Margaret Eleanor Garmon and had eleven children, died in 1835 at the age of 102. (4)

The Howells settled in the community of Warsaw (now Gwinnett County), where Evan farmed his land and later operated Howell's Ferry across the Chattahoochee River at the present site of the Bankhead Highway bridge. His brother Isaac and Alston H. Green ran the Green & Howell Ferry on the Chattahoochee River south of Montgomery's Ferry, in the vicinity of the present Six Flags Over Georgia amusement park. (5)

Evan's eldest son, Clark Howell (1811-1882), married Martha Ann Winn in 1832. She died in childbirth at the young age of fifteen. Clark then married Effiah Jane Park in 1838 and moved to Cobb County. They had eight children. He built the Lebanon Mills near Roswell and in 1843 served in the Georgia Legislature as a representative of Cobb County. (6)

After the death of his second wife, Effiah, in November of 1850, (7) Clark moved to Atlanta and purchased Dr. Crawford W. Long's incomplete house at the corner of Luckie and Broad streets (current location of the Equitable building and former site of the Piedmont Hotel). "I understand that was the first brick house in the city of Atlanta," Henry Howell said. (8)

After retiring from the Atlanta City Council, Clark Howell built a combination grist and sawmill along Peachtree Creek where it passes underneath Howell Mill Road, near Peachtree Battle Avenue. "When he bought the land from a farmer for the purpose of operating a sawmill, the farmer threw in significant extra land …which is extremely rugged terrain," Mr. Howell related. "The farmer said, 'This is not worth a damn, and you're gonna need the saw timber on it, so I'll just throw this in.'" (9)

The road running through Clark's property to the mill was called Howell's Mill Road. His brother, Charlie, also owned and operated a mill in the area. The road leading to his business, which ran down to the present West Paces Ferry Road, was also called Howell's Mill Road. Eventually these two roads were connected. (10)

Mary D. Hook became Clark Howell's third wife, and they had two children. Howell became a member of the first Inferior Court of Fulton County and went on the bench January 10, 1861. (11) Henceforth, he was known as Judge Howell.

***

In 1853, eleven years after James McC. Montgomery's death, Martin DeFoor and his son-in-law, Thomas Moore, bought one thousand acres of Standing Peach Tree land from the Montgomery heirs. DeFoor moved his family into the two-story Montgomery home and took over the operation of Montgomery's ferry, changing the name to DeFoor's Ferry. (12)

DeFoor's father, James, had left Amsterdam, Holland, and settled in Abbeville, South Carolina, where he and his wife had about fourteen children. Their son Martin, born on September 17, 1805, (13) married Susan Tabor, daughter of the Rev. John and Elizabeth Tabor, in Franklin County in 1830. (14) Their neighbor was James Moore (1798-1856).

Thomas Moore's father, James Moore (1798-1856), was sent to Belfast,

Ireland, in the 1700s by the king of England because he was a British sympathizer. He went to work for the Earl of Dunseath of the Southerland clan and married the Earl's daughter Ann. They emigrated to America in 1825 and settled in Abbeyville. (15) In 1837 James Moore and Martin DeFoor moved their families to DeKalb County and "settled in the Panthersville District," (16) where Moore operated "a sawmill and a gristmill down around the Bouldercrest Road. That's down below the present city of Decatur on Entrenchment Creek," Virlyn Moore Jr., a descendant of both families, explained. (17)

The families merged when Moore's son Thomas (1828-1914) married DeFoor's eldest daughter Elizabeth in 1848. Two years later they moved to the Bolton area and "built a one-story house ...on Chattahoochee Avenue and DeFoor's Ferry Road [located on the current site of the Peppermill Apartments]." They had one son, James. (18)

Thomas Moore built a gristmill in Buckhead on Peachtree Creek in 1854. "He dammed up Peachtree Creek and the mill was about where Moores Mill Road...crosses Peachtree Creek," Virlyn Moore Jr. explained. "The mill was about 100 yards downstream, and all that flat land where the Westover Apartments are now was the millpond." (19)

"Those mills were fascinating things," Mr. Moore continued. "A millwright was a skilled engineer." To generate water power to operate the mill, a large pond was created by damming up a creek. That "back(ed) up all this tremendous power into a mill pond. All these old mills were three-story jobs. They operated from centrifugal force." A chute went under the mill that set the mill wheel in motion; a plug was pulled, which opened the dam, and "the water would go shooting the shoot." The water hit "tub-like thing(s)" attached to upright poles, which made the mill's wheel revolve, turning the grinding stone. "The millstones were on the second floor and "the grain was stored on the third floor. The grain would be put on the wheel and ground." Thomas Moore's millstone "was cut in New York and transported to Savannah and up the Savannah River to Augusta. It was carried by train to Social Circle then by wagon to Atlanta." This millstone is now housed at the Atlanta History Center in Buckhead. (20)

Thomas Moore died on April 2, 1914, the day after he "was thrown from his buggy near Bolton when a Marietta interurban car frightened his horse." He was buried in West View Cemetery. (21)

***

On August 28, 1853, the Buck's Head Post Office was reopened and operated until March 25, 1861. (22) Rial Bailey Hicks (1827-1902), its postmaster, married tavern owner Henry Irby's oldest daughter, Sarah Jane (1837-1924), in 1854. As a wedding present, Irby gave the couple twenty acres of land and "a boy Andy." Later, Hicks became a schoolmaster and wore "a tall hat and a swallow-tail, long-tail coat the schoolmasters wore in that day," Sara Hammett (Mrs. Binion) Jordan, Hick's great-granddaughter said. (23) Hicks built his home at the present junction of Ivy and Old Ivy roads, which in the 1920s became known as Atlanta Heights. When the Hicks' daughters, Mary Ophelia (1858-1933) and Alice, were young girls, they were given a horse-drawn buggy, which they used to visit neighbors. When the Hicks went into Atlanta, "The family would ride to Tenth Street, then the northern outpost of Atlanta, and leave the horse and surrey in the wagon yard. Then they boarded the horse-drawn streetcar to go into town," Mrs. Jordan said. (24)

***

Small churches without full-time pastors were served by circuit-riding ministers who went from community to community, ministering to the congregations within their denominations. In each locale the preachers enjoyed the hospitality of families who offered them a place to stay, while they tended to marriages, burials, church services, and baptisms. The circuit riders also acted as a roving newspaper, bringing outside news to each district.

The Rev. William Joseph Rolader rode into Buckhead in the mid-1850s as a circuit-riding minister to conduct services at Sardis Methodist Church in their small, log cabin sanctuary. Born in Germany on August 6, 1816, Rolader moved to America with his family in 1828 at the age of twelve. At eighteen he joined the Methodist Episcopal Church South. Rolader married Anne Gunter in 1842, and in 1856 he got his license to preach the gospel as a Methodist minister and became a circuit rider. (25) At an unknown date he became a permanent resident of the Buckhead community. The Rev. Rolader died on November 8, 1893, and was buried at Sardis Church cemetery. (26)

***

The tranquility of the Buckhead community was disturbed when a quarrel turned into a killing, as residents gathered at Henry Irby's store to celebrate Christmas day of 1856.

An argument erupted when Henry Norton, who had been drinking, and had a reputation of turning violent when he drank, demanded that Henry

Irby pay for a raffle ticket. Despite Irby's insistence that he had paid, Norton continued to challenge him until the quarrel ended in a fist fight. Rial Bailey Hicks tried to separate the two and urged others to help. Then Irby's thirteen-or fourteen-year-old son, George, rushed up, fired his pistol, and hit Norton on the "left side of his head." Norton died a few minutes later. (27)

The grand jury charged George Irby with murder on April 9, 1857, and he was tried and found guilty of voluntary manslaughter in the Fulton Superior Court. Despite an appeal to the Supreme Court of Georgia, the original sentence was upheld, and Irby was sent to a penitentiary, where he served two years at hard labor. (28)

CHAPTER TEN
1860-1861
Pre-Civil War Period in Atlanta

$\mathcal{I}$n the late 1850s Americans were embroiled in an argument that would tear the nation apart and plunge it into a war that would claim over six hundred thousand lives.

In 1856 a major debate centered on whether or not Kansas should be admitted into the union as a slave state. How she came to statehood could change the political balance of power in the country. Georgia favored slavery, and rallies were held in Atlanta with firebrand speeches from supporters of the slavery issue, fueling the controversial fires. (1) In the spring of 1856 The Atlanta Company of Emigrants for Kansas Territory was organized. Their objective was to raise money to send "Southern emigrants" to three Kansas counties to help sway the vote to admit Kansas as a slave state. A committee was formed to raise the necessary funds, and Henry Irby, Pinkney H. Randall, Bushrod Pace, Clark Howell, and M. C. Donaldson represented the Buckhead District. (2)

The presidential election of 1860 continued to fan the blaze of dissension. During a political speech on October 30, 1860, candidate Abraham Lincoln's opponent, Stephen A. Douglas, declared "that no State had a right to secede and those who seceded would be rebels and traitors." (3) Georgia disagreed and stood firm on her sovereign right to make her own decisions. The following day a group of concerned citizens met and organized the Minute Men of Fulton County, to uphold the state's rights of Georgia. (4)

On December 22, 1860, shortly after Abraham Lincoln was elected president, South Carolina seceded from the Union. Georgia governor Joseph E. Brown was opposed to secession and urged his fellow Georgians to support the Union "so long as they continue to stand by her rights...But should this Organization be broken down, and her constitutional rights be denied, and her equality in the Union destroyed, I would then advise her citizens to strike for independence out of the Union." (5) On January 16, 1861, the Georgia State Convention convened at the capitol in Milledgeville to vote whether or not to follow South Carolina's act of secession. On January 21 the Georgia Legislature voted, and the state joined four of her sister states in leaving the Union.

Events moved swiftly in the early months of 1861. During a meeting in Montgomery, Alabama, in February, 1861, those states that had seceded elected Jefferson Davis president of the new Confederate States of America, and despite his opposition to his state's stand, Georgia's Alexander Stephens was elected vice-president. (6) Georgia's bid for the capital of the Confederacy was lost to Montgomery.

Before dawn on April 12, 1861, the Civil War began, when a mortar ball exploded over the federally-held Fort Sumter, located in the Charleston Harbor. Atlanta came under martial law on May 24, and Mayor James M. Calhoun was appointed civil governor. (7)

The final phases of the four-year Civil War were played out in Georgia. But before it ended, it came through Buckhead.

CHAPTER ELEVEN
1864
Buckhead and the Civil War

Bury th' Silva, th' Yankees are comin'!
- A cry from many Southern belles.

$\mathscr{B}$ecause Atlanta was a hub in the South's rail system, she quickly became a major supply and transportation center for the Confederacy during the Civil War. Georgia railroads became the lifeline of the battlefield, transporting crucial munitions, equipment, uniforms, food, and fodder to the armies in the field.

"Atlanta became a haven for refugees coming from elsewhere in the Confederacy where there was conflict," Civil War historian William Erquitt said. Atlanta also became a major medical center for those soldiers, both South and North, wounded in battle. "Over a dozen hospitals under direct Confederate supervision were established, and dozens of others sprang up in hotels, public and private buildings, and residences," Mr. Erquitt continued. One such hospital was set up at the Fair Grounds, now Memorial Drive at the Ed S. Cook School. (1)

In February, 1864, deserters from the Confederate Army had been frightening and robbing the citizens of Atlanta. After a Buckhead resident appealed to Major George W. Lee, of the Confederate Bureau of Conscription, to arrest the marauders, a house-to-house search was conducted by Lieutenant J. A. Caldwell and his men. (2)

Caldwell and his group went to the Wesley Gray Collier home at 2510 Peachtree Road (at current junction with Lindbergh), and without informing the Colliers of their mission, demanded entrance to the home and threatened to break in the doors and windows if not allowed entry. After sending his four frightened children and a servant to a back room for safety, Collier armed himself with a handgun and shotgun and waited for the intruders. When a man named Knight jumped through the window, Collier shot him in the stomach, and gunfire ensued. Collier was pursued out the back of the house and into the woods without injury. The soldiers placed their wounded colleague in Collier's buggy and left the area. (3)

Collier sent word to one of his brothers to go into Atlanta for help. In response, City Marshal Oliver H. Jones and his men tracked Caldwell's group and located them camped out around a fire, in the present Sixteenth Street vicinity. They found the wounded man, who later died, and Collier's buggy. Days later Caldwell's men were arrested and indicted for aggravated riot; they were found guilty. (4)

***

"In the spring of 1864 Gen. Ulysses S. Grant, commander of all the Northern armies, directed Gen. William Tecumseh Sherman to take the war into enemy country and destroy the Confederate Army and their war resources," William Erquitt explained. "The Atlanta Campaign was crucial to bringing an end to the Civil War." (5)

The Union's two main objectives were to take Richmond, Virginia, and to defeat the Confederate Army of the Tennessee in Georgia. Sherman's goal was to cut the railroads, destroy Atlanta, and cripple the Confederacy. "Gen. Grant had concluded that Georgia and Atlanta held the key to successful prosecution of the war. Georgia furnished the food on which the entire Confederacy, including Lee's Army of Northern Virginia, depended, and Atlanta furnished the guns, ammunition, wagons, clothing, and other supplies so essential for waging war. Gen. Sherman had observed that every wagon he had captured prior to the Atlanta Campaign bore the label 'Made in Atlanta.'" (6)

Brigadier General Francis Ashbury Shoup, Chief of Artillery for the Confederate Army of the Tennessee, had devised an alternate defensive line to the standard dirt and log earthworks of "artillery forts or redoubts, connected by infantry trenches and screened in front by rifle pits for individual soldiers." His *Shoupes*, as they were called, were to be made of heavily-constructed logs and dirt. The "two outer faces [of the diamond-shaped log forts] were to be pointed toward the enemy. Each fort was designed to be manned by a company of 80 riflemen." (7)

In the middle of June, 1864, Shoup visited Confederate general Joseph Egleston Johnston at his headquarters near Kennesaw Mountain and "urged him to authorize construction of his proposed defensive system at the point where the Western & Atlantic Railroad crossed the Chattahoochee River, a few miles northwest of Atlanta," on the Cobb County side of the river. Johnston approved the plan, and Shoup was sent immediately to the site to begin building the line of defense, using slaves from nearby plantations.

These fortifications became known as the Chattahoochee River Line. (8)

After Sherman's attack on Gen. Johnston's Army of the Tennessee at Kennesaw Mountain in late June, the Confederates fell back to the Chattahoochee River. By July 5 they were entrenched along their *Shoupades*. The war was at the doorstep of Atlanta and Buckhead. (9)

Sherman outflanked Johnston's River Line and sent his men across the Chattahoochee River at different spots north and south. On July 5, Gen. Kenner Garrard's forces were deployed to Roswell, where he took the town, destroying the cotton mills that furnished the South's military uniforms. "The mill workers were taken prisoner and taken to Marietta, where they were sent north by train," Mr. Erquitt explained. "Sherman felt they were a skilled and valuable resource for manufacturing." (10)

Fearing for the safety of Atlanta, Gen. Johnston quickly moved his troops across the river on the evening of July 9. "As they crossed the river, the Confederate forces destroyed the W & A railroad bridge and all other bridges within their lines." (11)

Federal troops quickly moved in and overran the Vinings area, and Sherman established his headquarters in Hardy Pace's house. Before the troops arrived, Pinkney Randall's son, Hardy Isaiah, put his wife "on the back of his horse and they rode out to Stone Mountain to get her out of the way," Luther Randall Jr. said of his ancestor. Hardy Isaiah "was made a first lieutenant in Company B of the Ninth Battalion of the Georgia Light Artillery on March 4, 1862." (12)

"It was from the top of Vinings Mountain at the old Randall-Pace Cemetery that General Sherman got his first view of the church spires and fortifications from the Pearl of the South, which was Atlanta," Mr. Randall remarked. "I think they used it [the house] as a hospital, and I think when they left they burned it." (13)

Around the 16th of July, Sherman relocated his headquarters at Power's Ferry (current intersection of Power's Ferry and Mt. Vernon roads) and issued this:

Memoranda to Special Field Orders, No. 36...Peach Tree Creek is considerable of a stream, but fordable at all points east of the main road from Buck Head to Atlanta. The first real lines to be found will be on the Old Peach Tree road [*sic*], which starts at Turner's Ferry, keeps near the Chattahoochee, crosses Peach Tree [Creek] at Moore's Mill and on a main ridge by Buck Head, Buchanan's and Pinckneyville. Our first line must be in front of this road, leaving it clear for communication, General Thomas, the right, General Schofield, the center, and General McPherson, the left. General Thomas will move substantially on Atlanta, General Schofield on Decatur, and General McPherson, with General Garrard's cavalry, is charged with the destruction of the [Georgia] railroad between Decatur and Stone Mountain. (14)

Three Union corps of the Army of the Cumberland (15,000 to 20,000 men in each corp) entered Buckhead. On July 16, 1864, the 20th Corp, led by Gen. George H. Thomas, crossed the river at Paces' Ferry. As his troops moved toward Buckhead, they engaged a contingent of Gen. Joseph Wheeler's Confederate cavalry and skirmished along Pace's Ferry Road (in the current Mt. Paran Road area) and around Brown's Pottery (Old Howell Mill Road and West Paces Ferry/AMOCO station and I-75), pushing Wheeler's men east towards Atlanta. The first night Thomas' men camped in the area of the pottery, and the following evening "the 20th Corp made its major encampment in the vicinity of [present day] Andrews and Habersham, with federals reaching as far back as [today's] Northside Drive," Mr. Erquitt said. (15)

Gen. Oliver O. Howard and his Federal 4th Corp crossed the river at Power's Ferry and moved into the Buckhead area behind the 20th. "The Federal 4th Corp continued through the encampment of the 20th on their way through Buckhead and across Peachtree Road and found desirable camping in the rolling hills and lowlands of [today's] Pharr Road, with elements reaching as far as Piedmont Road," Mr. Erquitt continued. (16)

"Federal troops [Gen. John M. Palmer's 14th Corp] headed toward Peachtree Creek, moved along various roads including Howell's Mill and Ridgewood roads." Another group crossed Nancy Creek and "took the high ground on which Westminster High School now stands, then formed a line along the present Margaret Mitchell Drive and drove toward Peachtree Creek. By noon of July 18, Palmer had taken most of the ground north of Peachtree Creek and Wheeler's defending cavalry burned the three bridges over the creek at Ridgewood Road, Moore's Mill and Howell's Mill. Wheeler was then withdrawn east to Atlanta to oppose [Gen. John B.] McPherson's flanking movement near Decatur, leaving only the three Confederate brigades of Claudius W. Sears, John Adams and Daniel H. Reynolds to defend the western end of the Peachtree Creek line against Palmer's XIV Corps." (17)

"There were huge masses of men, horses, and equipment that came through Buckhead, and they required vast amounts of water for drinking and cooking, and woods for shelter. Hence, Buckhead swarmed with men in blue trying to satisfy their needs while making their way to the Battle of Atlanta. Even the smallest of creeks and tributaries became infested with these blue coats," Mr. Erquitt asserted. (18)

On July 19, Gen. Johnston's Confederate troops were entrenched south of Peachtree Creek. "Johnston believed his smaller army could turn on the Federals along Peachtree Creek, outflank them, and turn them back across the river. Then he proposed to turn on Sherman's other divided army, which was approaching Decatur, and defeat them," Mr. Erquitt explained. (19) Confederate president Jefferson Davis, "frustrated by Johnston's failure to stop Sherman's advance, relieved him of command and replaced him with the more aggressive John B. Hood." Hood had lost the use of his left arm when he was wounded at Gettysburg, and after having his right leg ampu- tated at the thigh from a wound received during the battle of Chickamauga, continued to command his troops in the field while strapped to his horse. To ease the pain, he used the opiate laudanum. (20)

During the day of July 19, fighting took place around Moore's Mill and to the west of Peachtree Creek, around the present Northside Drive and West Wesley Road. The Confederates of Hardee's Corps crossed Peachtree Creek at Peachtree Road, then burned the bridge. Wood's 3rd Division of Federal forces followed, and fighting ensued around today's Piedmont Hos- pital. (21)

"Hood, now in command and briefed by Johnston's staff of his tactic, moved the Confederates from their camps down a line that ran east, then south," Mr. Erquitt related. "These entrenchments ran along Crestlawn Cemetery, through Peachtree Hills, along the high ground to the Temple [the current intersection of Peachtree Road and Spring Street], reached as far east as Highland Avenue, turned south, and extended to the Georgia Railroad. The line facing north consisted of Gen. A. P. Stewart on the left and Gen. William Hardee on the right. On Gen. Hardee's right were Gen. Frank Cheatham and the Georgia Militia, whose right extended across the Georgia Railroad. Wheeler's cavalry remained along Peachtree Creek and supported skirmishes to repel the Federal advance." (22)

Meanwhile, Gen. Joseph Hooker's men of the 20th Corp had "moved south along Howell Mill Road," toward Peachtree Creek near the present Morris Brandon Elementary School, while "Gen. Davis S. Stanley's 4th went east toward Buckhead, arriving in the late evening, having cleared the area of all hostiles. The 4th Corp camped in the low ground near Bagley Park [now Pharr Road]," Mr. Erquitt said. (23)

On July 20 the Union forces linked up and attacked the Confederate forces about 4:00 in the afternoon, near Peachtree Creek, around the present vicinity of Piedmont Hospital, along Tanyard Branch at Collier Road and around Northside Drive, along the present golf course and Bitsy Grant Tennis Center. "For more than two hours, the fighting raged around Andrew J.

Collier's Mill on the Tanyard branch of Peachtree Creek. By nightfall, Hood, badly beaten in his first engagement, withdrew his troops from the field." (24) When the Battle of Peachtree Creek ended, both sides had sustained heavy casualties and "the Confederates were defeated," Mr. Erquitt explained. (25) One of the Federal officers at the battle was Benjamin Harrison, the future president of the United States. (26)

After the Battle of Peachtree Creek, the war moved south into the city, where the Battle of Atlanta was waged on July 22. On September 2, 1864, Atlanta mayor James M. Calhoun formally surrendered the city to Brigadier General William T. Ward, Commander of the Third Division, 20th Corp. (27) Following the fall of Atlanta, Sherman's men pressed south on his infamous march to the sea.

***

When the smoke cleared after the Battle of Peachtree Creek, it was discovered that Meredith Collier's house on Peachtree had survived the combat. The house was so well built that when "the Yankees came and threw five cannonballs at the house, they couldn't tear it down because of the tongue and groove construction," Collier's grandson, Merrill Collier, said. The Collier family had fled south to escape the war. (28)

Hardy Pace died in 1864, after Federal troops crossed through his land on their way to Atlanta. He was buried in the family cemetery in Vinings and was survived by several children. His son Solomon and grandson Hardy Isaiah Randall continued to operate Pace's ferry after the war and, through an agreement with Fulton County, the county paid them a monthly fee of ten dollars for maintenance and operation of the ferry and equipment. There was no charge for the ferry service. (29)

When the Federal troops were in Buckhead, they invaded the Rial Bailey Hicks' home. "They went upstairs in my grandmother's home and ransacked it," Sara Hammett (Mrs. Binion) Jordan said. "One came down the stairs with a blanket over his arm and had on Hicks' tall hat and tail-coat that he wore as a schoolmaster. He came down the stairs jauntily. As he went out the front door, he tipped his hat to her [Sarah Jane Hicks]. My grandmother told me about how they would hide dishes and bury them in the ground or in the well." (30)

Rial Bailey Hicks mustered into the Confederate Army on April 27, 1864, and served as a first lieutenant in Company C, 2nd Regiment Georgia Reserves. (31) Three of Henry Irby's sons also served in the Confederate Army; James Early survived the war, but George and William were killed. (32)

Thomas Moore's mill did not survive the war. It was first torched in

40

1861 by hotheads who opposed his stand against secession. He felt "there was no way we could beat the North because of the number of people they had, and their manufacturing," Virlyn Moore Jr. explained. The mill was rebuilt, and when war broke out, Moore was exempt from serving in the army because, "He was a manufacturer and was grinding meal and so forth to supply the army; he ground sixty thousand bushels of corn for the Confederacy." (33) As the invading Union army moved toward Atlanta, the Moore family sought refuge in the city. They remained there several months "and had to live in a hole for ten days" while Gen. Sherman's artillery shelled the "residential section of Atlanta," Mr. Moore explained. When they returned home they discovered that the mill had once again been burned down. "The Confederates probably burned down the bridge to keep the Federal forces from coming. We had a sharp battle right there at Moore's Mill." (34)

After the war, Moore's mill was once again rebuilt, and was operated until 1901, "when the site was rendered untenable for mill use by the establishment of a city sewage disposal plant upstream." (35)

***

"While there was no wholesale destruction of private property in the Buckhead District comparable with what occurred in Atlanta and some other areas, the war caused much suffering in the District, aside from the numerous casualties among its young men serving the Confederate cause. Food was scarce. Raiding parties confiscated livestock and crops, and some houses, mills, and bridges were destroyed. Indeed, the District, along with most of the Atlanta area, presented a grim and depressing scene during the winter of 1864-1865." (36)

Today there are a few remnants left in the area which remind us of the skirmishes and the fierce battles which took place in Buckhead in July of 1864. Bits and pieces of artillery, minie balls, sabers, belt buckles, and other artifacts of war are now gone from the surface of the landscape. Left are "Trenches, parapets and earthen works [which] scar the countryside of woods and neighborhoods, and we can look upon them as footprints of history," Mr. Erquitt reflected. (37)

CHAPTER TWELVE
1865
Lumber

"It went like snow in the heat."
- Henry Howell

In March of 1864, Capt. Evan P. Howell (b. 1839), eldest son of Judge Clark Howell, mustered out of the Confederate Army and moved his family to Buckhead. (1) Prior to the war, he attended the Georgia Military Association in Marietta (2) and the Lumpkin Law School (now the University of Georgia Law School). After graduation in 1859, he moved to Sandersville, Georgia, and established a law practice. When the Civil War began, Evan enlisted and "was elected a sub-lieutenant. He fought at Gettysburg...down all the way to the Battle of Atlanta and finally surrendered outside of Macon," Barrett Howell said. (3) Evan Howell also fought in the Battle of Peachtree Creek, (4) where he commanded Howell's Artillery. (5)

After the war, the Evan Howells "were so desperately poor that they literally took the front door of the mill down to set on trestles to use as their dining room table when they were getting started after the war," Henry Howell related. "And there is a wonderful picture of Evan's wife, Julia, in great finery, with a marvelous silver plate and a sideboard, that was taken, I believe, on their twenty-fifth anniversary...The idea was that she was gonna show, doggonnit, that they had made it, after being reduced to eating off the front door for a table, within twenty-five years." (6)

Evan "desperately needed to be able to earn money," Henry Howell said. "There wasn't an awful lot of demand for lawyers at that point, but there was a lot of demand for lumber to rebuild Atlanta. So he took over the operation of his father's grist and sash mill." Evan would load his wagon with lumber at the mill and drive his team to Atlanta by way of Howell's Mill Road. "He'd seldom get much further than Collier Road before people descended on him and completely bought it out, and he'd go back and saw some more. It went like snow in the heat, there was so much demand for it," Henry Howell mused. "That's how they managed to get enough money to ultimately buy *The Atlanta Constitution*." (7)

***

At the end of the Civil War Solomon Jerome Cheshire and his brother Napoleon bought a large tract of land along what is now Cheshire Bridge Road, and established farms. Jerome's portion of the tract spread west to Piedmont Road and included the present Lindbergh Plaza and former Mooney's Lake property. Napoleon's land lay on the east side of Cheshire Bridge Road (once Service Merchandise at I-85). "They cut through Cheshire Bridge Road to their farms, and the bridge over Peachtree Creek connected the two farms," Jerome's granddaughter Margaret Cheshire (Mrs. Hilton) Dickerson explained. (8) At one time part of this road ran through Buckhead, as evidenced by a Historic Marker at the intersection of Piedmont and East Paces Ferry roads.

The Cheshires' father, Hezekiah (1786-1870), was born in St. Mary's County, Maryland. He married Susan Watson, of Lawrence County, South Carolina, in 1814, and had eleven children. After Susan's death, he married Sarah E. Goodwin, a woman twenty-six years his junior, in November of 1836. This union produced nine children. (9)

Hezekiah and Sarah's first son, Solomon Jerome (1837), was named after Jerome Bonaparte, Napoleon Bonaparte's brother. "Hezekiah had met Jerome Bonaparte when he came to Baltimore…when he was five years old." Mrs. Dickerson explained. Hezekiah "evidently liked him, because he named my grandfather Jerome and the next son Napoleon." (10)

Hezekiah moved his family from Lawrence, South Carolina, to DeKalb County around 1850, after a business deal went sour. "A friend or partner left, and left him to pay off a note," Mrs. Dickerson continued. He brought his family to the area to be near his in-laws, the Solomon Goodwins, and built a house on Highland Avenue where the Post Office now stands. (11)

Solomon Goodwin came to DeKalb County from Lawrence, South Carolina, in 1829, and built a plantation-style home on Peachtree Road in the present community of Brookhaven. Today, much of Brookhaven sits on his property, including the old Veteran's Hospital and the Brookhaven Country Club. (12) "For many years the home was a railway stop called Goodwin's, 11 miles from Atlanta." Travelers through the district also watered their livestock at Mr. Goodwin's water trough. (13) It is said that if Mr. Goodwin took a liking to a visitor who had stopped to water his horse, his hospitality would include refreshing mint juleps served by his servant.

44

(14) The house, which is the oldest house still standing in Atlanta, was moved across the street near the Nancy Creek Church Cemetery (across from present-day Harris Teeter) where he and several members of his family are buried. During the Civil War, Union troops spared the house because "they were going through some things and an officer came in and found a Masonic apron," Mrs. Dickerson explained. (15)

During the war, Jerome and Napoleon Cheshire served briefly with Nathan Bedford Forrest's cavalry, but "they decided they didn't want to be that far from home and transferred to Wheeler's cavalry," Mrs. Dickerson continued. Following the Battle of Chickamauga in Tennessee, Jerome took a leave from the fighting, and returned home to send his parents, sisters, and a brother to relatives out of town, away from the impending Battle of Atlanta. "When the family returned, they discovered that their house had been in the middle of a battle and had been burned down," Mrs. Dickerson said. "In the yard were graves of both Federal and Confederate soldiers." Their remains were later moved to Oakland Cemetery and to the National Cemetery in Marietta. (16)

The Cheshire house was rebuilt, and later remodeled for water and electricity. "They'd still go out to the well and draw their drinking water 'cause it was better. It went through solid granite," Mrs. Dickerson said. (17) A rope bed, a chair and a spinning wheel from Hezekiah's home are on display at the Tullie Smith House at the Atlanta History Center.

***

Captain James L. Mathieson served in the 93rd Iowa Cavalry (Union) and found himself in Macon, Georgia, at the end of the war. The Scottish immigrant, who settled in Iowa when he was nineteen years old, was sent to Atlanta to be mustered out. While there, he received word that his wife had died as a result of a kerosene explosion, and his two children were living with their grandmother.

Mathieson decided to remain in Atlanta and became supervisor of the Freedmen's Bureau, which distributed food to the hungry. (18) He married Atlantan Frances Ward, a war widow, after "convincing her that Yankee soldiers could be good husbands." After the wedding, they brought his children to live with them. (19)

Mathieson, who served as a Postmaster between 1867 and 1870, bought a log house and a large piece of property in Buckhead on the west side of Peachtree Road, which ran from the present Piedmont Road to Mathieson Drive. The Mathiesons discovered that the house had been a part of Sherman's quarters during the war. The doors of the house, which were stained with blood,

45

had been put on saw horses and used as operating tables. (20)

**

On December 15, 1866, The *Daily New Era* newspaper announced that gold had been discovered in Buckhead on Nancy Creek near the Chattahoochee River, on land that belonged to Gen. A. Austell, B. Pace and Ed W. Holland. "Mr. Holland, who has had 30 years experience as a practical miner in Georgia, reports the yield of gold in a test made by him of this rock, at about $250 per ton." (21)

Shortly afterwards, Pinkney H. Randall bought Land Lot 200 and established a gristmill for grinding corn along the creek. From a small amount of gold that was found on his property near the mill, a ring was made for a family member, and to this day the family still owns the mineral rights to the property. (22)

Henry Irby was also bitten by the gold bug. When he heard there were possibly veins of gold running from Dahlonega through Buckhead, he became a prospector. No knowledge of his success survives, but his gold scales do. "He had a large interest, they say, in the Dahlonega gold mine that was mining gold for the United States government," Sara Hammett (Mrs. Binion) Jordan said. (23)

Mrs. Jordan also stated that, during the Civil War, Henry "buried a dish pan of gold coins or bars somewhere in the Buckhead area, but it was never found. It is said when the soldiers came from the north, they ransacked everything, and he wanted to hide it." (24)

At the war's end, Henry Irby was left with worthless Confederate money and a lot of land. (25) To buy the goods he needed for survival, Irby bartered away some of his land. "He bartered land for wheat," Anne Irby (Mrs. J. M., Jr.) Comer, his great-great-great-granddaughter said. (26)

"He was considered land poor. In those days people had more land than they had any use for, and he was a real estate salesman," Mrs. Jordan explained. "He would ride all over the countryside selling farm land for five cents an acre." Irby hired Rial Bailey Hicks to manage the store in Buckhead while he was on the road. (27)

Irby's wagon yard, located next to his tavern, became an important way station for travelers. "People from North Georgia would come to Atlanta for business in their oxen-drawn wagons and bring their families," Mrs. Jordan explained. "They would camp next door to Henry Irby's store and spend the night. The next morning the husbands would go in their wagons down to Tenth Street which, at that time, was the northernmost part of Atlanta." The men would go into Atlanta on the horse-drawn trollies, conduct their business, then "go back to the campgrounds, where their families had been visiting each other all day. Then they would spend another night, before heading home the next morning." (28)

***

The Sardis Methodist Church log sanctuary had survived the Civil War, and the community resumed their church meetings. "the soldiers came along here but they didn't bother us. There weren't many meetings during those four years, and there wasn't any need for church dinners and bazaars. The people gave the preachers money," Mrs. Elizabeth Susan Poss said in a church account. (29)

The log chapel was moved onto Silas Donaldson's property and used to store wheat. In its place, a two-story frame building was erected. "We got a notion to build a better church...Mr. Donaldson...and I helped build it...We farmers around here did the building with our own hands," James Collie, who was born in 1842, said in the church history. (30)

***

In April of 1868 the voters of Georgia approved a new state constitution and the relocation of the capital to Atlanta, the largest city in the state, from Milledgeville. (31) "[Evan Howell] was the man who headed up the campaign to get the capital moved to Atlanta," Virlyn Moore Jr. said. (32)

CHAPTER THIRTEEN
1870s
Citizens, Churches, and Calamities

"I remember the day of the cyclone,"
- James Collie

*B*uckhead in the 1870s was marked by the arrival of more residents, the death of some of the early settlers, the organization of two new churches, the establishment of black communities, a cyclone, and a double murder.

***

Hezekiah Cheshire died in 1870 and was buried in the Plaster family cemetery near the present Piedmont Road railroad crossing; his remains were later moved to the Sardis Methodist Church cemetery on Powers Ferry Road. After his father's death, Jerome Cheshire lived in the family home to care for his mother and sisters, and in 1874 he married Eliza Wood. (1)

Jesse Wood, Eliza's father, had moved to DeKalb County in 1823 from South Carolina, at the age of twenty, where he began acquiring land on the west side of Peachtree from the Pershing Point north to Brookwood Station. His home sat behind the present station, and a family cemetery and chapel were established on a hill between the present Center For Puppetry Arts and the old Mayfair Club on Spring Street. The Wood family remains in the cemetery were later interred at Sardis Methodist Church cemetery. (2)

Jerome and Eliza had three daughters and a son. Their son, Thaddeus Johnson Cheshire, "would ride his Indian pony up to Piedmont [Road], where the railroad goes across," leave the pony at Plaster's farm, and catch "the train down to Hunter Street School For Boys, which used to be a private school for boys. It was across from where the...Flatiron Building is," Margaret Cheshire (Mrs. Hilton) Dickerson said of her father. After school "he would come home and pick up his Indian pony and head back home." (3)

Thaddeus married Willie Russell Law, daughter of Willie (Foster) and Fred Law; Mr. Law arrived in Atlanta after the Civil War from Alabama, when he was sixteen, and "started a very successful haberdashery." Thaddeus and Willie Cheshire lived on Ponce de Leon Avenue near Boulevard and had one child, Margaret.(4)

* * *

With the slaves having been freed from their bondage under the Emancipation Proclamation, a new concept arose in the South—the creation of black communities. Some of these neighborhoods were established when property owners deeded their former slaves land for homes, schools, churches, and cemeteries. One such benefactor was Dr. James H. "Whispering" Smith (1804-1872), who had previously allowed his slaves and the slaves of nearby plantations to use a portion of his Buckhead land for worship and burial. (5)

"Back in those days, when slaves died, they just put them in the grave and put stones around them," Elizabeth Campbell (Mrs. Moses) Few, a New Hope Church member, explained. Mrs. Few is the daughter of Mattie (Hector), from Monroe, Georgia, and Ivery Campbell, who came to Atlanta in 1929 from Oconee County. (6)

On May 29, 1872, Dr. Smith wrote his final will and deeded three acres of land, which included the original slave cemetery, to his former slaves for a school and church on present-day Arden Road. (7)

"It showed what a tremendous person he [Smith] was, in that he indicated in his will that the grounds should always be a place for a church and a school," Mrs. Few said. "We are talking about five or six years after the slaves were freed. Black people were still in a hostile environment. There were still some of the old laws hanging around in the spirits and the minds of some of the people, who still didn't want black people to learn how to read and write." (8)

Eight days after writing his will, Dr. Smith died and was buried next to his home in his family cemetery at Harmony Grove, which is located on West Paces Ferry Road at the corner of Chatham Road. At one time a small white clapboard, Harmony Grove Church, which could seat between 150 and 200 people, sat on a knoll along the dirt road. (9)

The land Dr. Smith deeded became the site of the New Hope Campground. There, under a brush arbor of four poles covered with tree branches, worshippers came from miles around to throw their hearts and souls into praying, singing, and socializing.

"That's how gospel music got started," Mrs. Few explained. The spirituals "recall the era of slavery...these songs had dual meanings for the slaves who sung them, having not only religious meaning, but allowing the slaves to metaphorically sing of freedom and escaping to the North." (10)

The Reverend Roland Wishum is credited with being the driving force in bringing the first group of New Hope worshippers together. Though not a minister, he led the services and cared for the property. The New Hope congregation joined the African Methodist Episcopal Church movement, which was founded in 1793 by a former slave, Richard Allen of Philadelphia. (11) Eventually, the congregation built a wooden building, which doubled as a school until a proper one could be constructed, and a nearby spring provided water before a permanent well was dug. (12) The Reverend Joseph Woods became the first pastor of New Hope Church, and at his first service, Judge Clark Howell's wife, Mary, delivered the Catechism. (13) In 1887 the congregation bought additional land across the street for a new cemetery, (14) and a tabernacle was built next to the church in the late 1890s. (15)

Sarah Huff, born in 1857, remembered that the Camp Meetings were popular in the Buckhead community, and that preparations were made weeks ahead of time for these events.

Hams of the finest quality had been smoked and cured to perfection over hickory coals in the old log smokehouses the winter before. And the boilings and the bakings carried on in wash pots and big ovens behind the tented households have left memories of their lusciousness in the minds of all who were fortunate enough to have scented them. (16)

"My mother (Mrs. Julia DeFoor Pace) was a member here for 77 years before she died, and she worked up here and she loved it," Mary Daniel said. "Her parents were slaves of the Howells, and they all loved New Hope…This cottonwood tree was there, I don't know how many thousands and thousands have sat under that tree." (17) "At Camp Meeting time, we would all gather, maybe three hundred people out there…If you weren't a member of the church, they'd carry you in the woods…and pray with you and come back, open the door of the church and a few would join," Mrs. Daniel explained. "Everybody would bring food, and they'd spread it outside…The pulpit would be twelve to fifteen ministers. Some of them couldn't get in the door." (18) The meeting would come to a close after the congregation marched around the Tabernacle seven times and sang "The Year of the Jubilee Has Come, Return Ye Ransomed Sinners Home." The preacher would then go to the four corners and blow a trumpet, and then the worshippers would assemble and form a circle for the final blessing. (19)

On the afternoon of March 1, 1875, Atlanta was hit by a storm that spawned a cyclone and swept through Buckhead, destroying the Sardis Methodist Church building and cemetery. (20) The congregation, with the help of the Sardis F. and A. M. Masonic Lodge, built a new, two-story, wood-frame church, and the Masons used the second floor for their meetings. (21)

> "I well remember the day of the cyclone," said James Collie. Cal Garmon and his boy had started to town with a wagonload of cornshucks, when a terrible cloud came up. They turned back and stopped behind the church for protection. The cyclone...blew the church down on top of them. But the Lord was watching out for His own. Cal and his son were not hurt, though one of the mules was killed and the wagon was broken. Old man (Silas) Donaldson had seen them go behind the church for shelter and got to them as soon as he could. He saw the church by a flash of lightning, then by another flash saw the ruins of the church. (22)

***

On October 18, 1876, Evan Howell bought *The Atlanta Constitution* (23) and was responsible for hiring Henry Grady and Joel Chandler Harris as reporters. In the 1890s, Howell turned the newspaper over to his son Clark (1863-1936), who is known to the present generation of his family as Papa Howell. (24)

"When he (Evan) owned *The Constitution*, northern officers wanted to come and inspect the old battleground at Peachtree Creek," Viryln Moore recalled. "They got up there where Collier Road and Peachtree Road run together, one of 'em said, 'You know, somebody had a battery right here, and they were really blowing us to pieces.' Howell said, 'Well, that was my battery. I was defending my land.'" (25)

***

As Buckhead's white population grew, more houses of worship were established. On September 29, 1877, the Pleasant Hill Church was born when William Brown (1832-1897) deeded an acre of land on Paces Ferry Road, at the intersection of Mt. Paran Road, to himself and James Baxter as trustees of the Methodist Church South. A small, white frame sanctuary was built, and the congregation often shared a preacher with other churches, alternating Sundays. One of these early ministers was the Rev. William J. Rolader. (26) The church, which is still in operation, was renamed Paces Ferry Methodist Church in 1957, after it merged with West Wesley Church. (27)

William Brown, the Pleasant Hill Church benefactor known as "Uncle Billy," settled in Buckhead after the Civil War, in which he fought and was injured. He built his home on Paces Ferry Road, which was later the location of Franklin M. Garrett's home at number 3325. (28)

For several years prior to his death, Mr. Brown had been in charge of Fulton County road-working convicts. On August 23, 1897, while working on Powers Ferry Road, an argument ensued between Brown and convict Lon English over an old feud. English struck Brown in the head with a pick. He died three days later and was buried in the Pleasant Hill Church cemetery. (29)

***

In 1877 Rial Bailey Hicks bought Land Lot 99 from his father-in-law, Henry Irby, for four thousand dollars, (30) and when his children married, Hicks gave each child twenty acres of land. When daughter Mary Ophelia (1858-1933) married Seaborn L. Ivey in November of 1878, they were given land on the present-day Ivey Road. When Alice Hicks married Seaborn's brother Russell, they were given land on what is today Old Ivey Road. The original spelling was later changed to Ivy. (31)

Seaborn Lumpkin Ivey was the son of Hardy Ivey, who had a farm "at Cross Keys above Buckhead near Oglethorpe [University]," Sara Hammett (Mrs. Binion) Jordan said of her grandfather. Seaborn Ivey's paternal grandparents were Thomas B. and Sarah Adcock Ivey, from Walton County, Georgia. (32)

***

Henry Irby, Buckhead's premier tavern keeper and family patriarch, died on February 20, 1879, and there are two different stories surrounding his death and physical appearance. One account says he lost consciousness on the evening of February 20 and died two hours later. "My great-grandaddy Henry Irby…was a powerfully built man, tall and lean, and had no ailments he knew of," Mrs. (Ruth Walker) L. O. Williams said. "But my mother told me…that one evening he retired, apparently feeling well, but during the night was seized with severe pains, became unconscious and died within two hours. Mother always thought the trouble was acute appendicitis, which at that era of medicine was not known under that name and was not considered operable." (33)

Sara Jordan said that Irby, "a small man who bought his clothes in the children's department," died of pleurisy at the age of seventy-two. "I think Henry was buried on his property and later moved by [his son] Fulton to Sardis [Church cemetery]." (34)

After her husband's death, Sardis Irby went to live with her son Fulton at Cross Keys. Sardis died on November 22, 1896, at the age of eighty-four, and it is believed that she is "buried in an unmarked grave at Cross Keys," Mrs. Jordan said. Street names of Sardis Way and Fulton Avenue in Buckhead still bear witness to one of the community's first families. (35)

***

Buckhead was the scene of a grisly killing in the summer of 1879, when two of the community's early settlers were unmercifully attacked while they lay sleeping. On the morning of July 25, the bodies of ferryman Martin DeFoor and his wife Susan were found brutally murdered in their bed. The discovery was made by DeFoor's relative and next-door neighbor, Martin Walker, who found that both DeFoors had been decapitated by an axe, which was found in the fireplace. The couple was buried in the Montgomery-DeFoor Cemetery, which is located on Marietta Boulevard in Bolton. It was theorized that an intruder got into the house during the day, hid in an upstairs room, and committed the murders during the night. An investigation was made and suspects were arrested, but the crime was never solved. (36)

CHAPTER FOURTEEN
1880s
One-room Schoolhouses

*T*he rapid growth of the Buckhead community during the 1880s gave rise to one-room school houses, new churches, "jot 'em down" grocery stores, and general sundry stores.

On February 7, 1871, the Georgia Legislature passed the School Law of 1870, establishing free public schools. Twelve members of the Fulton County Board of Education organized their county's schools into five districts; Buckhead lay in the Fourth and Fifth. (1) The Fourth District ran "From Paces ferry road [*sic*] down to Mason and Turners ferry road [*sic*] up this road to Courseys and thence to old Barracks and round the City to Peachtree road [*sic*] and out to Buckhead," and included New Hope School at the New Hope A.M.E. Church [for black students], and Howell's Mill School. The Fifth District began "at Pace's ferry with the ferry road as a Southern boundary across Buckhead and thence to [the] Eastern border of the County with the Decatur wagon road as Southern lines," and included Mt. Olive [for black students] on Pharr Road, Liberty Hill School at Mt. Paran and Garmon roads, and Buckhead School [location unknown]. Because no list of schools by streets survives, it is hard to place the location of many of these institutions. (2)

The Fulton County School Board minutes of June 17, 1886, noted the monthly teachers' salaries. Mrs. Emma L. Williams at New Hope earned $22.50, W. W. Griffin at Howell's Mill was paid $50.00, Rev. John Pharr at Buckhead earned $37.50, Isabella B. Hall at Mt. Olive, $25.00, and Samuel Parks was paid $32.50 for teaching at Liberty Hill. (3)

George Donaldson, Silas Donaldson's son, began school at Pace's schoolhouse, on Paces Ferry road, (present 550 West Paces Ferry Road between Tuxedo and Moores Mill roads). There is no School Board listing for a Pace's schoolhouse; it is possible that this is Buckhead School. George Donaldson described Pace's as a typical one-room school, which was taught by his older sister, Jane, who was known as "Miss Jane." A brush arbor in the school yard was used for classes during hot weather. (4)

Liberty Hill School was opened on Mt. Paran Road at the present-day intersection of Garmon Road, and the school's well can still be seen in front of the house at 1475 Mt. Paran Road. This one-room schoolhouse, divided into two rooms by folding doors, was heated by a large fireplace located at the end of the room. When the weather was too cold to properly heat the school, the children were sent home. "The school session lasted six or seven months, and I got $40 a month!" Mrs. Manston recalled of her teaching at Liberty Hill School from 1898 to 1899. (5)

"We had a big foyer that went into the room, a big room called a cloak-room, where we put all of our coats," Annye Mae Cobb, whose grandfather Edward Marsh was one of the Pleasant Hill Church organizers, recalled. "It had a stove [to keep warm] and some of the older boys, [were paid to] keep the fire going and clean the school." During Miss Cobb's school days at Liberty Hill, one teacher taught all seven grades. (6)

Alice May (Cain) Bailiff recalled a one-room schoolhouse in the 1880s in the heart of Buckhead, on Peachtree Road at Bolling Way, where the students sat on benches instead of at desks. (7)

The Pleasant Hill Church on Paces Ferry Road operated a private school on the premises, and one of the teachers was Miss Ida Williams, for whom the Buckhead Library is named. (8) "The parents got together, found a location, took turns boarding the teacher, and chipped in to pay her meager salary. Some of the textbooks...[used] at that time were "Faye's Elementary Geography, Hyde's Language Books, Branson's Speller, Blue Back Speller, Roudebush Vertical Writer, [and] Beacon's Arithmetic." (9)

***

A popular present to newlyweds continued to be land. When Silas Donaldson's daughter Cora married Dr. George Gilford Chapman, he gave the couple a large parcel of property on Roswell Road, where they built their home (the present-day shopping center site across from Windsor Parkway) and reared five children. "My mother used to give a fish fry every 4th of July and just had all the neighbors from everywhere," Margaret Chapman (Mrs. Leon) Townsend, Donaldson's granddaughter, reminisced. (10)

Dr. Chapman practiced medicine in Buckhead for fifty years, and "He used to say, 'The black people were better to pay him than the white people.' They would always bring him sweet potatoes, all sorts of vegetables and everything to pay their debts, whereas the white people didn't pay as well," Mrs. Townsend said of her father. (11)

Silas Donaldson's daughter Jane gave up teaching school in 1886 and opened a country store on Roswell Road at the present corner of Blackland Road (current site of the Landmark Restaurant). In this store, which she operated until 1931, she sold everything from apples to washboards, food and clothing, to tools and hardware. She "had a bell on a rope strung between her house and the store. If she wasn't behind the counter, customers would ring the bell and she would soon appear to wait on them." Miss Jane's 'jot 'em down' store was known as 'The Little Old Store Beside the Road,' and the community was called Oak Shade. (12)

Marcell Cobb (Mrs. Lon) Simpson explained why these were called 'jot 'em down' stores. "You'd go in and stand behind the counter. You'd say, 'I want sugar,' and he'd go get it and set it down, and then when he finished [filling the order], he'd take a brown paper bag and turn it over. He'd write down the price for all that, add it up." (13)

Miss Jane "had lost money in a bank failure and vowed never to put her trust in such a facility again. So she hid her money in sawdust in a barrel in the store...then one night the store burned down and all the money in it except some gold and silver. With these blackened coins she rebuilt the place." (14)

***

George Powell was another large landowner in Buckhead during the late 1880s who owned a vast tract of land around Roswell Road, from Sardis Way north to East Andrews. His house was located on Roswell Road on the present site of The Vault, and he operated a wagon yard on West Paces Ferry near Peachtree. "When he was a young boy, he had a meat market and drove cattle from Roswell and Alpharetta down [to Buckhead]," to his slaughter pen on Roswell Road, Edith Adams (Mrs. George) Minhinnett said. And, like other landowners, he gave each of his children property when they married. (15)

CHAPTER FIFTEEN
1870s-1880s
As the Wheel Turns

*B*ecause of the fine quality and quantity of clay in the area, Buckhead became one of Georgia's eight main pottery-making centers during the late 1870s and 1880s. These family-owned-and-operated enterprises owned by Bowling Brown, Thomas B. Cofield, and W. W. Rolader were located along creeks, which provided the clay to make their stoneware.

One of the first potters in Buckhead was Bowling Brown, who came from Jugtown, Georgia, in the 1870s and established a pottery at Howell's Mill. The pottery was turned over to his grandson Ulysses Adolphus "Dolphus" Brown in 1888. (1)

Dolphus Brown later leased the Rolader's pottery factory on Moores Mill Road and set up shop as Brown's Pottery, (2) which his son, Horace V., operated until 1933. Bowling Brown's grandsons, Edward C. and Millard, along with Thomas Will Cofield, ran a pottery at 1442 (West) Paces Ferry Road. It lasted until 1911. (3)

Potter Thomas Will Cofield, T. B. Cofield's son, married Dora Holcomb and had nine children. Their daughter Lottke Marriah married Edward W. Cox, whose "family lived around Howell Mill Road and Moores Mill Road, so they named that Cox's Crossroads," Ruth Cox Adams explained. She said that the hill on Howell Mill Road, where the Jewish Home and West Paces Ferry Hospital complexes are today, was called Soapstone Hill. (Franklin M. Garrett says the community was named for Carr Cox, Postmaster at Howell's Mill September 7, 1881.) (4)

Edward Cox's father and his sons operated a tin shop on Howell Mill Road. "I think they did all the tin work on all the houses and everything in Buckhead," Mrs. Adams said. "My father [Edward Cox] built almost all the homes in Morningside, and my mother was a big worker in Sardis Methodist Church." (5)

Mrs. Adams fondly remembers visiting her Will Cofield grandparents on Sundays in the Cox's Crossroads community when she was a child. "We'd play horseshoes and she [Grandmother] would sometimes let me milk the cow, and I'd go with her to gather eggs." Mrs. Adams loved picking and eating cucumbers off the vine in her grandfather's garden, and eating apples from the trees in their yard. She also enjoyed the yearly family picnic in the yard. (6)

"One thing that tickled me so, was my grandfather was superstitious. If a black cat ever crossed the road in front of him, he was gonna' stop until another car come. And if a car didn't come in a few minutes, he'd turn around and go back round and go around a side street," Mrs. Adams mused about her grandfather Cofield, who was also a Fulton County policeman in the early 1900s. "My grandfather rode his horse through Buckhead for the police force." (7)

***

Rolader Pottery was founded by William Washington "W. W." Rolader (1852-1924), son of the Rev. William J. Rolader. W. W. married Arrie Cofield, T. B. Cofield's daughter, and bought fifty acres of land on Moores Mill Road in 1886 from Mrs. Clark (Mary) Howell Sr. for eight hundred dollars, (8) on which he built a small log cabin. The cabin, which was "covered with clapboards for insulation…[and] chinked with potter's clay," (9) was enlarged over the years to accommodate the family of eight children. It was acquired by the Atlanta Historical Society in 1991.

Rolader's pottery shop and kiln were located to the east of the cabin. The clay was dug up at the rear of the property, then crushed by "a mule going round and round in the grinder to grind it up," Donald W. "Pete" Rolader, W. W.'s grandson, explained. The clay was then screened, turned into pottery, and placed outside on planks to dry in the sun. "If it came up a shower, everybody'd run and take all the pottery inside the shop because the rain would ruin it." Once it had dried to the proper stage, the pottery was placed in the kiln "to be burned and hardened. The kiln would be fired late in the evening or afternoon, and we would stay up all night long stoking that kiln with cord wood to burn the pottery properly, and then it would be sealed up and kept for a day or two until the heat got out." The finished jugs, churns, flowerpots, whiskey jugs, chimney flu liners and milk containers were delivered throughout North Georgia. (10)

W. W. was also a farmer "who put the pottery-making on hold during planting and harvesting time," Pete Rolader said. (11)

Rufus M. Rose was a Rolader's Pottery customer who moved to Cobb County from New England before the Civil War. After the war, in which he fought, he returned home and became an apothecary. "But he could not find any alcohol, so he opened up a still on the creek, which is located on what is now called Stillhouse Road" in Vinings, William Dreger III said. (12)

When word of the still reached Atlanta, people went to Rose's business to buy their alcohol. "Later [Rose] opened up a dance pavilion…and it became a very popular place for the young people to come and dance and buy his alcohol," Mr. Dreger explained. When Rose realized he was making more selling alcohol than medicine, he went into the whiskey business and "marketed the liquor under the name of Four Roses." (13)

Mr. Rose lived at 537 Peachtree Street, N. E. (across from the current site of The Doctors Building), in a Victorian-style house, that was built in 1900. When Georgia went dry in 1907, Rose moved his operation to Chattanooga, Tennessee. (14) Years later James H. Elliott Sr. operated the Atlanta Museum in the home, and a large statue of a black horse stood at the side of the front yard. (15)

***

"The state Prohibition in 1907 initiated the demise of Georgia's folk pottery tradition, which had thrived in eight jug towns across the Piedmont area of the state since the 1820s. The Depression, mass production of metal and glass containers and the rise of commercial dairies [which reduced the demand for equipment used in home processing] finished it off. When Rolader closed his shop in the mid-20s [sic], he was one of the last Atlanta potters." (16)

CHAPTER SIXTEEN
1890s
President Benjamin Harrison
Looks for Buckhead

The Atlanta Constitution described the rapidly growing suburbs of Atlanta during the 1890s in an article that appeared on February 9, 1890:

> Wave upon wave, and surge upon surge. It is thus that the expanding surge of Georgia's capital increases its circumference day by day.
>
> Even the shrewdest speculators are scarcely able to keep track of the growth of the city and its suburbs. From Grant Park northward, the broad Boulevard is now completed a distance of one mile, and no city can boast of a finer drive...When the few open gaps are filled up it will be a continuous drive from Grant Park to Buckhead, as the city street and country road are one and the same. (1)

April 15, 1891, was the day the president of the United States *almost* visited Buckhead. During a trip to Atlanta by President and Mrs. Benjamin Harrison, he requested a visit to the site of the Battle of Peachtree Creek, where he had fought as a colonel in the Union Army. A party of City and State officials obliged, but they all headed in the wrong direction. They went northeast instead of northwest, ending up "At a point overlooking the Richmond and Danville Railroad," near the Piedmont Driving Club. After roaming through the woods over unfamiliar terrain, the presidential party discovered they were in the wrong place, and in frustration, they returned to Atlanta. (2)

***

In 1891 the City of Atlanta purchased 122 acres of the Standing Peachtree land along the Chattahoochee River at Peachtree Creek for twenty thousand dollars from the estate of Martin DeFoor, for a water reservoir.

Atop the knoll where Fort Peachtree once stood, a water pumping station was built, which was completed in 1893. (3) The total cost of the project was $809,069.74. (4)

Thomas Moore "was responsible for creating the Atlanta Waterworks," Virlyn Moore Jr. said. "The Atlanta Waterworks originally was an artesian well in the middle of Five Points. Then they moved out to the South River and the reservoir for the Atlanta Waterworks was a lake at Lakewood Park...had a racetrack around it...They produced enough water to supply Atlanta. So Grandpa Moore persuaded them to come out to Bolton, and he gave 'em a right-of-way through his land...about two or three miles on Chattahoochee Avenue [now Coronet Way]...He surveyed the fall of the river, so that's when Atlanta bought that land and put the pumping station right there." (5)

Ellen Newell (Mrs. Wright) Bryan said that her grandfather, Judge George Hillyer, while he was mayor of Atlanta, was responsible for moving the waterworks from Lakewood to Buckhead. "He was known as the 'father of the waterworks'...My mother [Ellen Hillyer Newell] went to Europe with her father before she was married, and before they could go to the museums, they had to visit the waterworks in every big city, because he wanted to see what the waterworks in Atlanta should be like." (6)

**

As the population in the Cox's Crossroads community (around the current Moores Mill and Howell Mill roads) grew, Center Congregational Church and Rosserville School were established to meet their religious and educational needs.

The driving force in organizing the Center Congregational Church around 1887, is said to be Rev. Howell E. Newton, who had grown up poor and "had never worn a pair of 'store shoes' until he was 14 years old." His first formal education occurred when he was 23 years old, and he practiced as a lay preacher for years before entering the Atlanta Seminary in 1901 at the age of 50. (7)

The congregation initially gathered for services at individual homes, but when the membership increased, they met in an old building on Howell Mill Road. On January 23, 1895, Harriet M. Cox deeded a piece of land to the church Trustees for seventy-five dollars. She returned the money immediately, and the building was moved onto the church property. A small, white frame church with a belfry was built between 1897 and 1900, and a parsonage was erected next to the church ten years later. After a fire destroyed the church on June 13, 1941, it was rebuilt in the spring of 1949. (8)

The Church minister, Rev. Lorenzo Dow Rolader, and his wife, Mary Elizabeth (Haley), lived in a one-room log house in Cox's Crossroads, which also was called Minerva, Rosserville, and Rarytown. Nearby, the brother of the Rev. William J. Rolader built a grocery store at the corner of Northside Drive and Moores Mill Road (now the City of Atlanta water tower). (9)

To educate the children in the Cox's Crossroad's community, Fulton County opened Rosserville School on December 5, 1899, on Howell Mill Road, and E. F. Childress was paid fifty dollars a month to teach. (10)

***

On the eastern side of Buckhead, black citizens of the community organized Piney Grove Missionary Baptist Church. Church history states that the founding goes back to February 26, 1826, when "the land for the Piney Grove Baptist Church was purchased." (11) This would date the establishment before the Civil War.

On September 19, 1899, Piney Grove Church Trustees Aaron Hight, Dan Hewit, Sam Robertson, Edgar West, and Willis Arnold bought Land Lot 47, which is located on the present Canterbury Road, between Lenox Square and Lindbergh Plaza, near the Southern Railroad, from John W. Mayson, for fifty dollars. The original deed misidentified the Land Lot as 58; a November 12, 1913 quit-claim deed corrected the error. (12) The Piney Grove congregation worshiped under a brush arbor near an old slave cemetery on their acre of land until they built a wood frame sanctuary, and the Rev. Reese served as the first pastor. (13)

***

During the last part of the century, Peachtree Park encompassed the land now running from approximately Piedmont Road and the Southern Railroad, north out Peachtree Road, to the present Brookhaven community. On June 3, 1890, the Peachtree Park Post Office opened, with Carlos N. Peek serving as the first Postmaster; he was succeeded by Mrs. Annie L. Barford and Seaborn O. King. The post office was renamed Roxboro in 1899 and was closed on September 5, 1903. In 1915 part of the property was subdivided by the McKenzie Trust Company into a residential neighborhood. (14)

CHAPTER SEVENTEEN
1900
Turn-of-the-Century Buckhead

"Buckhead was country in those days."
- Sara Jordan

"The census of 1900 listed approximately 236 heads of families, both white and black, still predominately farmers, farm laborers, blacksmiths, carpenters, and a couple of potters" in Buckhead. (1)

The new century spelled the end of the most famous landmark in Buckhead when Henry Irby's log tavern was torn down in 1900. (2) In its place James Silvanus Donaldson, who had bought the property from Perry Humphries, who had bought it from the Irbys, built a building which would continue to be an important site in Buckhead's history. (3)

Perry Humphries owned property in the center of Buckhead and lived in the midst of his domain in a house located on the present Sardis Way (current Bank South location), and the park at the five points was his front yard. (4) He owned a blacksmith shop on Peachtree Road (now Buckhead Plaza) run by John Dobbs, a black blacksmith. "John, swinging his hammer under the big sweet gum tree was a familiar sight." (5)

Humphries also owned a wagon yard and a slaughter pen. "Mr. Humphries bought and sold or slaughtered all kinds of animals...and each week day you could see his two-mule team pulling a load of meat to Atlanta." At his wagon yard, "Mountaineers...drove their cattle, hogs, and turkeys down from the hills [and] camped for the night...There was a rough, empty house on the yard where the men slept on hay—others slept in their wagons. There was a charge for the men, the mules and the animals—something like five cents a head for the mules, and a correspondingly low amount for the men and the stock." (6)

***

The Rial Bailey Hicks family sold their house on Ivey Road and moved to 2725 Peachtree Road (behind the present-day Garden Hills Theater).

"The house was a two-story wooden house…with beautiful parquet floors and crystal chandeliers," Sara Hammett (Mrs. Binion) Jordan said of her great-grandparent's home. When Mr. Hicks died in 1902, "his Buckhead property was divided into ten parcels, one for each living child and his widow, Sarah Jane Irby Hicks." May Otella Hicks (Mrs. James Silvanus) Donaldson moved her family into the home to care for her mother and inherited the home when her mother died. It was torn down in 1982. (7)

Mary Ophelia (Hicks) and Seaborn L. Ivey built a home on her inherited parcel of land at 2737 Peachtree Road and moved from their home on Ivey Road. On this property, Ivey "operated a sawmill and sold wood for fireplaces in Buckhead," Mrs. Jordan explained. "They had a lovely garden and farmed vegetables for the household," and they had an annual barbecue. Ivey also owned land on West Paces Ferry Road. He later sold the land to John W. Grant. (8)

Edna Corrine Ivey (1882-1979), Seaborn's daughter, married George W. Hammett in 1906 and moved onto Cain's Hill Place. The following November, their daughter Sara (Jordan) was born. Hammett operated a wagon yard in Buckhead. "Today you would call it a parking lot," Sara Jordan explained. (9)

Seaborn Ivey sold his Peachtree Road land to Beverly DuBose Sr. in 1919 and moved to Piedmont Road, on the site of the present Peachtree-Piedmont Crossing Shopping Center. "Grandpa sold that land to Beverly DuBose and he wanted to pay Grandpa in Coca-Cola stock. Well, Grandpa refused it, he wanted the money," Mrs. Jordan mused. (10) The property is now the parking lot for Second Ponce de Leon Baptist Church.

***

Buckhead resident Robert Dorsey opened a grocery store in the heart of Buckhead on the corner of Peachtree and East Paces Ferry roads, and delivered groceries in his horse-drawn buggy. The Dorseys lived on Piedmont Road, where they reared four children. After going out of business around 1907 because of unpaid grocery bills, the family moved to South Georgia. "He had quite a lot of wealthy customers," Dorsey's daughter Agnes Dorsey Roberts said. "That was his trouble; they didn't all pay him, and he went broke." (11)

***

Annye Mae Cobb remembered that, during this period, Garmon Road "was just a little trail, like an old-fashioned wagon road." She and her sister

68

Marcelle (Mrs. Lon) Simpson and their other siblings attended Liberty Hill School. Their father, William R. Cobb, son of William and Muhuldy (McDuffey) Cobb, came to the area after the Civil War. (12)

***

Ruby Spruill (Mrs. George) Chapman, who was born in 1897, recalled that George Brumbelow operated a blacksmith shop on the point at Peachtree and Roswell roads (the park). He had wooden benches in his shop, where customers could wait for their repairs. (13)

Mrs. Chapman is the great-granddaughter of Samantha (1805-1835) and James Power (1790-1870). Power emigrated from Ireland and settled along the Chattahoochee, where he established Power's Ferry in 1835. Their son Samuel married Margaret Samantha Spruill, daughter of Lizzie (Ball) and William Spruill, and became Ruby Spruill Chapman's parents. (14) Ruby married George Chapman Jr. son of the Buckhead doctor. (15)

***

The Axson C. Minhinnett family moved from Roswell to Buckhead at the turn of the century and settled on Wieuca Road, when it was still a dirt road. (16) Minhinnett's grandfather and father were craftsmen who had left London, England, and after a brief stay in Philadelphia, settled in Roswell, Georgia, in the mid 1800s. (17)

Axson Minhinnett operated a general store in the center of Buckhead in the two-story building that he rented from James Sylvanus Donaldson on Roswell Road (site of Irby's Tavern). He paid seventy-five dollars a month for the upstairs space, and sub-leased part of it to a Masonic lodge and a small restaurant. (18) On the ground floor of the building, Minhinnett operated a soda fountain that "was the community's first cool drink emporium. Here was dispensed Coca-Cola and, presumably, sarsaparilla, gayola, ice cold lemonade and homemade ice cream." (19)

When Axson C. Minhinnett Jr. married Myrtice Power around 1913, her father George Power gave the couple land on Roswell Road, where they built a home called The Big House (present site of The Vault). A. C. Jr. was an attorney, who worked in the tax office at the courthouse in downtown Atlanta. (20)

CHAPTER EIGHTEEN
1903-1910
Buckhead Retreat

"We're goin' t'Buckhead for th' summah."
- Said by some vacation-planning Atlantans.

*T*he new century brought many changes to rural Buckhead, propelling it into a new destiny as many of the civic leaders of Atlanta moved their families to the community. Some, who lived in today's downtown, bought large tracts of land in Buckhead and built summer cottages, which later became permanent homes. Many moved to the "suburbs" along the Peachtree Road corridor, between Eighth and Fourteenth streets, to get away from the noise of city life. When the noise followed them north with the extension of the trolley to Fourteenth Street, these suburban pioneers once more looked for the peace of the country.

Many of these Buckheadians, such as Jack J. Spalding, Robert F. Maddox, John W. Grant, John M. Slaton, Phinizy Calhoun, and John K. Ottley lived on vast pieces of land, on which they operated small farms where they raised cows, chickens, goats, horses, and mules. Their large gardens produced fresh vegetables for their tables.

These new Buckhead residents were not the idle rich. They were the bankers, mayors, governors, doctors, lawyers, and businessmen, who gave both their time and money to civic and social organizations in order to make Atlanta a better place to live. In moving to Buckhead, they joined a community of farmers, ferrymen, mill owners, and potters, whose roots ran deep in the community.

The trolley line was extended to Buckhead in 1907, creating a major change for the small rural community by allowing workers to easily get to and from their jobs in Atlanta, and students to travel to the city for school. The trolley with *Buckhead* on it provided not only transportation, but later it was also a source of amusement for many of the Buckhead children.

***

Jack J. Spalding (1856-1938), a lawyer and founder of King and Spalding law firm, bought Reuben Arnold Sr.'s Victorian gothic-style home (built in the late 1880s) in Deerland Park, (where Piedmont Hospital now stands). He moved his wife, Elizabeth (Hughes), and their two sons and a daughter from the corner of Peachtree Street and Fourteenth Street to their new home, which was located on the site of the Battle of Peachtree Creek. Their nearest neighbor was Col. William Lawson Peel, who lived across the street on the present Darlington Apartment property. Spalding, born in Morganfield, Kentucky, to Susan (Johnson) and Ignatius A. Spalding, married in 1877 and moved to Atlanta in 1882 to practice law. (1)

"At the time they moved north…[Atlanta] used to stop right there at Fifteenth Street, where the Christian Science Church is," Spalding's grandson and namesake, Jack Spalding, explained. "The Colliers owned everything north of that, right on past Brookwood Station, and they wouldn't sell an inch, so that kind of forced the town to grow over towards Inman Park and towards West End. When 'Wash' Collier died, the land came on the market." (2)

"My grandfather kept two cows and a mule till the day he died. He had an acre of garden [for] vegetables, and had another acre on which he raised feed for the cows," Mr. Spalding said. "There was also a barn in the back with a privy for the servants." Deerland Park had its own train flag stop. In 1912 the Spalding's son, Hughes, married Bolling Phinizy from Athens, and the newlyweds moved next door to his parents' home on Peachtree Road and raised their four children, Jack, Hughes, Bolling ("Bobo"), and Phinizy. (3)

Peachtree Road, from Brookwood bridge to Buckhead, was widened "into an 80-foot boulevard" on property donated along both sides of the road by property owners. The work was completed at the end of March 1908. (4) "My grandfather Spalding was on the County Commission then, and he said the reason Peachtree north of Fifteenth Street is six lanes instead of the traditional four is because he had traveled and seen the boulevards of Europe and insisted on widening Peachtree, making a monumental avenue out of it," Jack Spalding explained. (5)

***

Some Atlanta families escaped to the coolness of the Buckhead forest during the hot summers and built cottages, which they also used as weekend retreats throughout the year. Before long, these vacation homes were replaced by grand versions of Tudor and Colonial homes, and Italian villas, many designed by noted architects Philip T. Shutze and Neel Reid.

The first of these new residents to have a cottage in Buckhead was James L. Dickey Sr. (1847-1910), who bought 405 acres of land on (456 West) Paces Ferry Road, in 1903, from Dr. James H. Smith for six thousand dollars. (6) In 1911 Mr. Dickey built a replica of George Washington's home, Mount Vernon, which he named Arden.

The second resident along unpaved (West) Paces Ferry Road was Robert Foster Maddox (1870-1965), president and Chairman of the Board of First National Bank. Maddox was the son of Nancy (Reynolds) and Col. Robert Flournoy Maddox, who came to Atlanta from LaGrange, Georgia, in 1858, and founded the Maddox-Rucker Banking Company in 1879. Through subsequent bank mergers, this bank has been named American National Bank, First National Bank of Atlanta, and Wachovia. (7)

Robert Foster Maddox purchased seventy-five acres of land for a summer home and farm across the road from his friend, James Dickey, in 1904 for $6,578 (8), and built a small, two-story, greystone and shingle country home. At the time he and his wife, Lollie (Baxter, daughter of Nathaniel Baxter of Nashville, Tennessee) and their two sons, Robert Jr. and Baxter, lived with his parents on Peachtree Street at Ellis Street, now the site of the Ritz Carlton Hotel. (9)

"Mr. Dickey was my father's best friend," Laura Maddox (Mrs. Edward D.) Smith said. "Papa always said that the only thing that came between him and Jim Dickey was Paces Ferry Road." (10)

Mr. Maddox later told a newspaper reporter:

When I bought my place on Paces Ferry Rd. [*sic*] in 1904 I had no idea I would ever live there. There were only two or three stores. I built a small house on my 75 acres and kept a few cows and chickens. I would go out in the summer and back in the winter. But soon it became a very desirable section. (11)

***

John Marshall Slaton (1866-1955) built his home on the west side of Peachtree Road, in 1908, in the center of Buckhead, on an eighty-five acre tract of land. His wife, Sarah Frances (Sally Fanny) Grant (1870-1945), inherited the property from her father, William Daniel Grant, in 1901. (12)

Mrs. Slaton's grandfather, John Thomas Grant (1813-1887), who was born in Grantville, Georgia, was a graduate of the University of Georgia and later a state senator. He was also a railroad engineer who "laid out the railroads and built them and financed them, and that's how he made his money," William Rudolph said of his great-grandfather-in-law. "'Dearie' (Mrs. John W. Grant) used to tell us that he was really one of the deciding forces on making Atlanta the terminus." (13)

John Thomas Grant married Martha Cobb Jackson, who was the daughter of William H. and Mildred (Cobb) Jackson, and a granddaughter of Georgia governor James Jackson. The Grants had three children: William Daniel, Mildred Lewis, and John Thomas. (14)

John Thomas Grant's son William D. (W. D.) (1837-1901) was born in Athens, Georgia, and acquired his Buckhead land before the Civil War. During the war he served as a captain in Gen. Nathan Bedford Forrest's Brigade in Tennessee and Kentucky and was superintendent of defenses around Atlanta. He married Sarah Frances Reid (1839-1920), daughter of William and Martha (Wingfield) Reid, and they had three children—John William; Sarah Frances; and William Reid, who died at birth. (15)

Sarah Frances Grant's first marriage to her relative Thomas Cobb Jackson, a lawyer in practice with his father, Capt. Henry Jackson, ended in scandal and suicide. The Gate City Bank in Atlanta closed its doors on January 22, 1893, because of a shortage of cash, and Lewis Redwine, an assistant cashier and a friend of Jackson's, was accused of embezzlement. The following day Jackson, who was terribly depressed over the bank scandal, sat in a buggy in front of his father's house and shot and killed himself with a revolver. Redwine was captured two days later, tried for his crime, and served time in the penitentiary. (16)

Sarah Grant Jackson then married John Slaton, son of William Franklin Slaton, who was a Civil War veteran from Meriwether County and superintendent of the Atlanta Public Schools in 1870. John Slaton served as president of the Senate in the Georgia Legislature and was elected governor in 1913. During his term as governor, Slaton became an integral force in the Leo Frank case. (17)

The Slaton farm fronted Peachtree Road in the heart of Buckhead at Pharr Road, N.W., and their tudor-style house, which was called Wingfield after Mrs. W. D. Grant's mother, sat where the Slaton Manor retirement apartments are now. The driveway meandered through the woods, from Peachtree Road to a rear fieldstone portal on Andrews Drive, which is now the entry for the house at number 2993 at the corner of Slaton Drive. (18)

Mrs. Slaton, who "never had any children but was very interested in all sorts of civic activities," was known for growing prize-winning roses, niece Betty Slaton (Mrs. John) Wallace said. (19) The Slatons operated a farm with cows and horses, and "had a riding rink in the back, where they had harness racing," Buckhead resident, William Dreger III, remembered. (20)

***

Another newcomer to Buckhead was Dr. Methvin T. Salter, who moved to 3225 Peachtree Road from Whitehall Street in 1910. He built his home across from Chief George Mathieson on the site of the present Maier & Berkele Jewelry Store. (21)

***

On May 21, 1910, four years after the death of Wesley Gray Collier, the executors of his estate, Walter Pemberton Andrews and Eretus Rivers, sold five hundred acres of the undeveloped Collier land, from Peachtree Creek north to the present Andrews Drive, to the Peachtree Heights Park Company, for $375,000. (22) The following year, Peachtree Battle Avenue was developed, and roads and avenues were created with names that are still an integral part of Buckhead: Habersham, West Wesley, Rivers, Cherokee, Vernon, Muscogee, and Habersham Way. This development, which was called Peachtree Heights Park, was described as a residential "section excelled nowhere in beauty and desirability." (23)

Around 1910 Walter P. Andrews (1865-1935) and his wife, Leontine (Chisolm), built a stucco and half-timbered, English-style cottage home on Peachtree Road (the present-day site of the Cathedral of St. Philip). On the grounds he had "a stable, kennels, and a building over the natural spring on the property. The latter was the site for a famed annual barbecue held by the Andrews for state legislators from around 1910 to 1923." (24) In the 1920s the Andrews' estate was sold and the house was repositioned to face Andrews Drive. They moved to Florida, where Andrews died in 1935; Mrs. Andrews returned to Atlanta, where she lived until her death in 1962. (25)

Andrews, who was a lawyer by profession, moved to Atlanta in 1891 from Montgomery County, North Carolina, and went into practice with Hoke Smith. Andrews became a leading force in state political circles when he served on Governor Joseph M. Terrell's staff from 1903 until 1907, co-managed Woodrow Wilson's Georgia presidential campaign, and served terms in the Georgia Legislature as a state representative and senator from 1915 until 1918. Andrews was also a United States "presidential commissioner to the Mediterranean and Balkan states for the Panama-Pacific Exposition of San Francisco (1915), and was appointed a special ambassador to Italy, Spain, Portugal, and Turkey." (26)

***

On a Sunday afternoon in August of 1910, Mr. and Mrs. C. S. Honor rode through Buckhead, returning from the funeral of their infant son, and found "children playing in the street." With approval of the Sessions of First Presbyterian and North Avenue churches, they established a Sunday School program as a memorial to their child, and held the first class in an empty Buckhead store on September 23, 1910. This school later led to the formation of the Peachtree Presbyterian Church in 1919. (27)

CHAPTER NINETEEN
1900-1910
More Children, More Schools

"Black students rode to high school in the white ladies' cars."
- Helen Few

$\mathcal{F}$ulton County continued to build more schools in Buckhead in order to accommodate the growing number of children in the community. A school was built prior to 1911 on Balloon Road (now 3720 Peachtree Dunwoody Road), but because of incomplete school records, it is impossible to determine the name of the school, or if it was for white or black students. (1) Over the years, the school property changed hands many times, and for a period, a Mr. Sawyer operated a still in the house. The Stanley P. Meyersons bought the property around 1946 and modernized the home for themselves and their four children. The house still exists as a private home. (2)

***

R. L. Hope Elementary School was built on Piedmont Road off of Peachtree Road (behind the present Nikko Hotel), in 1909, on land donated by Dr. Richard Lucien Hope. One hundred ten children were served in the two classrooms, and there was "a room for teaching domestic science, fitted up with a handsome range and other conveniences for instruction in cooking." Miss Ida Williams was the school's first principal, and Miss Willie McNeill the first teacher. (3)

"[The school] was a wooden school building that had four teachers. The sixth and seventh grades were both taught by the principal, Ida Williams. She was a fair lady, but a firm disciplinarian. She wasn't afraid to use her switch if it was necessary," Joseph K. Heyman, who attended with his siblings Dora, Herman, and Joe, reminisced. "We had no running water in the school, and the school had a well behind it, the kind of well you put a bucket down and rolled a crank to get it up...We had two outhouses back behind the building, one for girls and one for boys." (4) The frame school building was replaced in 1925 with a large one-story brick building.

Orphaned at the age of eleven, Dr. Hope came to Atlanta from the Dahlonega area to live with an aunt and later attended medical school with the help of a brother. He began buying land in Buckhead. Dr. Hope, who lived on his twenty acres of land at the present Piedmont and Rock Springs roads, is credited with persuading the "Rev. Peter Marshall to come to Atlanta as pastor of the Westminster Presbyterian Church." (5)

***

New Hope Elementary School, established by the Fulton County Board of Education in 1910 at New Hope Church on Arden Road, became an important element in the black community of Buckhead. Children from Irby Alley, in the center of Buckhead, and the Happy Hill community at Collier and Howell Mill roads, attended the school, which met in the church. Later, classes were moved into a one-room schoolhouse, which was erected in the churchyard, and a second room was subsequently added. "They had one teacher. She would sit between the rooms," Mary Daniel (1904-1995), a former student, remembered. There was no running water, and the "facilities" were outside privies. (6)

Mrs. Daniel walked three miles each day, six days a week, to New Hope to attend school. In the winter, "It would be cold, we'd have on socks or stockings over our shoes, and sometimes it would be so cold you couldn't get the socks or stockings off." (7)

Helen Few and her brother, Milton, lived on Northside Drive with ten siblings and their parents, Mamie (Moses) and William Few, who came from Oconee County, Georgia. When the Few children attended New Hope School, there were two teachers: "One teacher taught first through fifth grades and the next teacher taught sixth and seventh". Ms. Few remembers when Arden was a dirt road, where the only home belonged to Walter C. Hill. (8)

After elementary school, the New Hope graduates went downtown to Washington High School, and the chauffeurs of the "well-to-do" in Buckhead often drove the students to school in "the white ladies' cars," Ms. Few said. Many of these drivers would wait for the students at a certain point to take them downtown for their classes, that began at 12:00 and ran only half a day. (9)

CHAPTER TWENTY
1912
Johnson Town

"It was a real nice, friendly community."
- Janie Johnson

*M*ore black neighborhoods were developed in Buckhead, and the citizens of both colors lived side by side in relative harmony with general respect for each other. There was often a mutual dependency, based on one's need for help in the home and on the farms, and a need for jobs.

In 1890 and 1891 the Suburban Land Improvement Company developed the Peachtree Park Subdivision, across from the present Lenox Square, and attempted to sell (1) two hundred and forty-three lots, measuring 23 feet by 143 feet, along Fulton and Atlanta avenues, Peachtree Park and Lakeside Drive. (2)

The Peachtree Park enterprise met with only modest success because of its location and the lack of transportation, and by 1904 only forty lots had been sold. In 1912 this neighborhood took off in another direction when a black South Georgia couple, Columbus and Callie Johnson, bought from D. N. Williams, for six hundred dollars, fifteen lots, which encompassed a square block along Railroad Avenue from Central Avenue (now Oak Valley Road) to Fulton Avenue (now Lenox Road). (3) "There was a house on the property when my grandfather bought it," Johnson's grandson and namesake, Columbus Johnson, said. When the Johnson's four children grew up and married, "He built four more houses on the property for the families." (4)

Another Johnson grandchild, Anna Smith, described her grandparent's home as, "a big house...had about four or five big rooms...and it was fixed real nice, but they had to go to the toilet outside." (5)

Soon, other black families moved into the community and it became known as Johnson Town "because my grandfather was named Johnson," Columbus Johnson said. "Some people just called it 'Black folk's town'...

[but] they called it Johnson Town 'cause it was Johnson's town." (6) Some of these new residents bought property and built homes; others bought homes or rented. The street was filled with "hipped-roofed cottages, modest shot-gun dwellings, and bungalows." (7)

The religious needs of Johnson Town were served by Zion Hill Baptist Church on Railroad Avenue. The wood-frame church "was a Methodist church when it was first built. It turned into a Baptist church later," Mr. Johnson explained. (8)

Carter Elementary School educated the children of Johnson Town and the surrounding communities of Willistown and Piney Grove. It is not known when the two-room Fulton County school was built, but it was there in 1919 on the corner of Wright and Wolfe avenues. A larger, four-room building later replaced the small school. (9) Those students who continued on to high school rode the trolley downtown to David T. Howard School in Summerhill, or to Washington High School.

Parthenia Jetter and her brother, Cornelius Sawyer, grew up in the nearby Piney Grove neighborhood. They first attended school at Piney Grove Church, and "from there they moved us on to Johnson Town to Carter School," Parthenia Jetter said. (10)

It has been said that Johnson Town was created in order to provide servants and workers for the affluent white Buckhead families. Some Johnson Town residents became entrepreneurs within the community, operating grocery stores and a restaurant, which became a popular night spot, providing music, dancing, and drinks for the community.

"There were no servants for the rich people who lived in that area," Mr. Johnson said. "So they got together and created this place for the blacks...The Withams, the Elliots, the Ottleys ...and...Havertys." (11)

"Everybody knew everybody, and there wasn't all this crime and stuff," Janie Johnson said. "We would just go off, pull our door up, didn't have to lock 'em. There wouldn't be nothing disturbed when you'd get back." (12)

"It was nice," Leonard Walker remembered. "It was a community and everybody in the community knowed each other and raised each other...it was a place to grow up where everybody took care of each other...A community where everybody stuck together. It was like a town full of relations...My granddaddy, Henry Walker, owned apartment buildings and couple of duplexes, so he was sorta like a king pin that kept the community together." (13)

"It was good, nice," Parthenia Jetter said of the Piney Grove and Johnson Town communities. (14)

John K. Ottley III, whose grandfather's home was across from the black community (now Lenox Square Mall), remembered going to Johnson Town in the mid-thirties with his grandfather, John K. Ottley, to collect rents for houses he owned. He "was in property management and managed a lot of real estate in Bagley Park and Johnson Town. At that time you went weekly to collect the rent in cash." He said Johnson Town at that time had dirt trails instead of streets, and "there was no sewage system, no indoor plumbing of any sort. I imagine the original homes down there had wells." (15)

The black community of Willistown was located to the west of Peachtree Road. "'Cross the street just about one-half mile from Peachtree, down Peachtree-Dunwoody," explained Janie Johnson, whose family moved to the community from Thompson, Georgia, in the early twenties. (16) Willistown "was just a little community of about ten families, and that was also created for servants in that area," Columbus Johnson added. (17)

CHAPTER TWENTY-ONE
1911-1916
Buckhead for Sale?

$\mathscr{I}$n the spring of 1911, a rumor spread that Buckhead was going to be purchased by Robert F. Maddox and John W. Grant. In rebuttal, Mr. Maddox responded, "'It's all a joke. I certainly would like to buy the property, and remove certain rough board shacks, which have recently been erected on it — negro restaurants, barber shops, livery stables, etc., but I am afraid the price would be rather high.'" The rumor started at a luncheon given by Mr. and Mrs. Sam Inman, when Maddox was teased about buying the community. (1)

***

In 1911, Fulton County constructed two alms houses on Wieuca Road, in the present Chastain Park, to shelter the poor. The large, red brick building (now Galloway School) housed the white citizens of the county, and a white frame structure (now Arts and Crafts Center) housed the black citizens. (2)

***

The newly-built white clapboard Buckhead Baptist Church sanctuary on (West) Paces Ferry Road (present-day site of Buckhead Market Place), constructed under the direction of James S. Donaldson, was dedicated on November 19, 1911. Organized by Dr. Charles W. Daniel, Pastor of the First Baptist Church of Atlanta, Mr. John M. Green, and Mr. W. W. Gaines, the small congregation first held tented revival meetings on the present site of The Lodge At East Village Grille, at 248 Buckhead Avenue, across from the library. This was later the site of the City of Atlanta Fire Department, Station 21. (3) When the congregation outgrew the church facilities, Sunday School classes were held in various buildings around Buckhead. (4) The Rev. A. T. Peacock ministered to the congregation from 1911 until 1915; succeeding ministers were Chauncey L. Foote, J. S. Edenfield, W. J. D. Upshaw, J. H. Fuller, Dr. J. Weston Bruner and Geoffrey C. Hinchelwood. (5)

***

The development of Buckhead as a permanent and viable residential community continued, as more homes were built on roads such as (West) Paces Ferry, Andrews, (West) Wesley, and Peachtree. Some of the large land holdings in Buckhead were subdivided, creating new roads and home sites.

Sixty-one acres of the Benjamin Plaster estate were sold to American Securities Company of Georgia in 1911. The property was subdivided, and the new neighborhood was called Peachtree Hills Place. After later merging with Peachtree Terrace and Peachtree Hurst subdivisions, the area is known today as Peachtree Hills. (6)

***

Following the death of James Dickey, Sr. in the spring of 1911, shortly after building his home, Arden, his three hundred-acre estate on (West) Paces Ferry Road was sold to Charles Black's Tuxedo Park Company for $75,000. The Dickey land was subdivided into large tracts and sold at auction for prices ranging from $2,000 to $2,500 per lot. (7)

The Atlanta Journal extolled this new development of large wooded lots, which "average 250 feet in width and from 700 to 1500 feet in depth...[with roads and driveways] winding along by an enchanting stream and through attractive woods...The future of Pace's Ferry Road in the light of present and projected development is as firmly fixed as that of Peachtree." (8)

***

In 1912 Robert F. Maddox, who had served as mayor of Atlanta from 1909-1910, built a permanent English Tudor-style home, called Woodhaven, on his (West) Paces Ferry Road property (the present-day Governor's Mansion site) for sixty thousand dollars. "They decided that they wanted to have a bigger, more important place. [So] they jacked up [the country home] with mules and moved it to the left," Maddox's daughter, Laura Maddox (Mrs. Edward D.) Smith, explained. (9)

"Of course our place and our way of life were self-sustaining to a large extent," Mrs. Smith explained. "We grew our own vegetables...We had an enormous laundry, a big old thing in the basement that you would hang sheets on...We had a maid...a cook and a butler and a chauffeur...about five house servants." A big lunch was served daily for the help, and "the men all ate on the back porch and the women all ate in the kitchen." On the property there was a house for the laundress, and another for the white caretaker, who oversaw the maintenance of the yard and the small farm. There were five servant's quarters in the house. (10)

Mrs. Maddox had a beautiful garden with "five grass terraces, carved out of a hillside...covered in flowers, and the area around the garden pool at the bottom served as a sort of amphitheater." Statues representing the four seasons had been purchased by Mr. Maddox in Italy and were placed around the pond. (11) "My mother loved gardening, and our garden was one of the most famous gardens in the South," Mrs. Smith said proudly. (12)

When Mrs. Smith was nine, her father had a miniature English Tudor-style playhouse built for her, which they named Villa Lauretta. "It had a bedroom, a living room, dining room and kitchen. Everything in sort of three-fourth size, and I could sleep in the bed...Mother had miniature-size silver, china, glasses; it must have taken her forever to collect it all. In the kitchen, I had a little miniature waffle iron, running water, electric stove. Only thing it didn't have was a bathroom...it was charming. It had window boxes Mother had filled with flowers, had a little brick walk. I loved to take care of that little house. I had my friends over to parties...I [also] had a pony and a pony cart, and I grew up with a magic childhood," Mrs. Smith reminisced. (13)

***

William Bailey Lamar (1853-1928), a former United States Congressman from Florida, and his wife, Ethel (Toy Healey), widow of Charles A. Healey, built a home on (801 West) Paces Ferry. The large two-story, cream-colored stucco home they called Villa Lamar sat on two hundred acres of wooded land that was once the site of the old Hardy Pace home. (14)

"Supplies [for the home's construction] were unloaded in Vinings for everybody in this neighborhood out here and brought over by mule," Reuben A. Garland Jr., whose family later owned the Lamar property, explained. "It was a heck of a lot closer to Vinings than Brookwood Station, or the Terminal Station." (15) The Lamars moved to Washington, D. C., in 1914, where he became a judge and commissioner to the Panama-Pacific International Exposition in San Francisco, and Villa Lamar was sold to Sanders McDaniel (1867-1934) and his wife, Anne (Henderson) (1867-1934). Mr. McDaniel was the son of former Georgia Governor Henry McDaniel. When McDaniel's daughter Harriet married Rembrandt Marshall, they moved into the house with her parents. "During the McDaniel/Marshall ownership the house is said to have been known as Hollywood and Twin Oaks," Franklin M. Garrett said. (16)

In 1958, when the last member of the Marshall family had died, the property surrounding the house was subdivided, and Kingswood Subdivision was created. Reuben A. Garland Sr. and his wife, Fauntleroy (Moon), bought the house and moved the family from a home on Peachtree Road, north of Lenox, where they had resided since 1937. The house that the Garlands renamed Newcastle, (17) sits today at the corner of West Paces Ferry and Kingswood roads.

***

James W. Morrow bought twenty acres along (966 West) Paces Ferry Road in 1914 and built a large home of rock quarried from the rear of the building, and a stable for his horses. The house burned down about 1929, and in 1932 John Ogden bought the property and built a home that looks like a castle. Pace Academy bought the property in 1950 for a private school. (18)

Another new resident of Paces Ferry was Mrs. Howell Jackson, who built a summer home on fourteen acres at number 490. Later, owners of this property were the Nym McCulloughs and the Reuben Arnolds. (19)

***

Peachtree Road was also developing into a residential street on both ends of the central business district. Along the west side of Peachtree Road, just south of (West) Wesley Road, Hudson Moore bought a lot at number 2672 from Charles T. Hopkins, in 1913, and built a two-story Tudor-style home. (20) The following year John B. Whitman began building a Neel Reid-designed home at 2662 Peachtree Road; it was completed by Whitman's son-in-law Charles Dannals Jr. (21) Jacob N. Hirsch bought a lot at 2652 Peachtree Road from E. Rivers and built a home in 1916. (22)

***

On Peachtree Road at Fulton Avenue (Lenox Road), north of the Buckhead business district, John K. Ottley, president of the First National Bank, built a summer home in 1913, on property which now encompasses Lenox Square Mall. The Tudor-style home, which was named Joyeuse, "started out as a summer home, a place to get out from town for weekends," Ottley's grandson John K. Ottley III explained. Eventually the Ottley family moved to Joyeuse from their home on Peachtree Road at North Avenue (present-day site of North Avenue Presbyterian Church). (23)

Joyeuse was a large estate, with horses, stables, and a playing field on the East Paces Ferry Road end of the lot, where children in the neighborhood came to play. "The place was big enough that they had one or two golf holes in the front yard...[where John Ottley] used to go out and practice golf," Joseph K. Heyman recalled of his neighbor." (24)

Mr. Ottley also had the Ottley Station at the Southern Railroad tracks at the rear of his property, where he could flag down the train for a ride into downtown Atlanta. The family enjoyed picnicking along the creek in their backyard, where they would "have lunch and dabble their feet in the water," Mr. Ottley said. (25)

"Down Roxboro there's a little street called Canter Road and another called Marian," Mr. Ottley continued. His grandfather named one street Canter Road because he used to ride his horse down there, and Marian was named for Ottley's second wife. (26)

"Dad always liked the outdoors, and he had a great interest in hunting," Mr. Ottley said of his father. "He (John Jr.) went hunting many afternoons after school with the sheriff of Buckhead." (27)

**

In 1913 the Arthur Heyman family moved to 3350 Peachtree Road from their home on Washington Street, which was located "about where the south parking lot of the Atlanta Fulton County Stadium sits," son Joseph K. Heyman said. Arthur Heyman's father was a peddler, who came to America in 1852 from Essen, Prussia, and settled in LaGrange, Georgia, to be near the railroad. Arthur Heyman graduated from the University of Georgia in 1888, received his law degree in 1893, and moved to Atlanta to practice law. He worked for the firm that became known as (Hugh) Dorsey, Brewster, (Albert) Howell and Heyman, now called Heyman and Sizemore. (28)

In 1896 Arthur married Minna Simon of New Orleans, and the newlyweds lived in the home Arthur built on Washington Street. "He had a very green thumb and liked to do things in the yard, and somewhere along the line must have persuaded my mother that they wanted to have a place out in the country," Mr. Heyman explained. In 1913 they built a house that fronted on (3348) Peachtree Road a bit south of the present GA 400 highway. "We had a beautiful grove of trees in the back...which we used for a picnic area." He said he found Indian arrowheads and Civil War bullets on the property. (29)

"My family was the first Jewish family anywhere out on the north side of town...I was the only Jewish student at (R. L. Hope)...I was probably the only Jewish child that most of those other children knew," Mr. Heyman explained. From R. L. Hope, he went on to Fulton High School. "My dad had his law office in downtown Atlanta, not too far from where the school was located, and I'd drive down with him in the morning," and return home by streetcar. The trolley fare to Buckhead "was seven cents, and six cents more to ride the extra mile that I had to ride to get to my house. On days when I didn't feel very flushed, I would get off in Buckhead and walk that last mile." (30)

***

Buckhead resident, George Mathieson, James L. Mathieson's son, became chief of the Fulton County Police in 1913, a job he held for thirty-two years. He joined the force in February of 1900 at a salary of fifty dollars a month. "He was supposed to supply his own horse, pay for his uniform, feed himself, his family and his horse on that." Patrols were done on horseback, and the patrol uniform consisted of "broad-brimmed black hats and uniforms with small "Peter Pan" collars and bright badges." In 1911, when horses were replaced by motorized vehicles, Mathieson rode a motorcycle, "and after becoming chief, he...used...the first car in the county police service—a four-cylinder Oldsmobile." (31)

George Mathieson married Annie Belle Carroll in 1907, and they had a daughter, Mildred (Mrs. Russell Mitchell Timmons). His sister Daisy married Joseph L. Hammett, and they moved next door to the Mathieson's "large two-story wooden house" at 3236 Peachtree Road. "They owned property on what is Mathieson Drive," Sara Hammett (Mrs. Binion) Jordan remembered. (32)

***

In 1914 the Cam D. Dorseys moved to Buckhead from the Prado in Ansley Park, and built a home on Wesley Avenue (West Wesley). "My father had done a little better, and we wanted a larger home. Paces Ferry was just building up at that time and that was sort of *the* place," Sam Dorsey explained. (33)

Like many of the other residents in the area, the Dorseys had a cow and horses. "I had a pony, and when I grew older I had a horse and would ride horseback in that area," Mr. Dorsey remembered. His riding companions were the Hedley boys, Lawson and Phinizy Calhoun, and Lustrat Winecoff (whose family owned the Winecoff Hotel). "We used to like dirt roads to ride on...I remember they were grading Peachtree Battle and developing homes in Haynes Manor...they had the plows and the mules and everything, and we used to ride over in there." During World War I, the family moved to Pennsylvania for several years, where Mr. Dorsey served as an attorney for the shipping board. (34)

***

In 1915 Clark Howell, Jr. moved from his home on Peachtree and Fifth streets to Pinehill, his summer residence and weekend hunting lodge, built in 1895, on the corner of West Wesley and Arden roads. The man who had been the head of the Georgia Senate and several times Speaker of the Georgia House of Representatives built on land which was "part of the original purchase by Judge Clark Howell in the 1840s," Henry Howell explained. (35)

CHAPTER TWENTY-TWO
1915
The Leo M. Frank Case

"I would rather be the widow of a brave
man than the wife of a coward."
- Mrs. John M. Slaton

*T*he Leo M. Frank case, which resulted in one of the most vicious trials in the country, took place in 1913 and brought Buckhead residents and future residents together on opposite sides of the controversy. Before the episode was over, the last act would be played out in Buckhead.

On the Saturday afternoon of April 26, 1913, Mary Phagan went to the National Pencil Co. on Forsyth Street (once Rich's Store for Homes/now the Atlanta Federal Center) in Atlanta and collected her weekly wage of $1.20 from Leo M. Frank, the plant manager. Three hours later, the body of the raped and strangled thirteen-year-old girl was found in the basement of the building by Newt Lee, the black night watchman. James Conley, a black janitor at the factory with a prior criminal record, was arrested when he was found washing a bloody shirt in the factory. When questioned, Conley accused Frank of killing the girl. (1)

Leo Frank, who was arrested and brought to trial on July 28, 1913, was defended by Luther Z. Rosser Sr., Reuben Arnold, and Henry A. Alexander, who continued to proclaim their client's innocence. The prosecution was headed by Hugh M. Dorsey and Frank A. Hooper Sr.; Judge Leonard S. Roan presided over the trial. (2)

The trial was conducted amid hostile spectators, who jeered Leo Frank and cheered the prosecution, further inflaming the anti-semitic rhetoric. The most damaging evidence came from Jim Conley, who testified that Frank made sexual advances to Mary, and when she tried to thwart him, he struck her and she fell and hit her head. Conley said he was ordered by Frank to carry the body to the basement, write a note "from Mary" accusing Newt Lee of molesting her, and was paid two hundred dollars to burn her body. When he refused to destroy the body, Conley said Frank reclaimed the money. (3)

The defense denounced Conley's story as a lie and asserted that after Frank paid Mary her wages, she left the factory. Despite circumstantial evidence, Frank was convicted and sentenced to death.

On March 10, 1914, an editorial appeared in *The Atlanta Journal*: "Leo Frank has not had a fair trial. He has not been fairly convicted and his death without a fair trial and legal conviction will amount to judicial murder." (4)

Leo Frank's lawyers sought a retrial, and when they were denied, they applied to Gov. John M. Slaton for a commutation of Frank's sentence to life in prison. After reviewing the case records, the governor commuted Frank's sentence on June 21, 1915, and the prisoner was transferred from Fulton Tower to Milledgeville State Prison. (5)

Angered by the governor's decision and fueled by Thomas E. Watson's further denouncement of Frank and Slaton in his newspaper, *The Jeffersonian*, an angry mob of twenty-five armed men from Cobb County, calling themselves the "Knights of Mary Phagan," abducted Frank from the prison in Milledgeville on the night of August 16. They took him to Marietta, where they hung him from a tree. (6) After the body was cut down, it was transferred to Greenberg & Bond funeral home and placed on view before being sent to New York for burial. (7)

Efforts to clear Leo Frank's name continued until 1985 when Alonzo Mann, shortly before his death at eighty-seven, confessed to the Georgia Pardons and Paroles Board that he saw Jim Conley carrying Mary Phagan's body in the pencil factory cellar on the day of the murder. As an office boy of fourteen at the time, Mann had been too afraid of repercussions to speak out, because Conley threatened him and said, "If you ever mention this, I'll kill you." (8)

With the help of Alonzo Mann's testimony, Leo Frank was granted a pardon on March 11, 1986.

In the fall of 1995 leaflets written by Leo Frank while he was imprisoned in the Fulton County Tower came to light. He said that on the day of the murder, Jim Conley "had been drinking heavily that day of beer and wine. He brought a flask of whiskey with him to the factory. He was a dissolute and lascivious character, had been arrested several times and was always hard up for money. He had no business at the factory that day, it being a holiday. He was shown to be a liar many times." (9)

***

Gov. John M. Slaton's brave decision to commute Mr. Frank's sentence put the Slaton family in imminent danger when an angry mob marched from Atlanta to Buckhead, threatening to kill the governor for his actions. The National Guard was called out to the Slaton's home on Peachtree Road, where they patrolled the community for several weeks to protect against mob violence.

Ellen Newell (Mrs. William Wright) Bryan witnessed the crowd's march from Atlanta to Buckhead from her parents' (the Alfred Newells) home on West Peachtree Street. "I saw the mob coming out here to kill Gov. Slaton. They shot out the lights as they went by…Everybody turned out the [house] lights and locked their doors…[the militia] stopped them just before they got to Gov. Slaton's house. They were going to lynch him." (10)

"My mother and father were living on Forrest Avenue, one house from Courtland, and my mother heard this mob screaming for Slaton and Alexander," Cecil Alexander, Henry "Harry" Alexander's nephew recalled. (11)

"Uncle Harry went out to the Governor's Mansion to be with him [Slaton]," Mr. Alexander continued. "The governor had called out the Guard, and they had ringed the house. He had a tough Scotch-Irishman who was commander, and he told the mob leaders, 'I know you guys, and that don't make a damned bit of difference. You take one more step toward the house and my men have orders to shoot to kill.' And they backed off." (12)

When the mob descended on Gov. Slaton's home, his wife stood by him and said, "'I'm staying right here with you. You did the right thing. I would rather be a widow of a brave man than the wife of a coward.'" (13)

"I remember seeing the soldiers as far out Peachtree as Piedmont Road," Joseph K. Heyman said. "I'm seeing them standing there at this intersection…in their olive drab uniforms, with their guns out and their bayonets attached to their rifles unsheathed." (14)

Gov. Slaton "did the right thing…he said he was going to commute the sentence because he had inside information and he knew that Frank was innocent," Betty Slaton (Mrs. John) Wallace proudly said of her uncle. "Everybody told him, 'Forget it, you're going out of office in another day or two.' It was right when the next governor (Nathanial E. Harris) was coming in. 'Put it off on him, you don't have to do it. Don't mess up your political career.' And he said, 'No, I can't do that. It's my responsibility and I know that he's innocent and I have to do it.'" (15)

At the inauguration of Gov. Nathaniel E. Harris, Slaton was warned not to appear, for fear that something would happen to him. "'No. I was here when I was inaugurated and I'm going to be here now,'" the governor said. (16)

After he left office, Gov. and Mrs. Slaton went on an extended trip. "[Their] trip had been planned for ages and they just went ahead doing what he had planned to do," Mrs. Wallace explained. "By the time they had come back, things had calmed down, so apparently, he was not in danger anymore. But he did not run away...He certainly did what was the morally correct thing to do, even though it did ruin him politically. He never held another public office. He was planning on running for U. S. Senate."(17)

"My father (Alfred Newell) managed Mr. Slaton's campaign for the United States Senate, and he lost on account of the Frank case," Mrs. Wright (Ellen Newell) Bryan said. (18)

"The family have always admired Uncle Jack (Slaton) that he took this stand, and it's proven now that he was dead right," William Rudolph said of his uncle. "But of course it did not save poor Mr. Leo Frank...He [Slaton] did the best he could, and he very nearly lost his own life." (19)

Years later John F. Kennedy included the Leo Frank case in his *Profiles of Courage*. "John Kennedy used the story as a profile in courage for a man sticking up for what he thought was right even at the cost of losing his career," William Rudolph said. (20)

***

The Anti-Defamation League of B'nai B'rith was established because of the rampant anti-Semitism in the community, and the reawakening of the Ku Klux Klan. (21) Ironically, in a few short years, Buckhead would become the headquarters of the Knights of the Ku Klux Klan.

CHAPTER TWENTY-THREE
1917-1919
Drugstores, Estates, and Turtle-back Roads

*A*nyone who lived in Buckhead from 1917 until the mid-1940s could say, "I remember Jacobs' Drugstore," which was considered the heart and soul of the community. The owner of this famous establishment was an interesting man, whose drugstore in downtown Atlanta is credited with turning a medication into the most famous soft drink in the world, and making the penny an important coin.

Dr. Joseph Jacobs, born in 1859 in Jefferson, Georgia, did an apprenticeship with local physician, Dr. Crawford W. Long, the man who discovered anesthesia. Working with Dr. Long "prompted my grandfather's interest in pharmacy," T. Sinclair "Tory" Jacobs said. "In those days the doctors compounded their own medicines, and Dr. Long not only practiced medicine and made up medicines, but also made up cosmetics for the ladies." (1)

Joseph Jacobs, the oldest of thirteen children, wanted to be a doctor, but instead attended the University of Georgia, then attended and graduated from the Philadelphia College of Pharmacy in Philadelphia in 1879. After graduation Jacobs opened a drugstore in Athens, and in 1884 he moved to Atlanta. "He realized that Atlanta was the place to be," Tory Jacobs explained, and "he bought out the Taylor Drugstore at Five Points", on the corner of Peachtree and Marietta streets. (2)

Dr. Jacobs wrote to a friend, describing his reasons for moving to Atlanta:

> Atlanta's healthful situation and most salubrious climate the year round, added to her strategic position in the southeastern portion of our country for manufacturing, selling and delivering the products of pharmacy, appealed to me as a professional pharmacist manufacturer and merchant. And I noticed that Atlanta's people were appreciative of, and ready to support the efforts of earnest men worthily exerted. (3)

Dr. John Styth Pemberton's new medical elixir, Coca-Cola, which was being promoted as a syrup for relieving headaches, was sold in drugstores in the 1800s. In 1887 a fluke produced the most popular drink in the world, when a gentleman went into Jacobs' Drugstore, bought a glass of Coca-Cola, and asked Willis E. Venable, the soda fountain operator, who was a nephew of Dr. Long's first anesthetized patient, to add some water to the medicine so he could take it. Mr. Venable added soda water to the tonic, and when the gentleman drank the effervescent mixture, he was pleased with the flavor. Word spread about this new and tasty headache tonic being served at Jacobs' Drugstore, and by the next year the drink was being sold at the drugstore fountains throughout Atlanta. (4)

"My grandfather was peripherally associated with probably the two greatest contributions of pharmacy that ever came out of Georgia...anesthesia and Coca-Cola," Mr. Jacobs said. (5)

"[Dr. Jacobs] knew Dr. Pemberton and...he used to sell him ingredients of his various patent medicines. He acquired a considerable interest in Coca-Cola just to satisfy certain debts that Pemberton ran up with him, which he was not happy about. And eventually he [Pemberton] sold out that stuff [the syrup] to Asa Candler, who made Coca-Cola what it is," Mr. Jacobs explained. "Mr. Candler and he [Jacobs] were friends...Candler would say, 'Joe, you ought to get in on this, it's great,' but my grandfather said, 'It's bellywash.'" (6)

Margaret Cheshire (Mrs. Hilton) Dickerson also had an Asa Candler story. "When Candler first was here, my grandfather [Hezekiah] Cheshire lent him $200 to buy feed for his horses and he offered to pay Grandfather in Coca-Cola stock. 'Oh, no, don't do that, wait until you can pay me the $200.'" (7)

Dr. Jacobs also put the penny in the pocket of Atlantans. "Dr. Jacobs introduced the 'cut-rate' plan of drug merchandising to the local scene. Up to that time the nickel was the smallest coin in general circulation, not only in Atlanta, but generally throughout the South," Mr. Jacobs explained. "In order to make change, Jacobs ordered 3,000 pennies from Washington. Soon thereafter, when signs appeared in his store advertising items for 17 cents, 29 cents, 98 cents, and so on, something of a sensation was created in local retail circles...The penny was here to stay." (8)

In 1917 Dr. Jacobs opened a drugstore in the heart of Buckhead. When his son Sinclair married, he gave the newlyweds his house on Peachtree between Sixth and Seventh streets as a wedding gift and lived in a hotel until his new home on Roswell Road was completed. (9) The yellow brick house, called The Brambles, was four miles north of his store. (10) "It was a pretty big house and it had a big covered pavilion in the back where they had an indoor shuffleboard. He used to give parties and barbecues there." There were big pits where "two or three different animals" were cooked. "He had a sidewalk put in front of [his home]. It was the strangest thing in the world to drive out there and see this stretch of sidewalk that led no-where...just in front of the house," Mr. Jacobs mused. Dr. Jacobs died in 1929, at the age of seventy. (11)

***

Real estate developer Eretus "E" Rivers, the developer of Peachtree Heights Park neighborhood, also donated a parcel of land at the corner of Peachtree Road and Peachtree Battle Avenue for an elementary school. The three-story stone schoolhouse opened its doors in September of 1917 under the name Peachtree Heights School, and was renamed E. Rivers School in May of 1926, in honor of Mr. Rivers "as a tribute to his years of service on the Board of Education, to the community, and to Peachtree Heights School." (12)

***

John W. Grant Sr. made Buckhead his permanent residence when he replaced his summer cottage with a large white stucco and limestone English Country-style home on one hundred acres of unpaved (West) Paces Ferry Road in 1917. Grant named his home Craigellachie (now The Chero-kee Club), which in Scottish means 'Stand fast,' and is the family motto. The name comes from "the mountain in Strathepey, Scotland, that for gen-erations, had been the meeting place of the clan of Grant," John W. Grant III explained. (13)

John Sr., known to his family as "Big Papa," and his wife Annie (Hugh T. Inman's daughter), who was called "Dearie," (14) had five children: Margaret, Hugh Inman, William D. II, John W. Jr., and Annie Inman. Hugh Grant died in childhood of a burst appendix and his father, who was a trustee of Georgia Tech, donated fifty thousand dollars to the university for an athletic field as a memorial to his son. (15)

The building of the Grant home was begun in 1915, but was postponed during World War I, because of "a lack of building materials." It was fin-ished around 1917, complete with servants' quarters, a barn, and garages. John Grant's cousin, eminent architect Neel Reid, "redid these gardens in a more Georgian type thing, built a summer house down where they used to put the orchestra when they had lawn parties," William Rudolph explained. The Grants maintained Craigellachie as a working farm with horses, cows, and mules. "The mules were needed to pull things to cut all this grass." (16)

The original holdings of the Grants in Buckhead was several thousand acres, and William D. Grant, John's father, had operated a farm on Roswell Road around East Andrews (the present site of The Paces condos). When the Robert Candlers later built their home across the street on the corner of West Paces Ferry Road and Andrews Drive, "Grandmother Grant went over to call on Sarah, to welcome her to the neighborhood," William Rudolph said. "She told her, 'My dear, the reason all your shrubbery looks so good is that this is where my father-in-law's dairy barn was and you have many years of manure worked into the ground." (17)

Mrs. Grant said after the birth of her first son, John Jr., in 1902, "'It took me some time to forgive my husband because the day that my son was born, he was out here at this farm selling off his father's cows. I had to have the baby without him.'" (18)

"Dearie had a little electric cart called the 'Red Bug,' and she used to ride these paths so she could supervise what was going on on the place and see it firsthand," Mr. Rudolph said. (19) "Neither of my grandmothers drove an automobile, because both of them had had an accident," John W. Grant III contended. "The story was that [Dearie] ran into a cow in the 'Red Bug,' and my grandmother Connors ran into the ocean." (20)

John Grant Sr. cut a road through the south part of his property in order to develop saleable lots. "Of course he wanted to call it Grant Drive, because it ran right up to the gate of this house," Mr. Rudolph explained. "But in order to make the property more attractive, he needed an opening onto Peachtree Road. The problem was that Mr. Walter P. Andrews owned the property at Mr. Grant's southern border, where the Cathedral of St. Philip sits. He offered Mr. Andrews just one big price after another, but he just wouldn't budge...So [Grant] thought up this deal...'We'll make it Andrews Drive for you, I just want to buy this property to get through here.' Mr. Andrews...was flattered that he was going to name it Andrews Drive, that's what he really wanted, so he deeded it over to [Grant] for nothing." (21)

***

Dr. F. Phinizy Calhoun Sr., an eminent Atlanta ophthalmologist, built the first house on (2906) Andrews Drive in 1917, which then was called Peachtree Heights Park, and moved his family from their home at the corner of Fifth and Peachtree Street. (22) The Tudor-style house, originally called Shadow Hill, was later renamed Rossdhu "after the ancestral home of the Colquhoun (Calhoun) Clan in Luss, Scotland on Loch Lomond." (23) Andrews Drive "was a two-lane asphalt turtle-back road (humped in the middle). It was very hazardous to drive on. Course there weren't many automobiles in those days, so you knew every family that came by," Dr. F. Phinizy Calhoun Jr. reminisced. (24)

Dr. Calhoun Sr., a native of Newnan and son of Dr. A. B. Calhoun, married Marion Crompton Peel, daughter of Lucy Marion (Cook) and Col. William Lawson Peel. At their home on Peachtree Road, where The Temple is today, the Peels "used to entertain the opera visitors. [They] began getting the Metropolitan Opera into Atlanta," and were active in the Atlanta Music Festival. (25)

"Life out at 2906 Andrews for us in the beginning was country life. We had a big barn on those seven acres and had cows, a few horses, and a caretaker and his family that lived in a little house right there next to the barn," Dr. Calhoun continued. "Underneath our garage…we even had cow stalls…used to milk our cows. We had hog-killing time in November, raised all the vegetables we ate, and used to have all kinds of wild creatures in the woods on either side. (26)

"My brother Lawson and I used to play in the woods and creeks down behind the house, and on the unpaved roads. Much of the gravel that was used on the roads in this part of town came from a big quarry right behind our house where we used to play. [Buckhead] was a wonderful place to grow up in. It was a wonderful boyhood." (27)

"I went to E. Rivers School, which was called Peachtree Heights School in those days," Dr. Calhoun said. "We had a little athletic field where we used to play sandlot football, which is where the apartment houses are now on Peachtree Road, north of the school. The streetcar tracks were in the middle of [Peachtree] road, with gravel along the tracks so that automobiles could go on either side. It was about one-and-a-half lanes wide. There wasn't much traffic on Peachtree Road then. The curve at [East and West] Wesley was called 'Dead Man's Curve,' and at night we could hear the crashes from our house…off of [West] Wesley Road, and Wyngate used to be a little farming community where poor white people lived." (28)

*****

Ruth Cox Adams's life in Buckhead during this period revolved around family, Sardis Methodist Church, and the two-room, wood frame Rosservile School on Howell Mill Road. "Everything we did was connected with the church," Mrs. Adams said. "When we were babies, our mother and daddy would not miss church, so they would lay us on the pulpit to sleep while the preacher was preaching," the granddaughter of potter T. B. Cofield and daughter of Edward Cox said. (29)

"My mother's family was musical. They played everything from the washboard, hand saw and all musical instruments…The Cofield family had an orchestra," and would entertain on the second floor of the Donaldson building at the Sardis Masons Lodge every month," Mrs. Adams explained. (30)

***

Atlanta historian Franklin M. Garrett remembers Buckhead during the late teens, when he rode his bicycle from town to visit friends. "Stores extended about a block [from] Paces Ferry Road both north and south." Along (West) Paces Ferry Road from Peachtree was the white frame house of Dr. C. M. Adams. Nearby, policeman Charles T. Maddox lived with his family in a home without running water; they drew their water from a well in the yard, and used an outdoor privy. Young Franklin Garrett and Harry Maddox "discovered a place in Nancy Creek where you could go in swimming and it was deep enough to dive off a rock on the edge of the stream…Went in without bathing suits." (31)

"I remember Buckhead being the intersection of sort of five points," Joseph K. Heyman said of this period. He remembered Jacobs' Pharmacy, Mr. T. J. Dumas' grocery store, and a blacksmith shop on (West) Paces Ferry Road, where his family took their horse to be shod and their wagon and tools to be repaired. Mr. Heyman recalled that his neighbors, Charles Wickersham, president of the Atlanta & West Point Railroad, and his son-in-law C. A. Kitchens, had homes on the corner of Peachtree and Piedmont roads (now the site of the Nikko Hotel). (32)

"During World War I the [streetcar] line was extended from Club Drive on out Peachtree to what was then Camp Gordon [now DeKalb Airport]." Mr. Heyman remembered. "We used to bring soldiers home," to treat them to a home-cooked Sunday dinner. (33)

***

Laura Maddox (Mrs. Edward D.) Smith reminisced about living in Buckhead in the late teens, when Metropolitan Opera parties were given at Woodhaven, and when Theodore Roosevelt once paid the Robert Maddox family a visit. "I remember walking…[and] kicking a stone to Buckhead, and there being a Confederate soldier buried in the woods on Paces Ferry near the shopping center," Mrs. Smith said. "Mrs. Cox, Tom Dickey's mother-in-law, had an electric car. I can remember as a child I was so thrilled when she would say, 'Do you want to ride with me to Buckhead or something?' I'd get in the car and she'd drive the little electric car up to Buckhead. I thought I was driving in the magic chariot." (34)

***

Powers and Lucille (Cooledge) Pace built the first house on Muscogee Avenue in 1918. Mr. Pace had moved from South Carolina to Atlanta, where his father was minister of the Jackson Hill Baptist Church in Druid Hills. Powers married Lucille Cooledge, daughter of Lily Mae (Holmes) and Frederick Jerome Cooledge, a distant cousin of President Calvin Cooledge, and went to work for his father-in-law, at the F. J. Cooledge & Sons Pane Glass Store. (35)

The Pace family had a cow, pigs, and chickens until more neighbors moved in. "[A servant] took our cow down in the morning and tied her up to graze where Peachtree Battle is now," Lillie Pace (Mrs. Paul) Scoville said. At one point Mother had 350 chickens, and one night...somebody, or a group of people, came in, and the next morning we did not have a chicken. We never heard a squawk or anything." (36)

"We built a playhouse and...my four brothers used to go out there and smoke rabbit tobacco," Mrs. Scoville said. "At the bottom of the hill, at the corner of Rivers and Muscogee, I built a treasure, a magic path...and fixed it all up and charged a penny, I think, for people to come and go through. I took pieces of broken glass and made little decorations around it, and little places to sit." (37)

"I remember the first boughten ice cream cone I ever had," Mrs. Scoville continued. The family's cow provided milk for ice cream for the Sunday dinner. "One day I rode into Tenth Street with Mother to the grocery store, and she actually bought me an ice cream cone. I was so overcome, that when I took the first lick, the ice cream ball rolled off on the floor. I bawled. I think the man gave me another one." (38)

***

Homebuilding continued on (West) Paces Ferry Road in 1918 when Alex Wylly Smith built his home at 231 Paces Ferry, and at 1080, the T. B. Dillards built a Mediterranean-style home. The Dillard home, designed by P. Thornton Mayre, was later owned by W. D. Manley, Lindsey Hopkins, and A. D. Adair. (39)

***

The Harmony Grove Church on (West) Paces Ferry Road at Chatham Road closed its doors in late 1918, because of declining membership. The small country church was torn down, and all that remains of this little religious enclave is the cemetery that sits on the hill. (40)

In 1919, Beverly Means DuBose (1886-1953) bought six acres of land on Peachtree from Seaborn L. Ivey, and moved his wife, Lula Dean (Jones), and children, Beverly M. Jr. and Elizabeth (Mrs. Vernon Skiles), from Fourteenth Street to Buckhead. (41)

The Suwanee, Tennessee, native was the son of Elizabeth (Egleston) and Robert DuBose, who was the Registrar and Treasurer of the University of the South in Suwanee. Following his graduation from the University of the South, Beverly DuBose moved to Atlanta and joined the Hartford Fire Insurance Company, Southern Department. DuBose later became president of the company, which was renamed DuBose Egleston, Inc. Thomas Egleston, DuBose' cousin and partner, was also founder of the well-known children's hospital, the Henrietta Egleston Memorial Hospital. (42)

CHAPTER TWENTY-FOUR
1920s
The Ku Klux Klan

"A social club...purely for amusement."
- The Fallacy of the Atlanta Origins of the K.K.K.

$\mathscr{D}$uring the Leo Frank debacle, the Ku Klux Klan once more raised its ugly head, having been quiet since the 1870s. The release of W. D. Griffith's Civil War epoch movie *The Birth of a Nation* in 1915 poured more fuel onto the Klan's flame by bringing the anguish of the war to the surface, rekindling old hatreds. (1) Quickly, Klan membership grew, and their hateful activities of threats, cross burnings, beatings, and hangings increased throughout the South. Buckhead became their headquarters, with meetings held at the Imperial Palace on Peachtree, the "sheet factory" on Roswell Road, and the Imperial Wizard's home on Peachtree Battle Avenue.

The "true" history of the organization appears in a booklet published in 1945, which stated that the Klan "was born around the fireplace of the law office of Judge Thomas M. Jones" in December of 1865 in Pulaski, Tennessee, by six Confederate veterans. "Captain John C. Lester, Captain John B. Kennedy, Captain James R. Crowe, Frank O. McCord, Richard R. Reed and J. Calvin Jones," all respected men in their community, "decided, because of the dearth of amusement and lack of other interests in their war-torn world and the period of adjustment to these new conditions, that they would organize a social club—one purely for amusement." (2)

They chose the comical name of Kuklos ("meaning circle or cycle") Clan for their club. The name was later changed to the Ku Klux Klan. (3) To go along with the original charade, "They also adopted outlandish costumes of long white flowing robes with masks and strange headdresses." And, "Since the object of the society was purely amusement they, somewhat in the spirit of Mardi Gras, invented for themselves outlandish names and titles such as Grand Cyclops, Grand Geni, Grand Magi, Grand Turk, and Scribe. (4)

"There being little else to do, they resorted to riding about at night; and began to harass and terrify insolent negroes who were annoying the community in their new-found freedom. They would pretend, and the negroes readily believed, that they were the ghosts of dead Confederate soldiers. (5)

"Before long definite beneficial effects were recognized by the community." As word of this "club" quickly spread throughout the South, "Klan Dens sprang up in every state." By early 1868 the group had a foothold in Georgia. By 1877 the Klan had faded out. (6)

After years in hibernation, the Klan awoke on "Thanksgiving night in 1915" when William Joseph Simmons and 33 of his friends gathered on top of Stone Mountain to resurrect the Klan. (7) On July 1, 1916, the Knights of the Ku Klux Klan was officially born. (8) The Klan bought Edward M. Durant's property on Peachtree Road (present-day site of Christ the King) in 1921, and established their headquarters in the beautiful, two-story, anti-bellum-style home, which they called the Imperial Palace. Nearby, Simmons built an art-deco-style home for himself on Peachtree Battle Avenue.

Colonel William Joseph Simmons had been "an itinerant Methodist minister, life insurance salesman…[and chairman] of Southern History at Lanier University." Under his leadership the Klan membership grew to six million. (9)

A Mr. Coleman built the three-story Cotton Exchange building at 3155 Roswell Road in 1920, in the heart of Buckhead, which he deeded to the Knights of the Ku Klux Klan. The building became the Klan's "sheet factory," operating until 1929, when Klan activity waned. (10) During the Great Depression there was a resurection of Klan activities, and once again the Klan occupied the premises from 1938 until 1943. (11) Today the building is an office condominium.

Dr. Hiram Wesley Evans, a Texas dentist, wrestled control of the Klan from Simmons in 1922 and moved into the Imperial Palace on Peachtree Road. (12)

In 1922, the Klan created a plan for a "non-sectional" college, to be called University of America, which was to be located on Howell Mill Road near Peachtree Creek, on a 143-acre campus. (13) The founders "foresaw the new university as being comparable to "Harvard, Yale and Princeton or any of the other big schools of the east." Its curriculum was "true American history, uncolored by the sentiments of sectionalism." (14) The stage they chose for the new campus, that was never developed, was the site of the Battle of Peachtree Creek.

The four acres of the Imperial Palace property was sold in 1939 to the Catholic church, and Dr. Hiram Evans attended the dedication of The Cathedral of Christ the King. (15) The State of Georgia revoked the Klan charter in 1947. "Subsequently, a number of other societies were organized, and the largest and most powerful was the Association of Georgia Klans. In 1949 this group was placed on the list of subversive organizations issued by the United States attorney-general." (16)

***

Some residents of Buckhead were eye witnesses to the Klan's actions in the community. Some knew nothing about the Klan or their activities, while others felt the organization was a community service that did its civic duty, by helping to keep law and order. Others were the object of their attention.

"Their headquarters (the "sheet factory") was right there on Roswell Road at Irby Street. That's where they did all the printing, everything was done up there," Ken Moss explained. He recalled that the Klan marched in full robes around Buckhead every Friday night during the 1930s. "They'd come out of the Klan building, go through Irby Alley. Couldn't see any black people at all, they'd all stay in the house. Then they'd just make a circle around, come out on Peachtree, come back and circle around back to Roswell Road...That was usually the route." (17)

"They really did some community service. If someone wasn't looking after their family, they went by and talked to him the first time. The second time they went back, they talked to him again. And the third time they brought him outside and tanned his can. They usually didn't have to go back the fourth time," Mr. Moss said. "They straightened out a lot of family abusers. I knew ninety percent of 'em, wasn't suppose to, but I did. It was a real civic organization at that time, none of the stuff they do now. They were kind of a vigilante-type thing. They dealt out justice that the police department couldn't do, or wouldn't. They didn't get out of line. In my opinion, it needed doing. You had [members] from every class. The average working man, the white-collar worker and the blue-collar worker. It wasn't just an elite group, it was the whole neighborhood, civic-minded people." Mr. Moss said that when he was a youngster, he used to don his grandfather's Klan outfit and parade about the house. (18)

Guy Patterson said the Klansmen marched on Saturday during the mid-thirties in full robes in order to clear Buckhead for white shoppers. "Used to see 'em about every week...Right over Pharr Road was a colored section, Bagley Park. The colored got to where they'd crowd in up there in Buckhead where people couldn't come and shop. Those Klansmen could blow a bugle or a horn or something, and by the time they walked to Buckhead they wasn't a colored person there, they'd all gone home." (19)

"The Klan would march on the [Bagley] park on certain nights and the kids would follow. And they were turned back because they weren't allowed," Ellie Patterson remembered. (20)

Many in the community knew the members of the Klan. Guy Patterson said that one day a Klansman approached Long Kellogg, an elderly black man and asked, "'Long, do you know who I am?' 'Sure. Youse one of them mens behind that old robe you had on there the other day. I knows who you is. Well, I don't think you'll bother me and my family til I bother you. I didn't get this old by hurting people.'" The Klansman told Mr. Kellogg his name so he would never forget. (21)

Mr. Patterson also told an intriguing story of visiting the Klan's hidden room in the "sheet factory," while working for Buckhead Lumber Co., at 35 West Paces Ferry Road. After he delivered an order of lumber to the factory and placed it on the third floor, he discovered a secret room used to initiate new Klan members. "They had a tricycle special built, three (wooden) wheels on it, neither one wasn't round. So that thing would buck…They'd have to ride that tricycle and it a bumping up and down …called 'riding the goat.'" At the end of the ceremony the new recruit was blindfolded and placed in a coffin and left in a dark room. (22)

Leon Townsend said, "We didn't know much about the Klan. Heard a lot about it. My father was against the Klan." (23)

Ruth Cox Adams said she did not recall seeing Klan marches or parades, but stated that the Klan took the law into their own hands and often settled domestic disputes. "I remember my daddy telling about them burning a cross in front of somebody's house one time. And they took the man out and beat him. He was a white man…because he had mistreated his family. If they heard of a man mistreating their family or anything, they would drag him out of the house, they were really bad." (24)

Jack J. Spalding recalled his childhood living on Fourteenth Street in the late teens. "I have a vivid recollection, one day going out in the front yard and there was a Klansman just riding up and down on a black horse [in full sheets]. It struck terror in my little Catholic heart. That was a great street. On one block there were four or five Catholic families and about six or seven Jewish ones." (25)

"My father [Hughes] was elected county attorney during this period…And the Ku Klux owned the [Fulton] County, they owned the courthouse. They owned City Hall…they elected Father anyway." (26)

When asked if any of the well-to-do of Atlanta were Klan members, Mr. Spalding answered, "Sure they were, and they wanted them, they needed them, they wanted their support. And people joined…for political preferment; that was a way to get elected. Of course the people who joined the

Klan to get elected were not the rich folks. The rich folks joined, I guess, to be on the right side. You know how people are, they want to be with the victors...People joined like it was a club, a popular club. You had to join really if you wanted a political preferment, any favors from the governor." (27)

"I never saw the Klan march," Dr. F. Phinizy Calhoun Jr. said. "I can remember, as a student, I guess in high school, being solicited to join by another high school student." (28)

"I remember when [the Klan] house was built, built one of the first houses on Peachtree Battle. It was a beautiful place," J. T. Tolbert said. "I never did care too much for [the Klan]. At one time it was very powerful. I think it was kind of like the labor union. Right after the Civil War, it did a lot of good. I had a grandfather who belonged to the Ku Klux Klan. The way the South was treated when Abraham Lincoln was assassinated, then those birds up in the North, took it out on the South...punishing them for what they did. I think if Abraham Lincoln had lived it would have been a different story. And the Ku Klux Klan was just something that had to be almost at that time. Then it began to get powerful. Money got involved...it wasn't needed any longer ...Sometimes things like that serve the need and then they ought to get out...I wouldn't walk out the front door to see 'em march now." (29)

"I never knew anything about it, except I was terrified of them," Laura Maddox (Mrs. Edward D.) Smith said. (30)

"The Ku Klux Klan house was across the street from our house...that big white house...I was not aware of any activities," Florence Bryan (William Mrs. Bonneau) Ansley said. "I don't remember seeing any sheeted group." (31)

"None of my family was involved in it at all. I don't know anything about it," Betty Slaton (Mrs. John) Wallace said. (32)

"I remember a sense of dread, seeing guys that you couldn't see their faces," John Ottley III said. (33)

"As far as the Ku Klux Klan was concerned, I never knew it existed, at that point in my life," Barrett Howell said. (34)

"And certainly that with me," Henry Howell said. "You just never would have known anybody that had anything to do with the Klan. We all knew the Klan house on Peachtree Battle...was reputed to have a tunnel going who knows where, but in terms of knowing anything about the Klan, it was nothing you ever heard or talked about." (35)

When asked about the Ku Klux Klan with respect to Johnson Town, Columbus Johnson said that the Klan never marched in their area. "They did go to Bagley Park, but not to Johnson Town. Too many rich people were in back of the blacks in Johnson Town. They didn't bother the blacks there because of that. We were all around rich people, wealthy people, that's how we got there, so they didn't bother our people." (36)

"Everybody was afraid of 'em," Parthenia Jetter said of the Klan. She said the Klan never went to her community of Piney Grove. "They went to Bagley Park [they marched and burned crosses]. When we heard they was coming, we come home." (37)

Janie Johnson was a member of the Johnson Town community and said, "All I remember, they burnt some crosses out there in the street." (38)

"One of the most poignant memories I have," Tory Jacobs said, was the night he and Jim Gallogly came face to face with the Klan. "One night his [black] chauffeur picked us up…after the [Boy] Scout meeting…[in] a four-door sedan, and we drove to…Jacobs' to get a soda, and the Ku Klux Klan was in robes and marching. This Klansman came over to the car, and the driver turned absolutely white. The Klansman told him to get out of there, we were interfering with the parade. So we [boys] were sitting in the back seat…it was pretty scary…he could see two little white boys back there, he spoke to the driver and the driver took off. This was about 1934." (39)

"Daddy was a big friend of Hiram Evans, he was the Grand Dragon," William Brand Jr. recalled. "Daddy belonged to the Klan…One time I saw a parade with around 200 people; they were marching down Peachtree there. It was a big deal, I thought it was rather foolish, people running around in sheets." When it was mentioned that some people felt that the Klan served the community by disciplining errant husbands, he responded. "They got into trouble in East Point. There was a barber out there that was staying drunk, wasn't feeding his family. Sometime he used to take drunk in his barber shop there for weeks at a time. They took him out and whipped his butt. It was in the wintertime, and he froze to death. They had a big trial over that. That was sorta the beginning of the downfall of the Klan. In the thirties sometime, before World War II." (40)

"We knew it was there, but we never did see any kind of demonstration…never saw a cross burned," Marcus Cook III said. "I never was aware of people mistreating blacks like they have been depicted in movies like *Mississippi Burning*," and that nature…It's not to say that it wasn't happening somewhere else or maybe somewhere in Buckhead…I always thought, 'there but for the grace of Go go I'." (41)

***

Buckhead as a center for the Ku Klux Klan no longer exists. Gone are men dressed in white robes and hoods, marching around the community; gone is the Imperial Palace. But the Klan is still alive and reminds us that hate never dies.

"You can still see them [the Klan] in Cummings in uniform. They don't wear masks. They wear those conical hats," William T. Dreger III said. "You see whole families, a daddy and a mamma and little kids, they all got on the same kind of robes." (42)

CHAPTER TWENTY-FIVE
1920-1924
Rename Buckhead?

"Buckhead it is, and Buckhead it will remain."
- Wilbur Kurtz

$\mathcal{D}$uring the early twenties, Buckhead looked "like a little western town...it was nothing really very elegant," Mrs. Hilton Stanaland (1915-1994) recalled. (1)

"Where the Peachtree Battle Shopping Center is, was all kudsu. It was just acres and acres," said Margaret Chapman (Mrs. Leon) Townsend, who lived in Peachtree Hills. "I used to skate down Peachtree Road from Buckhead to Peachtree Creek. I'd wait till a small truck came along, or some truck slowed up at Peachtree Creek, and catch a hold of it and go to [the center of] Buckhead and skate back." (2)

***

Mooney's Lake, which was a popular recreational spot for many years in Buckhead, was developed by Deuward S. Mooney in 1920, on property which sits behind the present Lindbergh Plaza on Morosco Drive. In 1915 the roofing contractor, who "usually wore a black hat and had a sizable mustache," built a spring-water pool for his children. It soon attracted others, and as the pool became more popular, Mooney added a second pool, a lake, and a pavilion where food could be bought, and people could dance to music supplied by a jukebox. The complex also offered horse-back riding, canoeing, and it had a miniature golf course and railroad. (3)

"It was a big area," William Dreger III said. "During the war [World War II] it was full of soldiers and sailors...[Sometime in the late 1950s] the buildings there burned. They suspicioned that the owner had burned it down for the insurance. He went out of business and never opened up again. Only recently, last five or six years, somebody confessed to having burned that thing...for years he lived under a cloud." (4)

R. W. Davis and Jacques Carter purchased the property in 1957 for apartment houses, plus fifty additional acres adjacent to it for the Broadview Shopping Center, now Lindbergh Square. The dams were broken and the water from the lake made its way down into Peachtree Creek. (5)

***

Phillips Campbell McDuffie (1885-1965) built his home at 7 Cherokee Road around 1920. The Henderson, North Carolina, native and son of a Baptist minister worked his way through Harvard Law School. "Somewhere along the line he met Fred Loring Seely, who built Grove Park Inn in Asheville, North Carolina, and founded *The Atlanta Georgian* in 1906. He said, 'Phil, I want you to come to Atlanta and I'll see that you have a job with *The Georgian* paper,'" Helen McDuffie said of her father. (6)

Once in Atlanta, Mr. McDuffie went to work for the newspaper. He met fellow instructor Helen Walker Bagley (1888-1968) while teaching Sunday school at a Baptist church near the capitol, and they were married in 1911. Helen was the daughter of Henry Clay Bagley, who came to Atlanta from Americus, Georgia, around 1893. "At one time [Bagley] was the largest peach grower in the state," Ms. McDuffie said of her maternal grandfather. "Helen, Georgia, is named for my mother...My granddaddy, was [also] in the logging business, and he went up to what is now Helen...and named the town." (7)

"Mother and Daddy drew the plans for this home [on Cherokee Road], and Neel Reid was the architect," Ms. McDuffie explained. "They had a beautiful, formal garden in the back, and they brought Neel Reid out on a stretcher to approve of the beautiful gazebo that was in the formal garden. He was dying." (8)

***

In 1921 there were eighteen homes on Peachtree Road, from Terrace Drive to Andrews Drive. In 1923 Thomas Jefferson Hightower Jr., owner of Hightower Tank and Box Factory, bought the Jacob N. Hirsch home at 2652 Peachtree Road (now Park Place condominium) and moved from his home in Ansley Park. Mr. Hirsch sold his home after one of his sons backed out of the driveway on a motorized scooter, and was hit by a car and killed. (9) The Hightowers moved to Buckhead because, "Atlanta was moving in this direction at that time, and a lot of their friends lived out here," George Hightower said of his parents. (10)

Charlotte McCrea Nutting lived with her parents, the Thomas Hilliard McCreas, in their Tudor-style home at 2672 Peachtree Road. She remembered when her neighbor J. Epps Brown, who lived on Peachtree at the corner of West Wesley, "bought his first car: an air-cooled engine Franklin, and—never having driven before—careened across Peachtree Road yelling 'Whoa,' and ended up in the Ku Klux Klan yard on the corner of East Wesley." (11)

Further south on Peachtree Road, G. W. Moor had a home and operated a coal yard next to the William Lawson Peel property (now the site of the Darlington Apartments). "The back of that property ran to the Seaboard Railroad and there was a side track, and they had a little stop there called Deerland Park. There was always a coal car on the side track to supply Mr. Moor's coal yard," Jack J. Spalding said. (12)

"There was a guano [fertilizer] plant on the railroad," Mr. Spalding continued. "They would run special streetcars out there for the help at the plant. They'd let 'em off at the bridge and they'd walk down the railroad track. They did it 'cause they smelled so bad. That would be a form of segregation now." (13)

***

(West) Paces Ferry Road continued to be a popular address. In 1923 Mr. and Mrs. Andrew Calhoun built Trygveson/Pink Castle at number 923. Designed by Neel Reid, this Baroque-style home sat on eighteen acres and the driveway was framed with two Baroque entrance piers. The home of the realtor became a traffic-stopper when drivers slowed down or pulled over to look at the beauty of this Italian villa. Following Mr. Calhoun's death, his daughter Louise and her husband, Roly Robinson Jr., moved into the home. After their tragic death in the Orly plane crash in Paris, France, on June 3, 1962, the property was subdivided and Pinestream Road was cut through from West Paces Ferry Road to Northside Parkway. (14) Today, the Baroque piers stand at the entrance on West Paces Ferry Road.

Architect Neel Reid designed a 16th-Century, English-style home for the Winship Nunnallys on (West) Paces Ferry Road in 1923. It was later bought by Mr. and Mrs. Hugh Hodgson. Today the subdivided property is the location of the Paces West condominiums on West Paces Ferry Road at Northside Parkway. (15)

The following year saw the construction of Villa Juanita next door to Robert F. Maddox's Woodhaven. This 8,000-square-foot Italian Romanesque villa, designed by Pringle and Smith, was built for Conkey P. Whitehead and his new bride, Julia (Murphy), while the newlyweds traveled. Later a gymnasium and indoor pool were built, and a second story was added to the house. The property had elaborate gardens, and the house was known for its parties. Mr. Whitehead was the son of J. B. Whitehead Sr., who was one of the founders of the Coca-Cola Bottling Company. The home was named for Julia, whose father, John Murphy, helped to found what was to become the SunTrust Bank (formerly Trust Company of Georgia Bank). (16)

"In 1929, the stock market crashed and the Whiteheads divorced. Julia retained the house, and Conkey lived on his yachts, a villa in Havana, and in a German castle until his death in 1940." (17) Mrs. Whitehead died in 1935 and left the estate to her sister Katherine Murphy (Mrs. Julian) Riley. When Mr. Riley died in 1950, she married his brother James and lived in the home until her death in 1985. (18)

***

Habersham Road was graded and paved from Peachtree Battle Avenue to (West) Paces Ferry Road; the construction of the two-mile stretch, under the supervision of James Sylvanius Donaldson, was done at a cost of forty thousand dollars. (19) Between 1925 and 1928 a large number of homes were built on the road; the first was built by W. A. Higgins, at number 41, around 1920. (20)

***

Peachtree Park and Macedonia Park neighborhoods were created in Buckhead in the early twenties. The Peachtree Park neighborhood was developed in 1921 by the McKenzie Trust Company, which bought a large portion of Peachtree Park, from Piedmont Road to Brookhaven on the east side of Peachtree Road. The land was subdivided into 550 home sites, and Mr. and Mrs. R. N. Sager built the first home in the development, on Martina Drive. (21)

The same year, Macedonia Park was developed on Pharr Road, N.E. when John S. Owens and O. F. Kauffman, the civil engineer who developed Peachtree Heights Park, subdivided the property once owned by Henry Irby and made lots available for purchase to black citizens. (22)

The transfer of the land began in 1871, when Irby sold fifty acres between Peachtree and Piedmont roads to Gemima Catherine Barnwell for $400. The following year she sold it for $500 to John Crawford, who then sold it to his brother Joshua D. Crawford for the same price. Joshua added to his holdings by buying the adjoining ten acres for $100 from Orpha

Stowers in 1874. In 1909 Mr. Crawford sold the property to John S. Owens for $5,000, and a small piece of land was given to the Mt. Olive M. E. Church trustees. (23)

The community's spiritual needs were served by Mt. Olive Methodist Church, Macedonia Baptist Church, and the White Lily Baptist Church. The Macedonia Park residents supported two grocery stores, one owned by Mamie German and the other by William Bagley, and restaurants were owned by Mattie Allen and Mary Bailey, while William Bonner operated a blacksmith shop on Pharr Road. (24)

At an undetermined time the community became known as Bagley Park, named for resident Charley Bagley, from Cummings, Georgia. (25) Tom Murray said there were about two hundred homes developed along the gravel roads in the Park, and that a church was located where the Woman's Club now sits on Pharr Road. (26) "The Bagleys were well-respected black people," Barrett Howell said. (27)

***

The business district in Buckhead expanded in the early 1920s, when Axson C. Minhinnett opened a grocery store on the eastern side of Peachtree Road, at number 2921. Later, his sister Mary and brother Gene operated the grocery store and a restaurant at that location (present site of Aunt Charlie's). (28)

***

George P. Murray rented space and opened the first hardware store in the 2900 block of Peachtree in 1921, about 140 feet north of East Paces Ferry Road, where Miller's Book Store used to be. "There were only seven brick buildings in Buckhead. It is the oldest surviving business in Buckhead," Murray's son Thomas M. said. In 1929 the Murrays bought a wooded lot one block south on Peachtree Road and built a new hardware store that opened the following year. By 1934 the block was completely developed. (29)

"In the old days we used to have girls ride horses into the store to see my daddy," Tom Murray said. "He'd pat the horses and the girls would say, 'Mama says that Daddy wants me to bring a pound of nails home.' So he'd give them a pound of nails, put them on the horse and they'd go on home." (30)

The Murrays rented a house on East Paces Ferry Road that sat on a hill behind the store. "The house was about two hundred feet off Peachtree—that bank must have been about thirty-five feet tall. It's flat now. It had two or three little houses on it. They came along and graded it down after the war (World War II) and put buildings on it," Mr. Murray explained. The house had no water, and Mr. Murray ran a pipe from the store to the house to furnish this utility. The family lived there until 1932, when they moved into a home on Wieuca Road. (31)

"In the summertime, when it would get slow, my dad would get a new ice cream freezer out of stock," Tom Murray reminisced. "The boys next door at the drugstore would mix up a batch of cream and bring it over there and get ice and freeze it, and we'd sit around and eat ice cream all day and just have fun." (32)

"Your mama [got] on the streetcar every Friday with the two of you [George Jr. and Tom] to take the money from the store to the bank," Jane (Mrs. George Jr.) Murray said about her mother-in-law. "There were no banks in Buckhead...took it to the First National Bank downtown." (33)

"There used to be five hardware stores in Buckhead. You know why we survived?" Tom Murray asked. "We've done everything from baby sitting, changing diapers, and loaning money to bank president's wives so they could go shopping at the ten-cent store. I have customers who tell me, 'Buckhead is the only place I can go and visit with the owners of the place. I'm recognized.'" (34)

***

Phillips C. McDuffie built a two-story brick building, in 1923, on the site of Henry Irby's tavern at the corner of West Paces Ferry and Roswell roads (present-day site of Laura Ashley), on land he leased from the Donaldson family. "The McDuffie building was the first one that Daddy built," Helen McDuffie said. "He had a lease on all the property...from West Paces Ferry up to the Buckhead Theater." (35)

***

J. T. Tolbert and The National Library Binding Company of West Spring-field, Massachusetts, opened a plant at 2395 Peachtree Road (until recently Oxford Too Bookstore) around 1924, because Buckhead land was cheap. The company "was just beginning to start really growing, and we really didn't want to get out any further," J. T. Tolbert, president of the company said. Mr. Tolbert, who was born in Grant Park, moved his wife and children to Springlake near the Bobby Jones Golf Course in 1945. He was active in the Buckhead Elks' Lodge and the Buckhead 50 Club. (36)

***

During this period an attempt was made to change the name of Buckhead to Northwood. Even the streetcars got into the act. "These cars started running with little metal plaques in the motorman's window which said 'Northwood.' The ladies who moved to Buckhead out on Paces Ferry obviously thought Buckhead was a creepy, crappy-sounding name, so they tried to get the name changed to 'Northwood'...It didn't go over," Jack Spalding mused. (37)

"I used to think it [Buckhead] was the ugliest name," Laura Maddox (Mrs. Edward D.) Smith said. "I was embarrassed to tell people I lived in an area outside of Atlanta called Buckhead. I thought it was a terrible name. Now it's a big name. The place to live is in the Buckhead area. I think the developers have decided to call it prestigious." (38)

Historian, Wilbur Kurtz, summed up Buckhead perfectly. Some years ago, after the Civil War, some people wanted to rename Buckhead. "An attempt was made to change the name of the locality to Irbyville, and it is so marked on certain County maps, but the name wouldn't stick—so Buckhead it is, and Buckhead it will remain." (39)

CHAPTER TWENTY-SIX
1920s-1930s
Dairies

*N*umerous dairies were in operation in Buckhead during in the 1920s and 1930s. C. W. Webb operated his dairy on Mayson Avenue (now Lindbergh Drive), and Byrd's Dairy was located on West Paces Ferry "about a half a block in from the Buckhead center...[Wilson's] garage was at one time where the dairy was," Annye Mae Cobb said. (1) William R. Cobb managed a dairy on Garmon Road, Ivon Rolader ran one on Howell Mill Road, Hoyle Adams operated his dairy on Peachtree Battle Avenue, Elmur Farm Dairy was near Randall Mill Road, Keys Dairy was on the present Morris Brandon School site, and Reuben Morris operated his dairy on Moores Mill Road in the late thirties and into the forties.

C. W. Webb's dairy was situated approximately where Sam's Warehouse is today, off Lindbergh Drive, across from the present Lindbergh MARTA Station. "Daddy rented [the property] from Mr. Smith," Sue Webb Stephens, one of the Webb's twelve children recalled. "Often the cows would roam out off the property. One neighbor's "wife would call us...she'd get those cows by the tail and swing 'em around and she'd bring those cows in." (2)

Mrs. Stephens, whose grandfather was a cousin of Dr. C. M. Adams, said you could buy "chicken on the feet," at Jones [grocery store]. She recalled riding the streetcar to town to shop at Rich's, J. P. Allen's, and Regenstein's department stores. "Mr. [Richard] Rich would always meet Mother at the door [of Rich's]." Mr. Webb moved his dairy to Sandy Springs in the 1930s. (3)

The Hoyle Adams family, also related to Dr. Adams, moved from Alpharetta to Peachtree Battle Avenue, where he ran a commercial dairy. His daughter Edith Adams (Mrs. George) Minhinnett said that her father "had one of the first little Model T Trucks," which he used to deliver milk to E. Rivers School, to private homes, and to the market. (4)

Edith Adams married Axon C. Minhinnett Jr.'s son, George, in 1933, and they moved next door to the senior Minhinnett's Big House on Roswell

Road, where George operated a nursery and bicycle shop. (5)

William R. Cobb operated his dairy on Garmon road, near Mt. Paran Road, and supplied milk, buttermilk, and butter to the downtown residents twice a week. Later he had a vegetable garden and sold the produce to local merchants. (6)

CHAPTER TWENTY-SEVEN
1925-1929
Buckhead, Such A Lovely Neighborhood

In 1925 the Beverly Hills phase of Phillips C. McDuffie's Garden Hills neighborhood was developed, through his Garden Hills Company. The Country Club and Brentwood sections were to be ready in 1941. The property where Garden Hills Elementary School and North Fulton High School were later built was also part of his master design. (1)

A brochure put out by the P. C. McDuffie Company touted the new Garden Hills neighborhood as "the GARDEN SPOT of Atlanta's wonderful Northside residential section where the appeal of nature blends with all modern luxury." The average lot sold for $2,750 and measured 60 feet by 200 feet, fronted with sidewalks. The project offered a playground and was also "equipped with every modern appliance for the health and happiness of all those who live in this community of happy home lovers. Here, under the blue skies and away from the noise and smoke of the city, the kiddies can grow into sturdy, rugged, happy boys and girls." (2)

A letter to Robert W. Barnwell, dated August 25, 1925, informed McDuffie that The Piedmont Company wanted to list the four completed homes in Garden Hills with his company. The homes were to be priced from $25,000 to $28,000. (3) By the end of the year, five homes had been built on or near Rumson Road. (4)

On August 17, 1987, McDuffie's Garden Hills was named to the National Registry of Historic Places by the United States Department of the Interior. (5)

***

"My parents moved out to the corner of West Wesley Road and Peachtree (the present site of Two West Wesley Condos)...about 1925," and bought the J. Epps Brown home, Florence "Poncie" Bryan (Mrs. William Bonneau) Ansley said. Judge Shepherd and Florence Cobb (Jackson) Bryan moved to Buckhead from their home at the corner of Peachtree and Twelfth streets to be near many of their friends. (6)

Shepherd Bryan was a lawyer and judge of the Superior Court of Fulton County, who had moved to Atlanta from North Carolina before 1900. He married Florence Cobb Jackson, daughter of Henry and Sally (Cobb) Jackson of Athens, and granddaughter of Confederate general T. R. Cobb. (7)

"[Buckhead] was a lovely neighborhood when we moved out. The block had lovely homes and nice big lots all the way from Muscogee Avenue to West Wesley," Mrs. Ansley said. "It was so easy to cross Peachtree then and people…parked up and down the street right in front of the house." (8)

Mrs. Bryan decided that the children in the neighborhood needed refining, so she organized a dancing school, which met in her home. She "hired Miss Margaret Mooring to come once a week on Saturday afternoons to teach us and the boys on the block," Mrs. Ansley said. The music was supplied from a "windup Victrola." (9)

The streetcar ran in front of the Bryan home. "The law was that you must stop when the streetcar stopped, because the people had to cross right in front of the cars. [It] was very noisy, but it made it very convenient because you could come and go, and friends could come to see you…and the men could go to work," Mrs. Ansley explained. (10)

***

Fred Leon Rand, an architect with Pringle and Smith, designed and built his two-story, Georgian colonial home on Piedmont Road in 1926. The home was called Leighton for Mr. Rand's hometown in Alabama. (11)

"Piedmont Road at that time was a very high-crowned, two-lane, asphalt road with little traffic," Mr. Rand's daughter Mildred Rand (Mrs. Alva) Lines said. "My brother [Dr. Edgar Rand], as a young boy, could take his Flexi Racer and go down the steep driveway right on across the road and not worry about it. We had a tennis court in the backyard, and many of the boys would…set up a ball game on the front hill. The tennis court became a Victory Garden during World War II. The neighbors would come for a 4th of July picnic." She recalled Minhinnett's hamburger stand, a yearly fall carnival at R. L. Hope School, and swimming in Mooney's lake. Mrs. Edward Knott had a tea room at 3095 Peachtree Road that had "absolutely marvelous food, and you could see all your friends on Sunday." (12)

Mildred Rand married Savannahan Alva Lines in 1940. Before the war Mr. Lines and Boisfeuillet Jones worked with the National Youth Administration, teaching skills to young people, and "helped start the…Atlanta Youth Symphony Orchestra (1945)," Mr. Lines said. The orchestra became the

Atlanta Symphony Orchestra in 1947. (13) During World War II, Captain Lines served in the U. S. Air Force in the Pacific, and "later [Gen. Douglas] McArthur sent me back to be part of the military government in Japan." Afterwards, he attended the University of Virginia and the School of Military Law at Yale University to learn Japanese, "to prepare for the occupation of Korea and Japan." After retiring from the military, Lines returned to Atlanta and started Imagers, Inc. (14)

***

Cam D. Dorsey bought a lot on Habersham, at Vernon Road, and built a home about 1926. His son Sam went to Camp Ashnoka, in Asheville, North Carolina, with many of his fellow Buckhead friends in the early 1920s. At the camp at Asheville School for Boys, "I was captain of the Red Midgets, and we played baseball, went swimming," Sam Dorsey reminisced. Serpentine Road was the original name of Vernon Road. (15)

***

In 1926 architect Neel Reid designed an 18th-century Baroque-style replica of a Venetian church for Mr. and Mrs. Joseph Rhodes at 541 (West) Paces Ferry Road. The home, that sits on the corner of Tuxedo Road, became known as Sante Stae. In the spring, this home is a traffic-stopper when the entrance is abloom with two rows of beautiful pink dogwood trees. (16) Further west on the road, the Gately-Loridans' Georgian Revival mansion was built in 1927; today the home is on Paces Forest Drive. (17)

***

Around 1927, after their marriage, Carol (Dean) and Frank Spratlin built a home at 2943 Habersham Road. About the same time, Mrs. Spratlin's sister Dorothy (Dean) and her husband, Joel Chandler Harris Jr., built a home on the east side of the turtle-back road at 2973. "Jake was on *The Georgian* at the time. Then he went...into [national] newspaper advertising, at *The Constitution*," Mrs. Harris said of her husband, the youngest of author Joel Chandler Harris' nine children. (18)

***

Hugh T. Richardson (1869-1951) built his home on property that ran from (West) Paces Ferry Road back to the present Broadland Road in 1927.

The Mississippian, who was the son of Louise (French) and Lee Richardson, came to visit the Cotton States International Exposition in Atlanta in 1895. "He and Mr. (John) Ottley came over to the Cotton States Exposition from Vicksburg and never went back," his daughter Louise Richardson (Mrs. Ivan, Jr.) Allen said. (19)

In 1896 Richardson married Josephine Inman, daughter of Hugh Theodore Inman, one of the promoters of the Exposition. Mr. Inman's grandfather Abednego, along with his brothers, Shadrach and Meshach, fought in the Revolutionary War. Inman's father, Shadrach W., "was ruined financially by the War Between the States, and moved to Atlanta [from East Tennessee] shortly thereafter, entering the cotton business," founding S. W. Inman & Sons. (20) After their honeymoon in Europe, Hugh and Josephine Richardson built a home next to her parents, on land given to them by Mr. Inman, at the corner of West Peachtree and Fifth Street. Richardson joined his father-in-law's firm, but in 1896, after the business dissolved, he started The Richardson Realty Co. The couple had four children; Hugh Inman, Lee, Josephine, and Louise. (21)

"What brought them [the Hugh Richardsons] out here, I believe, was the excavation of the Biltmore Hotel," Mrs. Allen explained. "I think they started with the steam shovels at 5:00 in the morning and would hoop and holla' and dynamite, and no one would know when they were going to dynamite, must have been a lot of rock down underneath." The Richardson property fronted (West) Paces Ferry Road, and the house, designed by New Jersey architect Aymar Embry, today sits on Northside Drive, which "was a continuation of Hemphill Avenue." (22)

"He [Mr. Richardson] had a great deal to do with the extension of Northside Drive past Fourteenth Street, and got the convicts to build the low rock wall that goes down Paces Ferry and down Northside Drive. That's when they worked the convicts," Franklin M. Garrett explained. (23)

The same year the Richardsons moved to Buckhead, Ivan Earnest Allen Sr. moved his family from West Peachtree to their newly-built Tudor-style home (designed by Pringle and Smith) at 2600 Peachtree Road (now 18 townhouses, one of which is the residence of former mayor Sam Massell). "I was in Boy's High School at that time and had a little two-door with a rumble seat in it, coupe, 4-cylinder Chevrolet," Ivan E. Allen Jr. mused. "I would leave there in the morning and go to high school…and I would always pick up two or three other fellas…we'd share the cost of the gasoline." (24) Ivan Earnest Allen, son of Susan Reese Harris and Daniel Earnest Allen, was born on March 1, 1877, in Dalton, Georgia, and moved to Atlanta in 1895 and became a forty-dollar-a-month typewriter salesman. In 1900 he opened Fielder and Allen, an office equipment store, which later became Allen-Marshall Company. Today this business is known as the Ivan Allen Co. He married Irene Susannah Beaumont and moved to 874 West Peachtree, where their son Ivan Jr. was born in 1911. Mr. Allen Sr. was civically active, and was one of the organizers of the Atlanta Retail Merchants Association, the Atlanta Chamber of Commerce, the Southeastern Fair, the Boy Scouts in Atlanta, and he raised money for the building of Oglethorpe University. In the political arena, some of Ivan Allen Sr.'s accomplishments include serving in the State Senate from 1919-1920, and as a member of the Agriculture and Industrial Development Board of Georgia (1943). He also served as chairman of a commission "to reorganize the state government (1929)," the first Forward Atlanta Commission, Georgia's Democratic Campaign Committee in 1940, and the Fulton County Board of Public Welfare. He died in 1968. (25)

Ivan Allen Jr. went into his father's business, following his graduation from Georgia Tech, and married Louise Richardson in 1936. During World War II (1942-1945) he served in the U.S. Army, attaining the rank of major. After returning to civilian life, he served as Gov. Ellis Arnall's executive secretary from 1945 to 1946, and in 1946 he became president of Ivan Allen Co. when his father retired from the business. (26) In 1961 Allen was elected mayor of Atlanta, serving two terms, and was instrumental in calming the waters of the city during the tumultuous Civil Rights movement during the early 1960s.

Louise Allen, who attended Rosemary Hall in Connecticut and Vassar College in New York, also made her mark in the community. She was a "Co-founder of Atlanta Speech School; founding member of The Westminster Schools board; chairman emeritus for life of Atlanta Historical Society," (27) and was the driving force that got the Atlanta Historical Society to buy the thirty-two acres of her uncle Edward Inman's Andrews Drive property, which is crowned by the Swan House. In 1969 the City of Atlanta honored her as "Woman of the Year." (28)

***

The Rufus C. Darbys moved to 3003 Habersham Road around 1928. His father, Rufus Clark Darby, owned Darby Printing Co. in Washington, D. C. "They used to do railroad tariff work," Judy Beers (Mrs. Rufus M.) Darby, explained about her husband's family. "When the Southern Railroad opened up offices here in Atlanta…[Mr. Darby sent his son to Atlanta] to open the printing plant and to do all the Southern Railway tariff work." (29)

***

One of the most famous homes in Georgia, The Swan House, was built in 1928 on Andrews Drive. Designed by Philip Trammell Shutze, it was built by Mr. and Mrs. Edward H. Inman and was first called Nevera when the Inmans lived there. It was renamed The Swan House because of "Mrs. Inman's love of the birds, evident in the swan motifs displayed throughout the house." Today the home is a major part of the Atlanta History Center. (30)

Louise Richardson (Mrs. Ivan Jr.) Allen reminisced about Sundays at the Edward Inman's during her childhood. "After church that whole connection of the family (the Inmans, Richardsons, and Grants) would come and have about a 45-minute visit on the screen porch. They [the elders] probably had a glass of ice tea, or the men had a highball." While they socialized, the children played outside. Afterwards, each family would retire to its home. (31)

***

In 1928-1929, Owen J. Southwell designed and built a home for M. M. Emmert at 591 (West) Paces Ferry Road at the corner of Northside Drive. The home changed hands several times, when it was bought by Leonard Richardson, and then later by Byron Reeves. In 1969 John H. Candler Jr. great-grandson of Coca-Cola Company founder Asa G. Candler, bought the property and renovated it. When he went bankrupt, the estate went on the auction block and was bought in 1975 by Fulton County Commissioner Tom Lowe and his wife Betty, a former state representative. (32)

CHAPTER TWENTY-EIGHT
1925-1929
A Surge of New Enterprises

"I remember Wender and Roberts."
- Everybody

*B*usinesses increased in Buckhead as the population continued to grow. Among these new enterprises were the community's first bank, a specialty grocery store, two drugstores, a restaurant, and a spring water company.

Fulton Bank was opened in 1925 by John Schley (Sly) Thompson and his wife Helen (Pace), on Peachtree Road, about four doors north of Buckhead Avenue. Buckhead's first bank later merged with Fulton National Bank in the early 1930s, and both Thompsons were made vice presidents and managers. (1) Mrs. Thompson, who was a descendant of Hardy Pace, "was probably the first woman officer of any bank in the southeast...She was a good banker, she knew everybody...She reigned supreme out here in Buckhead," Virlyn Moore said. (2)

***

Kamper's Grocery Store opened on Peachtree Road, between Pharr Road and Peachtree Avenue, in 1925. Its founder, German native Charles Joseph Kamper, came to Atlanta from Buffalo, New York, in 1872, and approximately two years later opened a grocery on Peachtree at Ivy Street, (where Crawford Long Hospital is now). He married Florence Edith Meakin, and their son Francis Edgar Kamper was born in 1883. (3)

The success of Kamper's Grocery was due not only to walk-in customers, but it developed a large phone-order business. Each morning Kamper's customers were called for a list of their needs, and their orders were then delivered to them by horse and wagon. (4)

Francis Kamper attended Boy's High School and worked in the store in the afternoons. "He really wanted to be a banker, but it wasn't possible for him to go to college," Nancy Kamper (Mrs. Henry) Miller said of her father. He later became president of Kamper's, and of the National Retail Grocers Association of the United States, and was also active in civic and church programs. He married Vera Matilda Reins in 1905 and had two daughters, Nancy Surrage and Vera Waller. (5)

As their customers moved north and east, Kamper's Grocery followed. They moved first to Peachtree and Linden Avenue; another store was opened on Peachtree at 10th Street, "one in the Emory area, I think Buckhead was the last one," Mrs. Miller said. (6)

The demise of many family-owned grocery stores occurred when "the chain grocery stores came in and they could buy in such quantities, they could undersell the prices that individual stores had," Mrs. Miller explained. Francis Kamper closed his business in 1945, "Father was getting old, and he decided he would just close down." He died in 1960. (7)

***

On the corner of Peachtree and Pharr roads, the current location of NationsBank, Harrison Anderson lived and operated a grocery store. He also sold gasoline, and his customers would pull their cars to the curb on Peachtree Road to be serviced. (8)

***

Two new drugstores were established in Buckhead and became very popular with the residents of the community. Judson L. Hawk opened his drugstore in Buckhead on Peachtree Road at Peachtree Avenue, now a McDonalds location, around 1925. Hawk had come to Atlanta as a young man about 1902 and worked as a curb boy at a drugstore on Peachtree Street near Linden Avenue (now Crawford Long Hospital), while going to school. After college, he enrolled in the Atlanta College of Pharmacy, and around 1915 he opened Hawk and Stephens Drugstore on West Peachtree and 14th Street. "Their slogan was 'Druggist to the north side,'" son Dr. Judson L. Hawk Jr., a pediatrician, said. "People said what a damn fool he was going so far north. That he would dry up." (9)

In order to compete with the large chain drugstores, Hawk and "four or five other independent druggists started the Bestmade Ice Cream Company by collectively making ice cream for each other." The company "grew to become Drugs Mutual, the wholesale drug house in Atlanta," Dr. Judson Hawk Jr. explained. Only the independent pharmacist could own stock. "That allowed a lot of independent stores to stay in business." Hawk be-

Heritage group wants to save cemetery

The Buckhead Heritage Society objects to a pending application to remove a historic African-American cemetery from Buckhead's Frankie Allen Park

An application has been made to the Urban Design Commission by Community Renewal LLC to remove graves from the Mount Olive Cemetery at 431 Pharr Road NE, adjacent to the park.

Mount Olive Cemetery is all that remains of the Macedonia Park neighborhood, which was one of Buckhead's few historic black communities. A public hearing on the application was scheduled to be held June 10, the day the Buckhead Reporter went to press.

"Buckhead Heritage is saddened to learn of an attempt to remove one of the last remnants of African-American history in Buckhead," said Christine McCauley, the executive director of

the Buckhead Heritage Society. "We hope the landowner will be amenable to finding some alternative solution that will not negatively affect the Mount Olive Cemetery."

The area, known as Macedonia, was settled by freed slaves after the Civil War. In 1921 developer John Owens created an African-American subdivision named Macedonia Park. Macedonia was a thriving community and included 400 residents, three churches, two grocery stores, barbers, a blacksmith and restaurants. In the 1940s Fulton County began to systematically remove residents by condemning and purchasing the properties in Macedonia to make way for a park.

Located at the entrance to Frankie Allen Park, the 0.22-acre cemetery contains approximately 45 marked and unmarked African-American graves.

Nik and Arte, formerly of Fishmonger Seafood Grill, bring you...

Teela Taqueria

Tac o' the Town

Sandy Springs Freshest Taqueria
Tasty a la Carte Food at Great a la Carte Prices!

Taco's With A Twist!

came president and chairman of the board of Drugs Mutual. When he retired in the 1960s, he sold the drugstore to two of his employees, Mr. M. L. Owens and Dr. Cecil McGahee. (10)

In the summer of 1927 Wender & Roberts Drugstore began operating at 3073 Peachtree Road, in the heart of Buckhead, when pharmacist William Max Wender bought the drugstore from misters Callendar and Bussey. Marvin Roberts, who was working for the drugstore at the time of the purchase, became the Roberts of Wender & Roberts. "It was an opportunity, it was a growing area, an area of affluence, and he felt the business opportunity there were good," William M. Wender Jr. said of his father. "He owned a store at the Georgian Terrace Hotel, and previous to that, on Capitol Avenue near the Educational Alliance about 1915." (11)

Mr. Wender came to Atlanta from Lithuania in 1904, when he was ten years old, and lived in the Boulevard Park area of the city. He married Freda Cristol of Atlanta, and their three sons, William Jr., Donald, and Robert all became pharmacists in the family business. (12)

"We all went to the Southern College of Pharmacy, which is now Mercer University College," William Wender Jr. said. "Don and I went into the business after the war, even though we had worked there since the thirties, when we were young kids. We caught curb, we had curb service. People came out from the Druid Hills area and the Atlanta area on Sunday afternoon to get their chocolate sodas. Cars used to be lined up, angle parking on Peachtree, for a block or more down. Then we graduated to a soda dispenser or soda jerks...People in Buckhead were very nice to us, they were very good customers...for five generations families are still trading with us...Wender & Roberts was more or less a meeting place in Buckhead for many years." (13)

"The independent stores in every section of town were the successful drugstores. They would give the personal service, and in those days that's what people wanted," Bill Wender continued. "They wanted their little boys on bicycles delivering the packages, of course we had motorcycles [after World War II]. Atlanta was an independent drugstore town...the pharmacist was there for years and you could go in...pick up something and say 'charge that to me,' and go out the door, no name." (14)

Wender & Roberts became a place where the elite met to eat. "In those days we had a literary crowd in Buckhead. Ralph McGill lived on Piedmont, Justice A. B. Martin...prominent writers from *The Atlanta Journal*, Col. Ed Danforth...a number of editorial writers," Mr. Wender recalled. "We met a lot of interesting people in Wender & Roberts." (15)

Dorothy Dean (Mrs. Joel Chandler, Jr.) Harris remembered that at Wender & Roberts "you could go in and sit down at a table and order a Coca-Cola from the fountain with crushed ice for a nickel, and a ... sandwich of peanut butter." (16)

"Wender & Roberts was the place to go. They had a soda fountain, booths, and it was a gathering place for the young people," Laura Maddox (Mrs. Edward D.) Smith reminisced. (17)

"John's mother (Mrs. John W. Grant Jr.)...looked out one day, and there was a mule running amuck in her front yard (on Chatham Road), which was newly grassed," Louise "Weezie" (Mrs. John W. III) Grant said. "She didn't know who to call, so she called Wender & Roberts Drugstore, and they took care of it." (18)

***

Sometime during the mid twenties, the Wieuca Inn, "a rambling building of white wood," was opened on Roswell Road at Wieuca, by an unknown Jewish immigrant from Eastern Europe. He left New York, with Birmingham as his destination, but when his train stopped in Atlanta, he looked around and decided to stay. "He opened up a hot dog stand at Five Points and started making some money," Cecil Alexander said. "He built a five- or six-story building at the corner of Peachtree and Harris Street, across the street from the Capitol City Club. He got the idea (the movies had just started coming on) of putting a movie on the roof of this building. His genius left him because he didn't realize that there weren't going to be enough hours of darkness during the summer. He lost everything on that movie adventure." With financial help from Henry and Aaron Alexander, he opened the Wieuca Inn, which became a popular spot to eat and dance. The name Wieuca got its name from the developer, who used his children's initials. (19)

My mother, Cecilia Tesler (Mrs. Walter) Kessler, spoke of going to a tavern in Buckhead with her friends. "That was Wieuca Inn on Wieuca Road," her cousin Mary Tesler (Mrs. Ike) Kadis said. "Sometimes they would have dances on Saturday night." (20)

"We used to go down that area to 'neck,'" Mary's sister Rose Tesler (Mrs. Herman) Mechlowitz confessed. "We used to go to Silver Lake (Oglethorpe). There used to be a chicken house on Roswell Road, and we used to go there on Sunday nights. It was a restaurant in a home. And their specialty was fried chicken." (21)

***

"My father, Ivon, and his brothers, Clark and Homer, started the Rolader Spring Water Co...about the time I was born in the middle 1920s," Donald W. "Pete" Rolader said. "The springs were located off West Paces Ferry

Road...in the subdivision that is now known as Kingswood." (22) Because of his business, Ivon acquired the nickname "Springwater." (23)

The five-gallon water jugs used to hold the water were washed and sterilized daily, filled with spring water, corked, sealed and "loaded on the water trucks and hauled into Atlanta and used for drinking water in the office buildings downtown," Mr. Rolader explained. "This was before there were...electric coolers or drinking water in downtown office buildings. We furnished the coolers that these jugs turned upside down on, then we had an ice service that followed around and kept ice in those things...[this lasted] until electric water coolers came in [around the 1950s]." (24)

"My granddaddy [G. E. "Ed" Chatham] and I built the body on the truck that [the Roladers] hauled that spring water," Ken Moss said. "They wore out about four or five trucks...It was real good water." (25)

Ivon Rolader and his brothers also operated a gas station and general store at the corner of Moores Mill and Northside Drive, which also served as the Rolader Water Co. office. "In that store we had everything from gasoline pumps, groceries to dry goods to feeds to auto repair garage, and even a blacksmith shop," Mr. Rolader explained. "That corner belonged to my father's uncle, who was a minister [L. D. Rolader] at the Center Congregational Church down the road. He had leased this store to my father when he came back from World War I." (26)

Pete Rolader and his brother Ivon Jr. ("Ike") grew up in the midst of a large family on Moores Mill Road. "Grandmother lived on one side of the street and on the other side of Moores Mill Road were cousins by the bushels," Pete Rolader explained. "We all practically lived as one big family." The children "rode bicycles and roller skated and even played tin can hockey on Moores Mill Road, and you wouldn't have to get out of the way for a car." (27)

***

"In January 1925 the Rev. J. C. Adams from the [Methodist] Sunday School Board of the North Georgia Conference, Mr. D. J. Cofer, a Buckhead resident, and 19 theology students from Emory University made a religious survey of a one mile radius from the business center of Buckhead." After finding many residents in the area who were Methodists, they decided to form a new church. Dr. and Mrs. Methvin T. Salter offered their home for the first organizational meeting, and nineteen people became the founders of Peachtree Road Methodist Church. Rev. E. H. Wood served as the first pastor. (28)

With a loan of $15,000, a lot on Peachtree Road (present site of the International House of Pancakes) at Sardis Way was purchased, and by

June of 1925 services were being held in the partially-built sanctuary. The following year the Church was faced with foreclosure and was rescued by Emory University's financial help. (29)

In 1941 the property was sold for $41,500, and the present lot at 3180 Peachtree Road was purchased. While the Great Hall was under construction, the congregation used the temporary buildings, which had been moved from the original site. In 1947 the present white, colonial-style Sanctuary was built. (30)

***

The congregation of the Peachtree Presbyterian Church, which was founded in 1919, moved from tent meetings into their new, gray-granite sanctuary at the corner of Peachtree and Mathieson Drive (now Wendy's) in 1926. The Rev. F. D. Stevenson served as the first minister. (31)

***

Covenant Presbyterian Church, the first church in Atlanta to move to Buckhead, opened its doors in its Gothic-style building at 2461 Peachtree Road, on the corner of Terrace Drive, in November of 1926. The church had its beginnings in 1874, when Reverend W. H. Crawford was sent by the Cumberland Presbyterian Church of Tennessee to Atlanta to preach to their new congregation. Lacking in support, the First Cumberland Presbyterian Church closed in 1877, but was reestablished in 1901. Services were held in a tent on Baker Street until their church on Spring at Harris streets was dedicated in 1904. Three years later the church was renamed Harris Street Presbyterian Church. It was renamed Covenant Presbyterian Church when it moved to Buckhead, and Wilson A. Eisenhard served as first pastor. (32)

***

In 1927 the Sardis Methodist Church congregation, under the direction of George Spruill, built a Georgian-style church on their property on Powers Ferry Road. "Reputedly, the basement of the present structure was dug out manually by women prisoners," it was stated in a news article. (33) "And they helped make the brick that was used in the construction," Guy Patterson said. (34)

***

On October 11, 1927, Mayson Avenue became Lindbergh Drive. The road, formerly named for James Lucas Mayson, owner of Mayson & Turner Ferry at the Chattahoochee River, was renamed for the aviation hero Charles A. Lindbergh. Five months after his auspicious flight in the *Spirit of St. Louis* from New York to Paris, Atlanta celebrated Lindbergh Day. He flew his famous plane to Atlanta and landed at Chandler Field amid a tumultuous welcome. A parade celebrating the event went along Peachtree Road through Buckhead. (35)

***

On December 1, 1929, lots went on sale in the newly created Haynes Manor, which had been developed by Eugene V. Haynes, "a former well-known jeweler turned real estate developer. (36) Lots in the 125-acre tract, that ran from Peachtree Road to Northside Drive, ranged in price from $1,250 to $2,500. The advertising brochure for the new community stated:

A prominent hill in Haynes Manor was the headquarters of Benjamin Harrison (during the Civil War), afterward President of the United States. On this very spot he was made a brigadier general, here, too, he fell wounded. (37)

CHAPTER TWENTY-NINE
Late 1920s
Their Hearts Were Young and Gay

*D*uring the 1920s, life in Buckhead was still relatively uncomplicated. Before the Great Depression hit and World War II exploded, a vivid imagination was the order of the day for many of Buckhead's youth, looking to entertain themselves. Horseback riding, home parties, tennis, and badminton were fashionable, and a fascination for the automobile put many home-built and store-bought models on the road.

Boy Scouting was a popular activity for many Buckhead boys; Troup 5 met in the Buckhead Baptist Church on (West) Paces Ferry Road, and Troup 45 met in the Peachtree Presbyterian Church on Peachtree Road. "They bought a barracks from...Camp Gordon and moved it down there [to the Peachtree Presbyterian Church] ...Our scout master was a wonderful man, John Wayt Jr," Joseph K. Heyman reminisced. Among his fellow scouts were George Hightower, Phinizy Calhoun Jr., Hugh Dorsey Jr., the McDuffie boys and McClarian Johnson. "We had overnight hikes...We took part in the Scout Jamboree contests each year. Some of our scout members were real expert in doing fire by friction, and they used to win that prize." (1)

While working on the biking merit badge, George Hightower and Phinizy Calhoun "had to take a trip that was fifty miles and had to do it in one day. The first time we went to Duluth, it was all dirt roads, and my seat broke off just as I was leaving up here at 'Deadman's Curve'...We didn't get credit for it because we didn't send a card when we got to Duluth, so we had to do it all over again." (2)

Before annexation in 1952, Atlanta "was surrounded by a group of sustaining communities," such as Buckhead, Bolton, Whittier Mills, Inman Yards, Riverside, Ben Hill, and Masons, explained Virlyn Moore Jr. The common factors were that each had a corner drugstore and grocery, a church, school, and a ball team. (3)

"Everybody had a baseball team. There were fifty baseball teams surrounding Atlanta," Mr. Moore said. "Buckhead had a half a dozen" that were sponsored by Y-Church Leagues and businesses such as the Rolader

Water Company. The boys from Rarytown "played ball for the Sardis Methodist Church." (4) The mecca for black baseball was the Moores Mill Road area, where "the New Hope (Church) Dodgers...beat most of the surrounding teams." (5)

***

Horseback riding was the vogue, and many Buckhead gentlemen enjoyed early morning rides along paths that traversed the woods around (West) Paces Ferry, Habersham, and Argonne roads. This group became known as the Saddle and Sirloin Club, and included Walter Hill, James Dickey, Robert Maddox, Trammell Scott, Phillips McDuffie, John Grant, Hugh Richardson, Ivan Allen, and Herbert Oliver.

"They [the riders] all met at different homes in the morning...during the week...and they'd have orange juice and coffee," Helen McDuffie said. (6)

"Daddy rode with them," Ivan Allen Jr. said of the Saddle and Sirloin Club. "Fell twice and broke his arm. He used Mr. Walter Hill's stable." (7)

"We rode horseback all through these woods," said Louise Richardson (Mrs. Ivan Jr.) Allen. "I remember riding with them two or three times. It was great fun." (8)

***

There was a stable in Garden Hills, where horses were rented. "Where the pool is now, used to be a riding ring," Helen McDuffie explained. "We'd go riding...all the way to Piedmont, then we'd cross Piedmont and ride till we hit the Southern Railway." Ms. McDuffie and her friends also played hopscotch, smoked rabbit tobacco, went on hayrides, and hunted possum in the woods. (9)

George Hightower played polo with a mallet and volleyball in the Garden Hills riding ring. He also went hunting in the meadowland that is now Bobby Jones Golf Course. "We would have a big dove shoot every New Year's day...eight to ten of us." (10)

Tom Murray remembers playing golf where Buckhead Plaza is today. (11)

Ellie Patterson and her friends waded in a creek in the present Garden Hills area, climbed cherry trees on Pharr Road and ate the fruit, swam in Mooney's Lake at night, and skated on Pharr Road in the middle of the street. "One car came by once in awhile," Ellie Patterson, whose family moved from Gainesville to their new home on Lexie Avenue (now North Fulton Drive) in 1925, said. She remembered the trucks of the City Ice

Delivery Co., at the corner of Peachtree and Pharr roads (present site of Super Cut), delivering chunks of ice to home ice boxes, and the Highland Bakery selling baked goods from their horse-drawn carriages. (12)

Roy Milling, whose family moved to Fulton Avenue (now Lenox Road) in 1925, said he and his friends "used to walk down to Peachtree Creek and build dams, dam it up to swim in two feet of water." They would float down the creek on a home-made raft from the Lenox area to Piedmont Road. (13)

Mr. Milling described Buckhead as "wilderness...could go almost in any direction on Peachtree and get into the woods real quick...It was a nice little country town. When you got up when you could get in trouble and drive the car too fast, you didn't get a ticket. The officer would just say, 'Have your dad call me.'" He recalled that "cabs used to set on East Paces at the corner of Peachtree and that's where the paper boys went to pick up their papers...[and] where you paid the supervisor." (14)

***

Woodhaven, the Maddox estate, was a gathering place for the young set, where they played badminton and attended Coca-Cola parties. "Boys would come over...from Boys High and Marist. They actually used Woodhaven as sort of a club...especially on weekends, [where] there would be as many as twenty cars parked in front of the house," Laura Maddox (Mrs. Edward D.) Smith explained. "We had a straw rug on the porch with black and white checks. The boys decided that it was exactly the size of a checkerboard and moved all of the furniture out. We got Mother's fine Victrola records, and the big size records were checkers and the small size records were the other checkers. They played checkers with Mother's Victrola records on the rug. (15)

"Papa had a marble bust of his father in the same room on a big pedestal. He was a handsome man, with a big white mustache. One night we decided that he looked too formidable, so we kissed him all over with his face with red lipstick, and got a cigar and put it in his mouth. Put a slouchy hat...and...an overcoat on him...and we fixed him up, and we thought he looked real snappy. My mother said the next morning Papa came downstairs and saw his father, and he nearly had a stroke," Mrs. Smith mused. (16)

When the Conkey Whiteheads, their next-door neighbors, had a party, young Laura Maddox invited her friends over. The group would sit in the garden and listen to the orchestra music, and often called over to the Whiteheads to make musical requests.

"Every time we made a request, they would play it immediately, and we'd call back and say thank you," Mrs. Smith continued. (17)

***

"T Model Fords were going out and A Models were coming in in 1929," George Hightower recalled. He and George Wood bought outmoded cars for $10 or $15, cut them up and built *cutouts*. "I had one called 'Feena'...You take the whole body off, have a frame and a motor and put the hood back on with a leather strap around it, lower the steering wheel down into your lap, and use a wood seat...two people could sit on it...behind it was the gas tank." The finished products were sold to their friends for $50 or $75, and raced on a racetrack near the airport and on Northside Drive. "J. L. Riley was able to make seventy miles an hour...and since we could drive at age fourteen without a license...we used (West) Paces Ferry Road as a race track every Saturday morning." (18)

Ivan Allen Jr. recalled a race around 1927, run to determine which vehicle was the fastest. "O. J. Sala had a big red Indian motorcycle and Dick Gallogly...had a LaSalle Roadster, a rumble seat, canvas top. On a Saturday morning, with permission of [policeman] Cal Cates, they raced from Buckhead down West Paces Ferry, and stopped at what is the four-lane down here (now Northside Parkway). All of the high school and college kids that lived around here were all lined up on either side of the road as they flashed by." The raced ended in a tie. (19)

Once, while George Hightower's parents were out of town, his two older brothers, Bill and Red, decided to deliver *The Atlanta Journal* to earn some extra money. Their friends piled into one of the brother's Ford, and they headed out to deliver the newspapers. After the car broke down, they borrowed both their parent's Leland Lincoln Touring Cars in order to make a faster delivery. "This route was way out in the sticks," Bill McCollough said in an article. "We drove up to one 'way-out shack' to deliver, and the owner came out and bowed, and said, 'Yes sir, what can I do for you?' When Red explained that he was the paper boy, the man almost fainted." The route ended when the Hightowers returned home. (20) "Dad found out about it when they got back, and he had a call from somebody raising cane because they hadn't had their paper delivered," George Hightower told me. The boys were grounded for two weeks. (21)

***

"There was the drive-in...corner of Paces Ferry and Peachtree (where Buckhead Plaza now stands), kind of back in the woods," Jack Spalding

138

James McC. Montgomery's Home
Standing Peachtree
Courtesy of Troy Anderson

Henry Irby
Courtesy of Carol M. (Mrs. Mike) Murphy and
Sara H. (Mrs. Binion) Jordan

Silas Donaldson
Courtesy of Mr. & Mrs. Leon Townsend

Mary Ann (Mrs. Silas) Donaldson
Courtesy of Mr. & Mrs. Leon Townsend

Old Howell Mill
Used with the permission of the Atlanta-Fulton Public Library

Rial Bailey and Sarah Jane (Irby) Hicks
Courtesy of Sara H. (Mrs. Binion) Jordan

Mary Ophelia Hicks
(Mrs. Seaborn) Ivey (at 16)
Courtesy of Sharon (Mrs. James) Matthews

Seaborn L. Ivey
(at 19 or 20)
Courtesy of Sharon (Mrs. James) Matthews

Thomas Moore
*Courtesy of The Atlanta
History Center*

John W. Grant
and Family
*Courtesy of Mr. & Mrs.
John W. Grant, III*

Intersection of Peachtree and Roswell Roads, c. 1910
Courtesy of The Atlanta History Center

New Hope School, 1910
Courtesy of Elizabeth C. (Mrs. Moses) Few

Robert Dorsey's Grocery Store, c. 1907
on Northeast Corner of Peachtree and East Paces Ferry Roads
Courtesy of The Atlanta History Center

Gov. John M. Slaton Home, *Wingfield*
Courtesy of The Atlanta History Center

Robert F. Maddox Home, *Woodhaven*
Courtesy of The Atlanta History Center

Former Ku Klux Klan Sheet Factory
Present Cotton Exchange Building, 3155 Roswell Road

Former Ku Klux Klan Imperial Palace, later owned by the
Cathedral of Christ the King
Courtesy of The Cathedral of Christ the King

Camp
Ashnoka,
c. 1920-1921
Courtesy of
Sam Dorsey

Bottom Row, L-R: Sam Dorsey; Phillips McDuffie, Jr.; Veazy Rainwater; Harry Harmon; L.W. "Chip" Robert, III; Brown Rainwater; Crawford Rainwater
2nd Row: Henry Hand; Fontain Weyman; Phillip Alston, Jr.; Wilbur Blackmen; Phinizy Calhoun, Jr.; Tom Holcomb; Hugh M. Dorsey; Paul Degive
3rd Row: Fred Stokes; Rufus Darby; Jack Glenn; Ivan Allen, Jr.; Ed Inman; Lawson Calhoun; Arthur Tufts; "Doc" Ballenger.
Top Row: Henry Degive or Larry Laurent; Tom Daniel; Darrell Ayer; Kels Boland; Tom Law; Joe Boland; George Adair; ?; Roy Collier

Buckhead Hardware Company, c. 1923
Courtesy of Thomas M. Murray

Harrison Anderson (L) in front of his Peachtree Road Store
(at Pharr Road), c. late 1920s
Courtesy of Carolyn Laudermilk

Rolader Pottery
Courtesy of Maybelle Tatum (Mrs. Daniel) Osborne

George McDuffie at 7 Cherokee Road
Courtesy of Helen McDuffie

R. L. Hope School, 1939
Courtesy of Mr. & Mrs. Alva Lines

Former Fulton County Alms House (white)
Present Galloway School, Chastain Park

Former Fulton County Alms House (black)
Present Fulton County Arts Center, Chastain Park

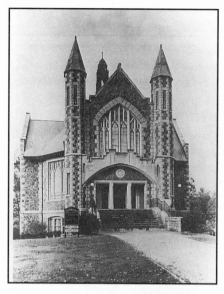

Original Peachtree Road
Presbyterian Church
*Courtesy of Peachtree
Presbyterian Church*

Original
Peachtree Road
Methodist
Church
from 1928-1942
*Courtesy of
Peachtree Road
United Methodist
Church*

Intersection of Peachtree and Roswell Roads, c. 1934
Courtesy of The Atlanta History Center

Rolader/Tatum Store
& Service Station,
Northside Drive and
Moores Mill Road
*Courtesy of Maybelle
Tatum (Mrs. Daniel)
Osborne*

Former Indoor
Badminton Court,
owned by Willian
T. Dreger, Jr.,
Lindbergh at
Piedmont

Mrs. Mary
Bloodworth's
Nursery/
Kindergarten

Charles Wilson and
Billy Bowen in front of
Lane Drugstore, 1937
Courtesy of Charles Wilson

Fritz Orr Camp, 1948
(L-R) Fritz Orr,
Victor ?, and
Ross Allen

Fritz Orr Camp Camping
Trip on top of Stone
Mountain, 1948
Frances Calder and
Susan Kessler (Barnard),
author of book (on right)
with Stormy

Intersection of
Peachtree Road and
Piedmont Road, 1940
Courtesy of Mr. & Mrs.
Alva Lines

Peachtree Road looking north at "Deadman's Curve" at
Cathedral of St. Philip, 1939
Courtesy of Mr. & Mrs. Alva Lines

Buckhead, c. 1948
Courtesy of the Atlanta History Center

recalled. "You got curb service…There was a blind black man, Blind Willie, and he'd come out and sing, (with his foot on the running board) he had a guitar, and he'd strum all these ballads…People would say, 'Meet you out at Blind's'." (22)

In the late twenties there was a private tennis court on Peachtree Road (current Burger King site) next to the National Library Binding Co. (until recently, Oxford Too); the owner is unknown. (23)

Miss Harriet (Hattie) Grant, sister of tennis player Bitsy Grant, remembered collecting her friends, Poncie Bryan (Ansley) and her sisters in the family Lincoln Touring Car and heading to the Brookhaven Country Club to swim. (24)

In the late twenties or early thirties, a three-day circus was held on Irby Alley. "They'd pitch a tent, bring two old mangy cats in, bring a small ferris wheel or something," Roy Milling said. The price of admission was twenty-five cents. (25)

***

Between approximately 1929-1933 concerts were held in an open-air theater band shell, which Phillips McDuffie built from a cut-out of a large hill behind the old Colonial Store on Keith Circle (now Buckhead Plaza). (26)

"It was successful…They had evening concerts," Jack Spalding recalled. (27) "I remember going there with Mother one time," Dr. Phinizy Calhoun said. (28) Mary Ann Bridges recalled Sunday concerts, and the audience either sat on benches or on the ground. (29)

***

The grade on Peachtree Road "is a continuous downhill from north of the junction of Peachtree and Roswell Road [from about Peachtree Methodist Church]," Jack Spalding said. "My mother was a very conservative driver, but she had the idea that if you were coasting…you could just fly like hell. And in those days you could pull your car out of gear, turn off your ignition and coast all the way from that church to Peachtree Creek. There were no traffic lights…For some reason or other, Mother thought that you were exempt from the law if you didn't have your foot on the pedal." (30)

CHAPTER THIRTY
1928
A Crime Spree

"Whiskey made me do it."
- George Harsh

$\mathcal{I}$n the fall of 1928, two young men from highly respected families, one a Buckhead resident, went on a crime spree that ended in murder. It began on the night of October 6, when E. H. Meeks was shot and killed while clerking at an A & P at 1004 Hemphill Avenue. Ten days later Willard Smith was held up at a drugstore, where he worked at 908 Boulevard, N.E. He was shot, and died shortly afterward, but the bullet he fired at the assailant helped solve the case. (1)

When Oglethorpe University student George Harsh sought medical treatment from a gunshot wound in his groin, the doctor reported the incident to police detective John Lowe. Harsh was arrested on campus on October 27, and his recovered bloody pants provided the evidence to link him to the crime. Harsh admitted shooting Meeks, and Smith then said that whiskey made him do it, "firing him to a craving for some thrill which could not be gratified by ordinary means." He also confessed to five other robberies and named Buckhead resident Richard G. "Dick" Gallogly, who lived at 2832 Peachtree Road, as his partner. (2)

Gallogly, whose family, the James R. Grays, owned *The Atlanta Journal*, was arrested in Athens, Georgia, where he was attending a football game. "Gallogly vehemently denied participation in the crimes and claimed that he went to the doors of the two stores only in an effort to prevent Harsh from carrying out his announced intention to rob the establishments." (3)

Harsh was tried, found guilty, and sentenced to death in the electric chair. Gallogly's first two trials ended in hung juries. While readying for a third trial, Gallogly plead guilty when he realized that Harsh was to be called to testify. He received a life sentence and was sent to Milledgeville. Harsh was retried and given a life sentence, which he served in Atlanta's

Bellwood camp. (4)

"The famous Dick Gallogly, the great murderer," Jack Spalding said sarcastically. "He was a rich kid, and a friend of his, George Harsh, used to go around holding up drugstores just for fun. His mother was one of the Grays; the Grays owned *The Journal*. The great thing about this case was it was a rich kid. Nothing his people could do to help him, and it ruined *The Journal* politically. Whenever *The Journal* endorsed a political candidate, the opposition would say, 'Well, this is a trade. If so-in-so is elected governor, he's promised to let Gallogly out of jail'…Finally, he was pardoned the day after (Gov.) Ed Rivers went out [of office]…The last night Ed Rivers sat up and pardoned everybody. [Gallogly] served a lot more time than he would have had he been a nobody." (5)

"My brother was a great friend of Dick's," Lillian Pace (Mrs. Paul) Scoville said. "That was such a sad occasion. Fred went away to W & L the year that they were picked up, and he was not in with the thing…It scared us all to death. Mother was just so grateful that Fred was out of town, so there could be no connection." (6)

"I knew Dick Gallogly and George Harsh very well," Ivan Allen Jr. said. "Played golf with [Harsh]. They served nine or ten years and were pardoned by Gov. E. Rivers…Dick Gallogly stayed here in town, and I think subsequently married. When [George Harsh] was pardoned from jail, he immediately went to Canada and volunteered in the Canadian Air Force, as they were developing the early planes to fight the Germans. After a few months, he transferred to England in a fighter squadron. On his first trip over Germany, he was a tail gunner in the plane, the plane was shot down, and he served five or six years in a German prison camp. Later on he came back and married and had a very fine family, and was living up in New Jersey the last time I heard about him. (7)

"While I was in office…a man walked in and wanted to see me about a private, personal matter," Mr. Allen continued. He said he was a neighbor of George Harsh's, and after filling in the details of his life after he left Atlanta, he said, "we think the people of Atlanta ought to know what a success he's been after that tragedy he went through." (8)

CHAPTER THIRTY-ONE
1929
Fritz Orr Camp

$\mathscr{T}$he Fritz Orr Camp, begun as an after-school program, was one of the finest camping experiences for boys and girls for over three decades. Fritz Orr, an Athens, Georgia, native, who had worked at the Athens Y Camp, at Mondamin Camp in North Carolina, and had taught math at the University School for Boys in Atlanta, was the camp's creator. In the fall of 1929, the married life insurance salesman found himself at the home of Charles B. Shelton at 2740 Habersham Road in the afternoons, teaching sports to Shelton's four boys. After other neighborhood children joined the boys, Mr. Shelton encouraged Orr to open an after-school camp. (1)

"He loved it, and it really seemed to be his calling," Polly Orr Bates said of her father. "He seemed to have a need to inspire and motivate...his goal with children was to bring out the best in them, to challenge them to do the most they could." (2)

Within eight years, the camp had grown to include an after-school program for girls, a nursery school, and a kindergarten. When it became apparent that a new campus was needed, a search was made for property, and Orr settled on a one hundred-acre parcel fronting Nancy Creek and West Paces Ferry roads. He purchased the property and then sold lots on the West Paces Ferry Road portion to repay the bank loan for the one hundred acres. (3)

"One of the early places he held the camp was on the front of Pine Hill, at the corner of Arden and West Wesley," Henry Howell said. "I remember my grandmother thought so much of Fritz that she bought two barns, I think they were five hundred dollars each ...that money was to help Fritz buy the land that was on Nancy Creek Road." (4)

A boy's gym and the football field, which became the focal point of the new camp, were built first, and used for winter camp activities. The boys arrived on campus to play football and basketball after having been picked up at school by Orr. "Then he'd take them home about supper time," Ms. Bates explained. (5)

"I have no memory that is much fonder than when he [Fritz] would issue football jerseys," John W. Grant III reminisced. "I loved football. Fritz was more than just a person who took boys and coached them...he focused on teaching sportsmanship." (6)

The Orr's home sat on a hill overlooking the camp, and "There weren't many neighbors," Ms. Bates said. "All my friends, especially their mothers, thought we lived in the country. Everyone loved to come, because there was so much to do. We had every animal you would ever have on a farm, I think my father was a frustrated farmer...Chickens, ducks and geese, goats, mules, donkeys, every kind of horse, pigs, sheep, guineas...A lot of people would give their children, at Easter time, a cute little animal. When the animals grew up they didn't know what to do with them, they'd bring them out there." (7)

The summer camp was opened in 1938, and the camp program transported the children into a world of sports and imagination, which gave the campers a lifetime of wonderful memories. Campers swam, shot rifles, learned archery, rode horses, canoed, learned about nature, tumbled, played tennis, and made things out of wood and clay. They watched Ross Allen, of the Ross Allen Reptile Institute in Silver Springs, Florida, wrestle alligators in the camp pool and milk poisonous snakes. Campers canoed the Chattahoochee River, climbed to the top of Stone Mountain, where they spent the night, took horseback trips to Kennesaw Mountain, and enjoyed an outpost camp at Rock Creek Lake in the North Georgia mountains. Campers had "sky hooks" to keep from falling off Stone Mountain, Pepsodent Toothpaste to ward off "wompus cats," and their favorite drink was "kikapoo joy juice".

"First job I ever had was a counselor at Fritz Orr Camp for eight weeks [around 1941]," Barrett Howell recalled. "I earned $25...bought a pair of cordovan wing-tipped shoes, cost about $15 of the $25." (8)

"My father was the driving influence," Ms. Bates explained. "He was everywhere, was always involved with all of it, and he was so interested in each child. It was a challenge to him to get the potential out of that child. He was such a competitor." (9) The ingredient that made Fritz Orr Camp so successful was the man who knew every child by name.

CHAPTER THIRTY-TWO
1930s
The Great Depression

"Ragged knees and overalls...."
- Pete Rolader

 $\mathcal{T}$ he stock market plummeted in October, 1929, ushering in the "Great Depression." Banks closed, or took extended holidays, businesses failed, huge amounts of money were lost in the stock market, and many families became impoverished when jobs were lost. It was estimated that there were 6,383 families in Atlanta and Fulton County on relief in 1931, and by 1932 there were over 11,454 families on the relief rolls. (1) In Buckhead, 600 families out of the 10,000 population were considered "destitute." (2)

To aid its citizens and relieve unemployment in Georgia, the state provided $2,147,000 for building bridges and roads, and a Central Relief Committee was formed to distribute money to those in need. (3) The City of Atlanta appropriated $6,000 to feed the hungry, and Fulton County established a "self-help plan" that put men to work on streets and roads, paying them in "scrip which called for $1.25 worth of plain but substantial groceries available at the county's commissary...Every man is given at least two days' work a week, 10 hours a day." (4)

To Pete Rolader, the Depression meant, "Ragged knees and overalls. I came along right in the Depression. My father ran the store [at Moores Mill Road and Northside Drive] trying to feed people who couldn't pay. Some could and some couldn't. Tried to keep your customers and keep business, let the fat fry the lean and keep 'em going. When he had to leave that store...thousands of dollars of unpaid grocery bills were on the books. We threw the books away and forgot about it...The people had just the bare necessities. We were, I guess, what you would call 'poor folks.' My father was a merchant, he worked night and day to keep things going and left us in pretty good shape. We wore overalls with holes in the knees. You didn't just go buy new clothes because you had a patch in your overalls." (5)

"Everything was awful tight," Ken Moss said of this period. (6)

"You couldn't find no jobs," Guy Patterson recalled. "When you did…well, I was making $7 a week until I went to the Post Office. Worked at Kamper's for $7 a week, the lumber yard [Buckhead Lumber Co.] for $7 a week, that's all they'd pay. But there were so many people out of work…just wasn't no jobs." (7)

"I know Buckhead was hit hard," Ruth Cox Adams remembered. "There was a lot of people suffered from the Depression…my daddy…always had a hand to reach out to help somebody in need, and I know that there were several families that he would carry old clothes and [food] to." (8)

"We didn't have any wealth," Sam Dorsey said. "Father was success-ful, he gave us a home, gave me a pony…I remember times were hard, they weren't hard for me, I was lucky…During the Depression, I remember they shut down the banks for three days, couldn't cash a check." (9)

"It was bad," Ellie Patterson recalled. Father walked to downtown, looking for work." (10)

"Maybe we got through it better than a lot of places…because we didn't have vast payrolls," Jack Spalding said of Atlanta. "The farm depression is what I remember. Boll weevil [early 1920s]. By the time the Wall Street Depression came, we'd been broke so long we couldn't tell the difference…so we had a real good head start surviving the Depression. Atlanta survived better than most places because it was a white collar com-munity …we didn't have steel mills, weren't dependent on cotton tex-tiles…That's when we began the Forward Atlanta advertising. The Cham-ber of Commerce…started advertising the advantages of life in Atlanta right at the depth of the Depression. Brought in a lot of new people and new industry. So the hard times weren't as hard here." (11)

The Bruce F. Woodruff family lived on Huntington Drive during the Depression, "and the back yard faced on the tracks going into Brookwood Station. The hobos would come off the train and make a track through our back yard. Grandmother [Mrs. Mary Hardwick Bloodworth] would always make them a peanut butter and jelly sandwich. They [the hobos] would put a mark on the driveway that we were friendly people," Bruce F. Woodruff Jr. said. (12)

Sue Webb Stephens recalled that hobos who rode the trains would camp nearby the railroad trestle and start fires to keep warm and cook. They would also beg food and water from the Webbs, who lived and operated their dairy on the present Lindbergh Drive. "Daddy would give 'em water, but no food. Said they made signs where they could stop and get food to eat." (13)

"In 1932, in the middle of the Depression, I was graduating from college over in Athens," Dr. F. Phinizy Calhoun Jr. recalled. "College was not expensive in those days. They were very glad to get you...I used to, more or less, support myself by playing in a dance orchestra." (14)

"Buckhead at that time was not a real rich section, everybody was doing their part, working sixty to sixty-five hours a week to get fifteen dollars a week to live on," Thomas M. Murray said. "If you had a job you were rich." (15)

On Christmas Eve, "all the parents on Highland Drive that were giving riding toys of one kind or another would get out and try 'em. And your mother had saved and bought a new coat and you and George were getting a wagon together from Santa Claus," Jane (Mrs. George Jr.) Murray said about her husband's family. "They got out to try it [the wagon] and her new coat got wrapped around the wheels and it just tore it up. She had to patch it and wear it." (16)

"We were probably too young to recognize the Depression," Roy Milling said. "We knew there wasn't any money." (17)

"The people who had money could afford a maid, but probably paid 'em five dollars a week and some toting privileges," Barrett Howell said. "Things were tough, there wasn't any money...didn't affect me...when World War II came along everything changed." (18)

During the Depression, a still was operated out of the former White Provision Co. building on Lenox Road, across from the present Lenox Square Mall. "Had the biggest liquor still I ever saw," Roy Milling recalled. "The vats were probably six feet across, three and a half feet deep. The reason he got caught, they were putting their waste in the septic tank and it was coming out in the field behind where we played baseball." (19)

At the Buckhead Seed Store, "people would come in and say that they were hungry. They didn't have anything to eat. If he [William Brand Sr.] would let them have something on credit [they said] that they would come back someday and pay," William Brand Jr. said. "Daddy said that there had been times when he was hungry, so when they came in he let 'em have stuff. And surprisingly, [some] would come in in a few years, say, 'I got some groceries from ya, and I come to pay my bill.'" (20)

"We had a home...[and] always had plenty to eat," Marcus Cook III said. "Seemed like we always had roast beef on Sunday ...We weren't wealthy, but we were comfortable and never wanted for anything. Occasionally, on Sunday, a homeless person would walk down the street and come to the door, and we would ask them to come in. Mother would bring them to the kitchen table and serve up their plate with a mound of food." (21)

"Nobody had any money...I mean money in your hand. I don't mean we didn't have enough to eat. We had servants. It was such an amazing life to think we lived as we did and yet nobody had cash…You didn't pay very much for help and food didn't cost much," Lillie Pace (Mrs. Paul) Scoville said. "We had a big garden and we ate what we grew. Mother canned and put up jellies and jams and the whole bit." (22)

"Mother made all my clothes. I remember my first boughten hat," Mrs. Scoville continued. "She would go to the ten cent store…and would buy a hat and dye it and then trim it. I remember one time I saved and saved and saved my money and I walked up to the corner and got the streetcar and went to town, and in those days you went clear down to where Rich's was, and I got a pair of white sandals for $1.95. I got on the streetcar to come home and it started pouring rain. And I didn't do a thing but take my shoes off and stuff 'em in my non-existent bosom…My first boughten dress was when I was twelve," which was purchased so she could attend a wedding. (23)

"Everybody was poor, but nobody knew it, because we didn't talk about it," Jane Murray said. (24)

CHAPTER THIRTY-THREE
Early 1930S
Colonial Dames of Buckhead

In the 1930s the population of Buckhead was 10,000, (1) and Guy Patterson thought it went from the Buckhead Theater to approximately Pharr Road. "You could stand on the corner over there and see nearly all of it." (2)

Among the people and places remembered by residents of Buckhead during this period were Mrs. Bloodworth's Kindergarten, the Buckhead Theater, Ken Moss' Blacksmith Shop, Colonial Store, "Old" Dr. C. M. Adams, who brought many of the Buckhead babies into the world, a pool hall on Irby Alley, Ma Bell's Hot Dog Stand on Peachtree at the corner of East Paces Ferry Road that "made the best hot dog in the world," Tidwell's Barbecue, Fulton National Bank, Kamper's Grocery, Buckhead Duck Pin Bowling Alley, Buckhead Hardware; Hawk's Drugstore, Wender & Roberts, and Pinkard's Cleaners.

***

Mrs. Bloodworth's Kindergarten became a landmark in Buckhead from approximately 1930 until 1952, when it was incorporated into the Atlanta Public School program. Mary Hardwick Bloodworth, a descendant of John Wesley Hardwick, was born in Atlanta and married banker Herbert Raines Bloodworth. When her husband "died of the hiccups" in 1905, leaving her with three small children to raise, she opened a small kindergarten in Druid Hills. Many of her "friends were wealthy and they readily brought their children to her," Bruce F. Woodruff Jr. said of his grandmother. (3)

Around 1930, Mrs. Bloodworth rented the office building that her friend E. River used while developing Peachtree Heights, and opened a kindergarten in Buckhead. She "retired when the City took over the Buckhead area [1952]," and died in 1957. Today the building is the City of Atlanta Administrative Building. (4)

The schoolhouse "used to have a picket fence around it, and my cousin and I used to be like Huckleberry Finn and paint that fence on both sides and splatter paint all over each other. It had a jungle gym on the front side, swings...Her maid...Willie [Scott]...was there the whole time that Grandmother had the kindergarten. My mother [Mary Hill Bloodworth Woodruff] would help out and play the piano for the kids," Mr. Woodruff explained. (5)

"My grandmother was a real teacher. She was an Aquarian ...Aquarians are the teachers, the humanitarians...she was a teacher by heart. She was a Christian Scientist to the core and was the proof of her religion," Mr. Woodruff explained. (6)

"They always had their graduation over at E. Rivers School and they put on a show with caps and gowns," Ellen Newell (Mrs. William Wright) Bryan, whose three children attended Mrs. Bloodworth's Kindergarten, explained. (7)

"It was a marvelous place," former student, Barrett Howell, said. "Many of us went there for one year and then graduated...and went on to E. Rivers across the street." (8) "There were no public kindergartens," Henry Howell added. "This was really the first socialization for most of us." (9)

***

In 1930 the Spanish Baroque-style Buckhead Theater (later renamed the Roxy) opened on Roswell Road at the five points. The theater and six stores, designed by architects Danielle and Beutelle, was built for $120,000. (10) The theater became a Saturday afternoon institution for the children in the community, and in the days of racial segregation, it was partially integrated. The black citizens of Buckhead bought their tickets at a counter at a separate side entrance on Irby Alley, then went upstairs and sat in the balcony.

"The Buckhead Theater is one of the few theaters in the greater Atlanta area...where blacks could go to the movies," John K. Ottley III said. (11)

"We had to come up and go through the alley to go to the theater...there were quite a few shanty houses...in this [Irby] alley," Milton Few commented. "The only way you could go in the front door was if you had on a maid's dress or a butler's coat." Irby Alley was named for Neppie Irby, a black woman. (12) William Brand Jr., whose father owned Buckhead Seed Store, recalled that "the colored sat up in the balcony, and a few times when the truck driver would be baby-sitting with me, he would take me to the movie. I had early integration." (13)

Tory Jacobs and his friends went to the Buckhead Theater on Saturdays to watch "the cliffhangers" and serials. "We used to ...get into trouble because we had these little firecrackers and we'd set 'em off and get the ushers all upset." (14)

Betty Slaton (Mrs. John) Wallace remembered the Saturday triple feature. "Hopalong Cassidy...Buck Jones...And then they had a continuing serial like Flash Gordon. Then they had another movie like 'The Thin Man,'" Mrs. Wallace said. "In the sixth grade it became quite popular to have a so-called 'date' to go to the movies from school. For a dime you and your date could go to the Buckhead movie and then go across the street to Jacobs' Drugstore and have a soda. Afterwards, the parents picked you up and took you home." (15)

***

In 1930 G. E. (Ed) Chatham and his grandson Ken Moss moved their blacksmith shop from Northside Drive at West Paces Ferry Road, to the center of Buckhead behind the Buckhead Theater. "At the time our shop was there on Irby Alley. We got dignified later and they named it Irby Street. It was a dirt alley," Ken Moss said. "There were ten negro houses, rental houses, and Mrs. (Neppie) Irby owned them." (16)

"You had wagons and horses coming from all over," Mr. Moss explained. "Around Buckhead there were a lot of pretty good-size gardens and farms. Down on Paces Ferry there was an old black man that had an ox that drove a two-wheel wagon or cart. I used to shoe the ox. What you did was cut a horseshoe in half, cause they have a split foot...John W. Grant used mules, all of them down there had horses. We used to shoe them and repair the wagons." (17)

Mr. Moss hunted squirrels and quail in the woods near his home on Mathieson Drive. "It was all woods from Mathieson Drive on over to Shadowlawn," he said. "We used to trap rabbits...[and] sell them to [Gene Minhinnett] for fifteen cents apiece. In the winter they kept these rabbits hung up all over the front of the store." On Sunday afternoons boys would sit on the rail of the elevator shaft next to Jacobs' Drugstore, which opened to a storage area in the basement. "We knew all fifteen or twenty cars that went by. Knew everybody that walked the street." (18)

Mr. Moss said that Burt Miller lived on East Paces Ferry Road "and had a liquor store on the ground level...[He] had a bear cage back of [his] liquor store...and an old black bear, old Mopsy. Town bullies and whatever would get in there and wrestle with the bear. If they beat the bear, he'd pay 'em so much. He put a muzzle on him so he couldn't bite. And he had a thing where he couldn't scratch'em. But he'd bear-hug 'em. That was in the thirties, early forties." (19)

When Mr. Moss moved to Roswell in the late 1950s, he used to demonstrate his skills to Cub Scouts and would tell them: "In the old days, the blacksmith was the most important man in town, because he built the cooking utensils for the houses, made the carpenter's tools, made the nails to build the houses with. He built the wagons, he made the plows, he shod the horses. The town that didn't have a blacksmith really didn't prosper." (20)

***

Because there was no public high school in Buckhead, white students made a daily fourteen-mile round-trip journey to Washington Street to attend Fulton High School. Concerned with the unwieldy situation, Mrs. Morton Rolleston, Phillips C. McDuffie, and Mrs. Alfred D. Kennedy approached other parents in the community, and a move was instituted to establish a high school in Buckhead. Parents petitioned the Fulton County Commission, who purchased ten acres in Garden Hills, in 1930, for a high school. The renowned architect, Philip Trammell Shutze, designed the school building in the Georgian-Classical Revival-style, and by September of 1930, North Fulton High School's doors opened for business, with W. Frank Dykes as the first principal. (21)

***

On the corner of Roswell Road and (West) Paces Ferry (the current Laura Ashley location), was Abraham Tesler's La Rosa dress and maid's uniform shop, which was named for and managed by his daughter Rose from 1930 until 1932. Mr. Tesler owned two other stores; "Fayge's store was on Peachtree and Tenth and was called Peggy's, and the one in Little Five Points was called Marilyn's for Mary," Rose Tesler (Mrs. Herman) Mechlowitz said. Mr. Tesler also "had a dress factory called Relset Manufacturing Co., our last name spelled backward." (22)

Charles K. Keith owned a large parcel of property in the middle of Buckhead (now Buckhead Plaza), on which he lived with his family in a small, frame house. Around 1931 Fulton County condemned part of his property and cut a street from Peachtree to West Paces Ferry Road, behind Lon Bridges' and Burt Miller's service stations, and named it Keith Circle. "They took it against his will and paid him for it," Tom Murray said. A Colonial Store was built on Keith Circle, and many who worked on Peachtree parked their cars on the circle. Mr. Keith got mad because they were parking on *his* street, and as a warning, he put roofing nails under the offending car's tires, resulting in many a car with four flat tires. (23)

Dorothy Dean (Mrs. Joel Chandler, Jr.) Harris remembered shopping at Colonial Store. "All [our] young group used to go over there and buy groceries...called ourselves 'The Colonial Dames.'" (24)

***

The Buckhead 50 Club was founded in the early thirties by fifty Buckhead merchants, and when it met on Wednesday afternoons, "Buckhead would close up,' Tom Murray said. The club is still active, and meets each month at the American Legion Club on Powers Ferry Road. (25)

***

Two more churches were added to the Buckhead landscape in the early thirties—Second Ponce de Leon Baptist Church and the Cathedral of St. Philip.

On August 3, 1930, Ponce de Leon Baptist Church held its first service in the partially-constructed sanctuary building at the corner of Peachtree and East Wesley Road. This move began when Ponce de Leon Baptist, established in 1902, decided to move north of the city because of encroaching business. The corner lot in Buckhead was purchased in 1929, and, under the leadership of Dr. Luther Rice Christie, the church merged with Buckhead Baptist Church. Following the final merger in 1932, with Second Baptist Church near the state capitol, the new church was named Second Ponce de Leon Baptist and was served by Dr. Christie until Dr. Ryland Knight was elected pastor in November 1932. (26)

The land on which the church sits once belonged to Mae Hicks (Mrs. James Sylvanus) Donaldson, daughter of Rial Bailey Hicks and granddaughter of Henry Irby. The family says that Mrs. Donaldson donated the land to the church. (27)

The Georgian-style sanctuary was completed in 1937, and the bell, which came from the original Second Baptist Church, was placed in the 150-foot-high steeple. (28) In 1949, the church bought the 5 7/10 acres of the adjoining Beverly DuBose property on Peachtree Road, which he had purchased from Seaborn L. Ivey, Rial Bailey Hick's son-in-law. (29)

The Cathedral of St. Philip moved to Buckhead from the corner of Washington and Hunter streets (present site of the State Agriculture Building across from the State Capitol) in 1933 to accommodate its parishioners. The church had its beginnings in 1846, when a group interested in forming an Episcopal church met in Samuel G. Jones' home "at the corner of Forsyth and Mitchell streets." The members of the newly formed Cathedral of St. Philip held services in one another's homes until a church was built in 1848. (30) During the Civil War St. Philip "was used as a hospital for Confederate wounded. When the Federals took Atlanta, they used the church as a stable for their horses, then a commissary depot and bowling alley." After the war, the small, frame church was replaced by a larger red brick structure. In 1895 it became the Cathedral of the Episcopal Diocese of Georgia. (31)

In 1933, under the leadership of The Very Rev. Raimundo de Ovies, Dean of the Cathedral of St. Philip, the church leased land at the point of Peachtree Road and Andrews Drive and built the Pro-Cathedral, which was opened for services on September 10; the property was later bought for $45,000. The 'little grey church' was used until Thanksgiving Day of 1959, when services were held in the new Hall of Bishops. The original church building was torn down and replaced by a Gothic-style church, which celebrated its first service on Easter Sunday in 1962. (32)

In 1989 the Cathedral bought the adjoining property owned by Dr. William Robert Dunn (formerly Walter Andrews' property) after the death of his widow. (33) The church, which sits at 'Dead Man's Curve,' on 'Amen Corner,' is considered "the largest Episcopal church in the country." (34)

***

The residential population of Buckhead expanded in the early thirties, as some people rented apartments, and others built homes.

In 1930, Fitzhugh Knox and his son Britton built an apartment house at 2260 Peachtree Road and later constructed apartments on Peachtree Memorial Drive. Mr. Knox came to Atlanta from Virginia in the early 1890s, married, and had nine children. He built his first home in Inman Park, then around 1909 he built a house on Piedmont Road between Seventh and Eighth streets, which today is the Knox House condominium. (35) "He was a noted lecturer," Janet Knox (Mrs. Thomas) Moore said of her grandfather, who died in 1940. "I feel that my grandfather was one of the founders of Atlanta from that period on…he was a number one realtor. He did so much for the [High] Museum…He started a library there." (36)

***

Sinclair Jacobs, who succeeded his father, Dr. Joseph Jacobs, in Jacobs' Drugstore, moved his family in 1930-1931 to 2933 Andrews Drive, in a home that backed up to James Gray's and Gov. John Slaton's property. "We used to play over there [Slaton property] and see this magnificent old Packard he had for State occasions, that had patent leather fenders," T. Sinclair "Tory" Jacobs, Sinclair's son, said. He remembered "secret places, caves, woods, and vines on which you could swing from trees and play Tarzan. Where I grew up there was lots of land and not too many people, and you felt safe." (37)

"There were black families living back there [between Peachtree Road and Andrews Drive] that had lived there from the days of slavery," Mr. Jacobs remembered. "These were sort of the family retainers of…James Gray, [who] was the publisher of *The Atlanta Journal*. He had the big house on Peachtree that later became Hart's Restaurant. They raised [and] slaughtered hogs. We would go and watch hogs being birthed, and later they would slaughter…and cook 'em." (38)

***

Architect Philip Trammel Shutze and Mrs. James J. Goodrum designed her Regency-style home at 320 (West) Paces Ferry Road, which was completed in the early 1930s (now The Southern Center for International Studies). Mrs. W. W. Rushton bought the home in 1957 and named it the Peacock House in honor of the birds she raised. The peacocks became a familiar sight as they wandered throughout the neighborhood, screaming a terrifying shriek that sounded like someone being attacked. (39)

William Rudolph lived around the corner from the Rushton house on Arden Road and often found one of the birds up in a tree in his yard. "They would scream and scream, it'd wake us up. The most hideous sound in the world. And you'd have to call the Rushtons. They would send the butler down here. He'd go knocking the peacock out of the tree, catch it and take it home." (40)

Mrs. Rushton, who was in the doll manufacturing business, had a daughter renowned for her "risque-type" reputation. One of the most famous stories occurred while a man was poised on a tall ladder working on the entrance hall lighting. "The fellow was in there fixing the chandelier, and she [daughter Wright] suddenly appeared minus any clothing on the upstairs landing. He got so excited that he dropped the chandelier," Franklin M. Garrett mused. (41)

***

In 1932 John Ogden, a founder of the Family Finance Corporation, bought James W. Morrow's twenty acres at 966 (West) Paces Ferry Road and built his "castle" of quarried rock on the site of the previous house, which had burned down in 1929. In 1958 the property was sold to Pace Academy, Inc. (42)

The same year, a two-story, neoclassical, Revival-style house was built at 400 (West) Paces Ferry Road for Mr. and Mrs. George Arthur Howell. It was designed by Sam and Joe Cooper (Cooper and Cooper). (43)

Judson L. Hawk moved his family to 277 West Wesley from Spring Street in 1933, eight years after opening his drugstore in Buckhead. "I remember a pool hall [on Irby Alley], but I was never allowed to go into a pool hall," Dr. Judson Hawk Jr. said. "That was off-limits as far as my mom and dad were concerned." (44)

At 341 (West) Paces Ferry Road, Mr. and Mrs. William H. Kiser built a Georgian mansion designed by Philip T. Shutze in the early thirties. The home, known as Knollwood, was modeled after Chatham, an "elegant 18th century Stratford County, Virginia, mansion built before the Revolutionary War." This replaced a brown-shingled summer cottage, which previously sat on the fifty acres. In 1952 the home was sold to Dr. and Mrs. Bernard Wolff; lots were sold off and new homes built. The present address for the home is 3351 Woodhaven Road, N.W. (45)

***

Early on the morning of July 6, 1933, John K. Ottley was kidnapped from his front yard at 3415 Peachtree Road (now Lenox Square), taken to Suwanee, Georgia, and held for ransom. Two men were waiting at the Joyeuse streetcar shed in front of his home when Mr. Ottley drove out his driveway on his way to work. On pretense of hitching a ride, a man called Grover and his young accomplice, Pryor Bowen, kidnapped Mr. Ottley at gunpoint, threw him into the back seat of the car, and then drove north on Peachtree to Suwanee. Along a dirt road near the Chattahoochee River, they bound and blindfolded Mr. Ottley and placed him on a log. While Bowen stood guard, Grover returned to Buckhead to deliver a ransom note to Mrs. Ottley demanding $40,000. (46)

With Grover gone, Mr. Ottley prevailed on Bowen to release him. "My grandfather persuaded the young man that if he would let him go, he would testify on his behalf and make it a lot easier on him, otherwise he would spend the rest of his life in prison," John Ottley III said. "So the teenage boy let my grandfather go…He got to a phone, called the police and then called his family to let them know he was okay." Bowen was arrested in Suwanee and Mr. Ottley, true to his promise, did not press charges. (47)

Meanwhile, in Buckhead, Grover delivered the note addressed to Mrs. Ottley, who was out of town, in care of the Ottley's caretaker. "Written on a square piece of letter paper in pencilled capital letters, with a dash between each word, it read:

Your husband has been kidnapped. We are holding him for $40,000.
If you notify the authorities, the police, the newspapers or anyone

else, he will be killed. Instructions later. Get the money immediately—today if possible. Do you want your money or your husband? The money in $5, $10, $20, $50 bills. Which shall it be? If anyone asks about him say he was called out of the city for a few days. When I contact with you I will be known as E. M. (48)

On his return to Suwanee, Grover "heard all these police sirens…he figured the jig was up. He escaped and no ransom was ever paid." Grover was arrested on August 5 in San Antonio, Texas, while picking up his mail. He was returned to Atlanta, where he confessed to the crime. It was discovered that Grover was actually William Randolph Delensky, an ex-convict, and "On September 13, Delensky was found guilty of kidnapping for ransom, robbery and carrying a concealed weapon. He was sentenced by Judge John D. Humphries to serve 21 to 28 years in prison, but was finally released in 1949. A couple of days later Bowen was given one year on the chain gang for his part in the abduction." (49)

"He [Grover/Delensky] would periodically write the family, and asked if they would testify for him to be granted a pardon or clemency," John Ottley III recalled. The family feared that one of the children would be kidnapped. (50)

CHAPTER THIRTY-FOUR
Early 1930s
Race Relations in Buckhead

"The community was very much together."
- Elizabeth Campbell (Mrs. Moses) Few

*T*here was an interesting relationship between the black and white citizens in Buckhead. Around West Paces Ferry Road, black citizens felt the whites were protective of and helpful to the New Hope Church community, while some residents of Johnson Town felt that, though they were shielded from Ku Klux Klan activities by their white neighbors, the business district was often less friendly.

The football field on the John K. Ottley estate (now Lenox Square) became a common meeting ground for the black and white children in Buckhead. Eugene Johnson said that, though the children played ball together, they "never struck up any strong relationships with the whites." (1)

"People here have been kind and supportive," Elizabeth (Mrs. Moses) Few, a member of New Hope Church, said. (2) "The community was very much together...your problems were my problems and our problems were their problems," Milton Few added.

"Ninety percent of the [blacks in Buckhead] served as domestic help in the homes of the white families as maids, butlers, cooks, and gardeners," Milton Few explained. "Most of the blacks were poor, but they were family-oriented and proud, always striving to get ahead. The old always encouraged the young to move up the ladder and try to achieve along with the whites...Learning was a must in the household. I started to work at four years old sweeping yards and floors in the neighborhood. At eight, I started working with my dad, a gardener, weeding flower beds at the homes of white families." At twelve, he went to work for the Jack Glenns. Proudly, Mr. Few said of his sisters and brothers that there were, "six teachers, one minister, one secretary, one nurse, one aircraft mechanic, one machinist and one homemaker." (3)

Mr. Few explained that white members of the Buckhead community often extended a helping hand to their black neighbors. "My brother-in-law [Dr. Asa Johnson] wanted to be a doctor and ended up as the only [black] medical doctor in this neighborhood," when he opened a private practice in an office attached to his home on Northside Drive. "He had both white and black patients." (4)

Dr. Asa Johnson was born in Buckhead in 1908. He was a member of New Hope Church and attended Morris Brown High School, Morris Brown College, and received his medical training at Meharry Medical College School of Medicine in Nashville, Tennessee. After serving as a medic with the rank of captain in World War II, Dr. Johnson started his practice in Buckhead. He married Bernice Few, who was a nurse, and had one child, Berneda (Haney). Later, Johnson opened an office in Marietta and became the first black doctor in that community, then he opened an office on Ashby Street in downtown Atlanta. (5)

Berneda Johnson Haney remembers "seeing white people sitting in the waiting room." If his patients were unable to pay for his care, "they would bring things from the garden for their payment." Dr. Johnson died in 1963. (6)

***

New Hope Church was also a magnet for many in the white community during the church's Camp Meetings.

"There was a special section for white people to come over there to attend their meetings," Pete Rolader said. "God knows they could sing better than anybody you know. We all enjoyed that, that was the social gathering of the blacks and whites." (7)

"Daddy would give 'em straw and things to put on the floor," William Brand Jr. said. "A lot of times we went down there and they would put us on a special place on the side." (8)

"We'd ride by [New Hope Church] and see if they were singing," Jack Spalding reminisced. "If they were, you'd just park and listen." (9)

***

The climate in the Buckhead business center was at times hostile for black citizens. "We were all business in Buckhead, get in and get out," Columbus Johnson of Johnson Town remembered. It was "kinda rough…We were black and there was prejudice there. We had to be very careful what we said and what we did. We had to walk very light in Buckhead." Johnson said there were always threats, and it was one such intimidation that forced him to leave home. "Some fellas threatened me...One of them thought I didn't call him 'Mister,' but he didn't hear me. They was always looking for trouble...I left the next night and went to Chicago. They were gonna get me for nothing. I had a cousin ...[who] used to save his money, didn't throw his money away. Someone asked for some change. He could change a ten dollar bill, but they beat him up and took his money. [They were] What we would call 'Red Necks.'" (10)

CHAPTER THIRTY-FIVE
1930s
Prison Camp in Buckhead

In the early 1930s Tony Chastain sold one hundred acres of his land to Fulton County for a prison camp (now the Chastain Park golf course), and a men's prison was built on the hill facing Powers Ferry Road, where the American Legion lodge sits today. After a fire destroyed the building, a new one was erected on the present site of the ball diamond at Lake Forrest and Wieuca roads. (1)

"One night when I was staying at my grandparents' [Mr. and Mrs. Charles W. DeFoor, on Piedmont Road], that prison farm caught on fire. Papa drove us over there, as close as we could get," Marcus Cook III recalled. "The...prisoners that they were not able to get unchained from their beds were burned to death." That night, while young Marcus tried to sleep, he saw from his window "the red glow in the sky, and the smoke, and my young mind was conjuring up the horrible visions of these people being burned to death." (2)

Guy Patterson was working for Fulton County as a maintenance man at the courthouse when he was offered a job as assistant to Mrs. Jesse Boynton, manager of the alms houses on West Weiuca Road. In December of 1935 he moved his wife and four children into the white clapboard building that served as the black alms house (the current Chastain Art Center), and was in charge of the forty black prisoners who were housed in the rear of the building. The women, serving time for offenses such as stealing clothing from department stores, and playing the 'bug' [gambling], worked in the alms houses, and on the prison farm, raising vegetables for the complex and for other prison camps in the county. "They'd work those ladies and they'd plow the mules down there just like a man," Guy Patterson said. The women also cleaned the cemeteries at Sardis, Mt. Paran Baptist Church and a church in Sandy Springs. (3)

"All of the golf course was cornfield," Marcelle Simpson remembered. "There wasn't more than five or six houses from there to Buckhead. The Negro women convicts tilled the corn. I used to ride my bicycle down there and sit on the bank and watch 'em." (4)

"They'd raise all the vegetables and stuff, and we could have all we wanted," recalled Margaret Chapman (Mrs. Leon) Townsend, whose family lived nearby. (5)

***

In 1940, prisoners at the Fulton County Prison Farm in Buckhead were put to work converting the farm into a park, and when it was completed in 1945, it was named North Fulton Park. The male prisoners were transferred to Bellwood and Bolton; the women's prison and nursing homes were closed in 1968. (6) Following the death of Troy Chastain in 1945, the park was renamed Chastain Memorial Park. On January 1, 1952, the park was turned over to the City of Atlanta. (7)

"Chastain gave the property for the horse stables," Marcelle Simpson said. "It went to the city, and I know at one time Mayor Maynard Jackson wanted to sell it." The deed stated that the property "would revert back to the Chastain estate," if the stables were discontinued. (8)

CHAPTER THIRTY-SIX
1934-1939
Trolleys, Clubs, and Snowstorms

"It wasn't too hard to find a place to park."
- T. Sinclair "Tory" Jacobs

In the mid and late thirties in Buckhead, horse riding clubs for children were in vogue, the community was hit by a snowstorm, trackless trolleys replaced the old trolleys along Peachtree Road, and a boy's camp was operated near the present Lenox Square Mall.

In 1936 the ladies of the Peachtree Garden Club took on the project of beautifying Buckhead. They persuaded the Fulton County commissioners to have sidewalks constructed along Peachtree, and to help clean the vacant lots and streets. Garden club members planted six hundred feet of privet hedge at Peachtree and West Paces Ferry roads. "This evergreen hedge, collected by Mrs. William Hill, was donated by Madames Reuben Garland, Hugh Dorsey, Cobb Caldwell, William Kiser, Floyd McRae, Bulow Campbell, Robert Maddox, John Slaton, and John Grant." (1)

"My mother was a member of Peachtree Garden Club," Jack Spalding said. "I remember one year they planted peach trees all along Peachtree, and the drought came and every damn one of them died." (2)

Betty Slaton (Mrs. John) Wallace belonged to a riding club with about eight other girls, who met at 10:00 on Saturday morning at the Highland Riding Academy on Roxboro Road. After their ride, the group went to one of their homes for hot dogs and hamburgers, then headed to the Buckhead Theater for the matinee triple feature. The evening often ended with spending the night with a friend. (3)

Betty Slaton lived with her parents in Brookhaven from 1930 until 1945 and attended R. L. Hope School. Her father, William Marshall Slaton Jr., was the brother of Gov. John M. Slaton, and manager of Hospital 48 Veteran's Hospital (later Lawson General) on Peachtree Road in Brookhaven. He worked for the Veteran's Association during World War I and become Southeastern Manager of all Veteran's Affairs after World War II. (4)

***

Aline Cocke (Mrs. Eugene) Cofield moved to Peachtree Way from Thirteenth Street with her parents, Erle and Elise Cocke, and her brother Erle Jr. in the fall of 1934, so she could attend North Fulton High School. "I wanted to go to North Fulton and we had to live in the county instead of the city," Mrs. Cofield said. (5)

Mrs. Cofield and her friends took dancing lessons at Margaret Bryan's Peachtree Street studio near the Fox Theater. "One Saturday night a month she had fifty-cent dances," Mrs. Cofield reminisced. "A lot of the [girl's] mothers would have buffet suppers…before we went to the dances. Occasionally, if the boy had been at your house for dinner that night, he would pay your fifty cents." She danced at Mooney's Lake, went on picnics and hayrides, bought ice cream from a parlor (where Fellini's Pizza now stands) at Peachtree and Rumson roads, hung out at Wender and Roberts, and swam in the lake at Brookhaven. (6)

***

Charles Wilson, whose father, Ray C., owned Wilson's Garage at 35 (West) Paces Ferry Road, lived with his family on East Paces Ferry Road, and worked as a curb boy at Lane's Drugstore in 1935. He recalled Woodall's Fruit Stand, "Marvin Martin's Service Station, Harrison Anderson's store, Bubba Gilbert's Gulf Station, Kamper's Grocery." (7)

Mr. Wilson remembered Atlantic Ice & Coal on Peachtree Road where you could buy twenty-five- or fifty-pound blocks of ice, or have it delivered to your home and put it in your ice box. "They would let kids around the area bring watermelons and leave them for a day or so to get cold. You would scratch your name on your melon and it would always be there when you came back to get it." (8)

The Lon Bridges family moved to Shadowlawn Drive in 1935, in the middle of Buckhead, and opened a service station there, which they ran as part owners with a Mr. McMillian until around 1950. After World War II the Bridges opened other service stations, including one on Peachtree Road at Maple Drive. "It was a good community to live in, nice people, friendly, nice shops around Buckhead," Lon Bridges Jr. said. (9)

***

The Valley Road area was developed in the 1930s. At the same time, more new homes were under construction along (West) Paces Ferry Road.

At number 105, the two-story, English Regency-style Thornton/Jones home, designed by Philip Shutze, was built in 1935. (10) The following year, Bolling Jones Jr. built a two-story, red brick Georgian-style home, with huge columns at number 1145. (11)

Dulcie (DeFoor) and Marcus Cook Jr. returned to their home in Buckhead in 1935 so that their son Marcus III could attend R, L. Hope School. They had built a home on Martina Drive in 1929, then left Atlanta the following year because of business. "I would go to sleep at night with the sound of the streetcars going down Peachtree Road...everything was peaceful," Marcus Cook III said. (12)

Mrs. Cook was the daughter of Charles Willard DeFoor, whose real estate partner was Charlie Black "of the Blackland Road development." DeFoor's father "may have been James, who may have been a cousin or brother of Martin DeFoor," Mr. Cook III explained. Charles DeFoor moved from College Park in the 1920s, into a home he built at 3666 Piedmont Road (now Piedmont Center One, Two, Three and Four). (13)

"We always felt like the intersection of Piedmont and Roswell was kind of the jumping-off place to the country," Mr. Cook continued. "Right down where the Lanigan Insurance Agency is [3610 Piedmont Road], and those couple of houses that have been turned into businesses, was kind of a crude baseball field with a backstop, and we would play baseball down there." (14)

***

A two-day storm of ice, sleet, and snow hit on December 28, 1935, crippling the metropolitan area of Atlanta. *The Atlanta Constitution* described the scene: "Sidewalks and streets strewn with the debris from broken trees; entire sections of the city in complete darkness; homes without telephones, radios, heat, or fuel; grounded airplanes; delayed trains; wrecked automobiles were some of the miseries inflicted on a housebound city." (15)

"Atlanta was just paralyzed for about ten days," Aline Cooke (Mrs. Eugene) Cofield remembered. "We had a coal furnace in the house...and a big fireplace in the living room...That's where we boiled the water and soup and Mother broiled steaks on the living room fireplace. And we all thought it was wonderful, we teenagers, a new experience. We put on our galoshes and went wherever we wanted to go. We didn't miss a single party." (16)

In 1937, following the death of Clark Howell Jr., the Clark Howell III family moved from their Peachtree Road home to Pine Hill, on West Wesley Road. "My grandfather, Papa [Clark, Jr.] Howell, died in 1936, we redid old Pine Hill," Barrett Howell explained. "We had a stable, a cow and horses, ponies, tennis court, and everybody rode all over everybody's land. Had bridle trails everywhere." Mr. Howell, who still lives on at the property, said, "We had a milk cow, and we never took from a dairy until after World War II. We had big gardens, vegetables, and chickens." (17)

Randolph A. Hearst, son of newspaper giant William Randolph Hearst, was sent to Atlanta as a reporter for his father's paper, *The Atlanta Georgian*. He met and married Atlantan Catherine Campbell in 1937; their daughter became the infamous Patty Hearst. The following January they moved into the home they built at 1154 (West) Paces Ferry Road and lived there until World War II, when they sold the house to Paul and Mildred Seydel and moved to San Francisco. The story goes that Mrs. Seydel "found the front door key hidden in a Christmas corsage from her husband." (18)

***

Henry Alexander moved to his new home at 3440 Peachtree Road (current site of Phipps Plaza) in 1939. Atlanta became home when his grandfather Aaron Alexander moved here about 1847 and settled around Marietta and Peachtree streets. Later, when Aaron took his family to see the new lot, he bought further north on Peachtree Street (now the site of the South Tower of Peachtree Center), his wife "got about where the Candler Building is now and said she wasn't going to live that far out," architect Cecil Alexander said of his great-grandparents. "He carried the day, though; he did build a house." (19)

Aaron Alexander's son Julius married and had two sons, Henry Aaron (also known as Harry) and Cecil Aaron, father of architect Cecil. Julius bought property in Buckhead at the corner of Peachtree and Wieuca roads, and when he died in 1917, his son Harry inherited the land. "Uncle Harry had a few guiding economic principles: One was to buy Peachtree property and hold it, and the other was to buy Coca-Cola stock and hold it. Both moves were successful," Mr. Alexander said. (20)

Henry Alexander was a lawyer who dabbled in politics, serving in the Georgia Legislature in 1909. "He also became one of Atlanta's first Republicans, and he ran for congress several times as a Republican," Mr. Alexander said. Henry married Lithuania native Marion Klinitzkava and had four children, Henry Jr., Rebecca, Esther, and Judith. (21)

Alexander's magnificent home in Buckhead, designed by Lodowick Hill Sr., was called Peniel, which comes from a passage in the Bible. (22) "I think my uncle had in mind one day it would be the governor's mansion," Cecil Alexander explained. In the 1940s he offered the property to the state. (23)

Frances Yudelson (Mrs. Harry) Kuniansky remembered that while the house was being built, many in the Jewish community rode out to Buckhead on Sundays to watch the construction. (24)

"Mr. Alexander...had a big sign up on Peachtree Road...[that] said, 'Vote for Alexander for Governor.' Then under it it had something called a 'Republican,'" Bill Dreger remembered. "And I didn't know what that was. I went home and asked my dad, 'What is a Republican? That's what Mr. Alexander is.'" (25)

***

Mr. and Mrs. William Wright Bryan (Ellen Newell) moved to Buckhead in 1939, because she wanted to live near the friends she had made in grammar school, Washington Seminary, and in the Lucy Cobb Institute in Athens. "I wanted Newell [their daughter] to go to school with the children of my friends with whom I had grown up," Mrs. Bryan explained. Their house on the east side of Peachtree Road at number 2413 (now The Gates condominium) was a Tudor-style home, with a huge front yard that had a joggling board made by her grandfather Judge George Hillyer. (26)

Mrs. Bryan's great-grandfather, Alfred Hope Colquitt, had served Georgia as governor and as a U. S. Senator. Her father, Alfred Colquitt Newell, was a night city editor for *The Atlanta Constitution* before moving to New York, where he worked for *The Brooklyn Eagle*, *The New York World*, and worked briefly as private secretary for Joseph Pulitzer. Following the birth of daughter Ellen (Bryan), the Newells returned to Atlanta, and he went into the insurance business. (27)

In 1932 Ellen Newell married *The Atlanta Journal* reporter William Wright Bryan, and seven years later they moved to Buckhead from Fifteenth Street. Mrs. Bryan said that their neighbors, the Shippleys, had a cow in their front yard on Peachtree Road. (28)

***

John Grant III fondly recalled the annual Christmas eve parties at Craigellachie, his grandparent's home, which was attended by over forty relatives. "They had real candles on the Christmas tree in the ballroom, where the present bar is at the Cherokee Club. You could not go in that room when you first got there. Just before dinner you would hear Santa Claus' bells ringing and that caused great excitement and everyone would run toward the music room. They kept those doors closed and you could kinda peek through the glass that had curtains on them. And if you got there quickly enough, you could see Santa Claus actually going out the door there on the west side." (29)

"My cousin Frank Owens and I played football in the front yard constantly," Mr. Grant III said. "And we would hit golf balls out to West Paces Ferry Road." (30)

***

Trackless trolleys, using overhead electric wires, and diesel-fueled buses began replacing the electric streetcars throughout Atlanta on June 27, 1937. The "Buckhead-Oglethorpe Line" was converted at a cost of $500,000. (31) "Before World War II came, they had converted over to buses, then after the war began, they went back to the electric cars [because of the gas shortage]," Mrs. Hilton Stanaland explained. (32) After the war, buses once again replaced the trackless trolley.

The trolley was considered fair game for many of the children in Buckhead. "The trolley car ran on tracks right down the middle of Peachtree…On Halloween…we'd grease the track and it made quite a slide from Lindbergh down to the creek,'" Barrett Howell explained. "You'd pull the poles off the lines so that guy didn't have any power." (33)

"We used to grease the streetcar tracks every once in awhile on the hill, and they'd have to dump all their sand in order to get traction," Ken Moss said. (34)

"When the streetcars were replaced with the trackless trolley…the kids would go out there and pull those things [the overhead lines] loose and they wouldn't run at all," Pete Rolader mused. (35)

John Grant III recalled watching boys riding their bikes along Peachtree Road, while hanging on to the streetcars. (36)

***

Bruno Stein leased some property on Lenox Road behind the present MARTA station, where he operated an after-school club for boys in the 1930s and 1940s. The children were picked up at E. Rivers once a week, by a driver in a station wagon, and taken to the campus, where they spent the afternoon working in the tool shop and playing games such as football and softball. (37)

"Bruno Stein had a little boy's play club, along the lines of Fritz Orr, not near as fancy or well-organized. He had leased some property on Lenox by Lenox Park apartments [behind MARTA], had a little shop up there with power tools and a little cleared-off area for playing football, softball," John K. Ottley III remembered. (38)

"They had shop, crafts, and things of that nature," Marcus Cook III said. "We would tramp around in the woods, some young people would ride horseback in there because it was very extensive woods." (39)

CHAPTER THIRTY-SEVEN
Mid to Late 1930s
Prohibition, Police, and Private Schools

"We left the keys in the car and the front door wide open."
- Bruce Woodruff Jr.

$\mathscr{T}$he police operating in Buckhead used Burt Miller's and Lon Bridges' service stations on Peachtree at the five points as their headquarters. "It was more or less their outpost. They had a shortwave radio and they'd park their cars over there and go in and sit. And when they had a radio call they'd get in their cars and go investigate," Thomas M. Murray said. "But the police in those days furnished their own automobiles, they didn't have county cars and they'd always ride four in a car." (1)

"We really didn't need any police," Bruce F. Woodruff Jr. said. We left the keys in the car and the front door wide open." (2)

Florence and Sam Inman recalled that, during Prohibition, you could buy bootleg whiskey at Burt Miller's service station right where the police had their "office." (3)

"I remember the middle to late thirties, Daddy's store [Buckhead Seed Company] was the Fulton County police headquarters," William Brand Jr. said. "There were always two or three police cars parked there, on Roswell Road [south of the theater and across the street from Jacobs's]." Chief Mathieson "and Daddy were big friends." He remembered an arena on Early Street, behind the Buckhead Theater, that had wrestling matches on Saturday nights. (4) Roy Milling said that the ring for boxing and wrestling was on the current site of the Johnny Rockets restaurant. (5)

***

Buckhead was enhanced by the opening of two private schools in the late thirties. The first was The Lovett School, which opened in 1936 on its new fifteen-acre West Wesley Road campus, under the direction of its founder and first grade teacher Eva Edwards (Mrs. William Cuyler) Lovett. (6)

Mrs. Lovett was born in Marshallville, Georgia, on January 14, 1873, to lawyer and Civil War veteran Joseph Ashbury Edwards and his wife Emma (Miller), who "was the first honor graduate of Wesleyan Female College." Eva attended Peabody College in Nashville, Tennessee, and after receiving her Certificate-Licentiate in Instruction, taught elementary and high school students in Fort Valley, Georgia, and later in Eatonton. (7)

In 1898 Eva married Dr. William Cuyler Lovett, a minister in the Southern Methodist Church, and two years later they moved to Atlanta, where she taught at Miss Willette Allen's Kindergarten. In the summer of 1916 she organized Mrs. Lovett's School for Children and operated it for five years, until she and her husband left Atlanta. They returned in 1926, after Dr. Lovett's retirement, and Mrs. Lovett opened The Lovett School at 32 Peachtree Place, with twenty students attending grades one through three. (8)

Around 1930 the expanding school moved to 921 Myrtle Street, and by November of 1936 they were in their Buckhead location. Mrs. Lovett retired in 1954, and "The ownership of the school passed into the hands of the Cathedral of St. Philip," with Sally (Mrs. Frank, III) Sellers as principal of the new organization. When the school once again outgrew its facilities, land was bought on Paces Ferry Road at the Chattahoochee River. The new Lovett School officially opened in September of 1960, with Dr. Vernon B. Kellett as its Headmaster. (9)

Mrs. Lovett "was really a remarkable woman...and a group of people, like Bill Kiser and his wife...Julian and Henrietta Hirshberg, John Sibley...Norris Broyles were the original people who invested in it, on a very small scale," Edith (Mrs. Herbert) Elsas said. "Mrs. Lovett was really a champion of the children and had very serious ideas about how children should be treated...she was a large woman (about six feet tall) and I think strict in a way that the children knew she was their champion." (10)

The second school to open was The Atlanta Speech School, which was founded in 1938 by Katherine "Kitty" Cathcart (Mrs. William G.) Ham, whose son was hearing-impaired. Mrs. Ham "took a group of handicapped children she had been teaching privately to a Junior League meeting...and urged the ladies to recognize the need for this type of service in Atlanta." The ladies agreed, and the project became the Junior League School for Speech Correction. Classes began in the Medical Arts Building, then moved to Villa Clare, the J. J. Haverty home at 2020 Peachtree Road (now Shepherd Center). The name was changed to the Atlanta Speech School in 1960. In 1967 the school relocated to its new quarters at 3160 Northside Parkway, N.W., and is now the Speech and Hearing Department for Emory University. (11)

***

New Hope Church built a new rock and wood sanctuary in 1936, which replaced the original wood building destroyed by fire in 1927. To raise the necessary money for the rebuilding, loans were taken out on some of the members' property, and monetary gifts were donated by many in the white community. "Mr. Clark Howell was named Honorary Trustee," Elizabeth Campbell (Mrs. Moses) Few said. "The church was honored in 1991 by the Smithsonian Institute," and Mrs. Few was honored by the Interfaith Broadcasters as an outstanding minister. (12)

"When they built the bottom here, they hauled all these rocks from a Confederate place around mid-town on…wagons to build the church…basement," Milton Few explained. "My uncle built the parsonage," said Helen Few, Milton's sister. (13)

***

In 1938, Christ the King Catholic Church bought the Ku Klux Klan property at 2699 Peachtree Road. The four acres lying between East Wesley Road and Peachtree Way cost $35,000 and included the anti-bellum-style Imperial Palace that served as the Klan's national headquarters. At the time of the purchase, the home was known as the Wesley Avenue Apartments. Fr. Joseph P. Moylan conducted Sunday Mass on the front porch of the house, while the first floor was being renovated for a chapel. (14)

The parish had been established in 1936 by Bishop Gerald P. O'Hara. Seven months later, on January 5, 1937, Pope Pius XI "issued a proclamation changing the Diocese of Savannah-Atlanta," granting it "Co-Cathedral status, equal in rank to the Cathedral of St. John the Baptist in Savannah." (15)

The thirteenth- and fourteenth-century, Gothic-style cathedral was built with Indiana limestone and designed by Henry Dagit and Sons of Philadelphia. It was dedicated on January 18, 1939. Present at the church's dedication was Dr. Hiram Wesley Evans, Imperial Wizard of the Ku Klux Klan. (16)

***

In the 1930s and 1940s the (Jackson T.) Hitt Sanitation Service was located next to and south of the Ottley home at 3393 Peachtree Road. Mr. Hitt lived in a "big, two-story, red brick house, they had all the garbage trucks parked behind. He was the only garbage man around Buckhead. His sons drove the trucks...He made lot's of money hauling garbage," William Brand Jr. explained. (17)

Lillie Pace (Mrs. Paul) Scoville recalled that the Hitt's trucks carried more than garbage around Buckhead. "They also used the truck for social events. Nobody thought a thing in the world about riding in that garbage truck." (18)

"A woman wanted a pig hauled off and gave the driver twenty dollars," Bill Dreger said. When Mr. Hitt's son found out about it, he got into an argument with the driver and the driver killed him. "The Hitts went out of business after the son was killed. [Afterwards], the county didn't have any garbage service, you had to contract with a private company to pick up the garbage." (19)

***

Prohibition ended in the spring of 1938, ending eighteen years of bootlegging. "Where Piedmont goes into Roswell Road, there was sort of a little tavern there," Mrs. Hilton Stanaland remembered. "During the days of Prohibition, they did a really good business. Not many boys had cars, and you'd have to have about three couples on a date so the boys could share the expenses and at some point, maybe one of the boys would disappear, nothing was said, but when he'd come back he'd have a flask of whiskey." (20)

***

As the third decade came to an end, Atlanta played host to one of the most famous movie premiers in the world, Margaret Mitchell's *Gone With the Wind*. On the evening of December 15, 1939, the stars of Hollywood and Atlanta's elite gathered at the Lowe's Grand Theater downtown to attend the long-awaited movie adaptation of Miss Mitchell's novel. Parties, parades, and pageantry heralded the event. Strobe lights lit up the sky as the huge crowd of onlookers waited to catch a glimpse of Vivien Leigh, Clark Gable, Olivia de Haviland, Leslie Howard, and Miss Mitchell alighting from their limousines.

"We were in the ROTC at North Fulton [High School] when *Gone With the Wind* premiered. All of us ROTC students were commandeered to stand on the streets and keep the people back on the sidewalks during the parade when Clark Gable and Vivien Leigh came down," Pete Rolader recalled. (21)

CHAPTER THIRTY-EIGHT
1940-1941
Buckhead Before World War II

*I*n the 1940s, badminton courts graced many yards, illegal slot machines were popular in secluded spots, children hunted small game and swam in the creeks in the Buckhead woods.

"Badminton took over Atlanta by storm in the late thirties, and everyone who had room in their back yard had a badminton court," William T. Dreger III said. In 1940 his father "built an indoor [commercial] badminton court on the corner of Lindburgh and Piedmont. It's that two-story green wood building that...[now] has an antique furniture store (Furniture Exchange) in it." Mr. Dreger Jr. was Bitsy Grants's tennis partner, and his hopes of becoming a professional tennis player were dashed when the Depression hit. [Mother] "couldn't figure that tennis balls were a good investment." (1)

***

Edith and Herbert Elsas moved to Paces Ferry Road in 1941, on land that was once a farm, and their nearest neighbors were the Ben Smiths and the Pleasant Hill Church. "We had electricity, no gas, no sewage, no city water. We had a spring," Edith and Herbert Elsas said. They shopped in the center of Buckhead, and voted at Mr. Lindsey's store (current Amoco Station) at the intersection of Paces and West Paces Ferry roads. (2)

Mr. Elsas's grandfather, Jacob Elsas (born in 1842), emigrated to Cincinnati from Germany in 1860 and became a peddler. During the Civil War, "He figured that there would be a great need for supplies and a need for exchanges of goods. So he came down behind the U.S. Army and settled in Cartersville," bought local products, and sent them North, where he bought goods needed in his community. In 1867 he moved to Atlanta and began manufacturing cotton jute bags at his company, Fulton Spinning Co., which was renamed Fulton Bag and Cotton. (3)

Civic minded, Jacob Elsas was one of the founders of Grady Hospital.

"He believed that people should pay for their illnesses if they could, but if they couldn't it should be provided by the public," Herbert Elsas said. "My father, Louis J. Elsas, was on one of the first Grady boards." Jacob Elsas also helped found Georgia Tech in order to educate "technical personnel, to supervise cotton manufacturing." (4)

***

Following the death of Mary Ann (Mrs. Lon, Jr.) Bridges's father, she and her mother came to Atlanta in 1941 and moved in with her Aunt Annie Belle and Uncle [Fulton County Police Chief] George Mathieson, in their home on Peachtree Road. She recalled a public golf driving range on Peachtree Road, before Peachtree Road Methodist Church bought the property, and that flirty high school girls were called "pinks" and the boys who hung around them were called "gels." (5)

Mrs. Mathieson loved to gamble and was particularly fond of the slot machines, which she was introduced to during a trip to Florida. Tom Murray said that while the Mathiesons and the George Murray Sr.'s were in Miami on vacation, Mrs. Mathieson went downstairs at the hotel to buy stamps to mail letters to their daughters. An hour later, the chief found her "pulling the dime slot machine. He said, 'Annie Belle, what the hell are you doing?' she said, 'Well, I put a dime in to get some stamps out and it gave me five dimes and I took them to the nice man at the counter and he showed me how to operate this machine.'" (6)

One of the hot spots for gambling was Black Bridge (now Vinings on the River Shopping Center, once Robinson's Tropical Gardens) on Paces Ferry Road across the river from Lovett School. "Annie Belle would take us out there and let me play the slot machines. One evening, when Chief Mathieson came home, he asked, 'What did y'all do today?' And I piped up and said, 'I got to go play the slot machines today at Black Bridge,'" Mary Ann Bridges reminisced. "He said, 'Annie Belle, I raided that place today!' We had just missed it!" (7)

Mrs. Mathieson and Mrs. Murray would ride around on Saturdays, and in the evening the police chief would ask his wife, 'Well, where you been, Annie Belle?' 'Florence and I went up to Roswell...up a country road about a mile, and we found the nicest filling station. It had two slot machines in the back and we played about an hour or two.'" After getting directions to the gambling spot, the chief would raid them, Tom Murray mused over a typical story. Chief Mathieson was out to close down the slot machines, and "She never knew she was the lookout." (8)

Weyman Brown, grandson of potter Ulysees Adolphus "Dolphus" Brown and dairyman Reuben Morris, lived on Moores Mill Road amid his large family. He recalled hunting squirrels, spring fishing, and swimming in a pond behind the Rolader cabin. The family belonged to Center Congregational Church on Moores Mill Road, where Weyman Brown enjoyed ringing the church bell. "There was a rope on a pulley, and they let the children ring the bell, ride the rope up and down." He said that church baptisms and picnics were held along Nancy Creek, in a curve called Big Bend, at the junction of Paces and West Paces Ferry roads. (8)

CHAPTER THIRTY-NINE
1940s
Buckhead Goes to War

$\mathcal{A}$fter America entered World War II in December of 1941, short-ages of fuel, food, gasoline, and building materials were created. Americans were introduced to coupon ration books, which were needed to buy gasoline and food, and Victory Gardens were cultivated in the backyards of many homes. Air raid wardens patrolled residential neighborhoods, and school children collected tin foil, metal hangers, string and newspapers for the war effort. Buckhead suffered the same fate as the rest of the nation, as many of her young men and fathers went off to fight in the European and Pacific theaters of the war.

R. E. "Red" Dorough (1897-1973), the "unofficial mayor of Buckhead," became one of the most important men in the community. The Texas native opened a "drive-in sandwich and drink stand on Peachtree Road...[that] became the meeting place for politicians and would-bes." He also ran the Buckhead Billiard Parlor on Roswell Road, near the Buckhead Theater. (1) "Red was in real estate and insurance. He had an office there on Roswell Road just down the street from the poolroom," William Brand Jr. said. (2)

During the war, the fate of many a Buckhead citizen was in the hands of Dorough and William Brand Sr., who operated the Buckhead Draft Board from the second floor office over the Buckhead Theater. They alternated positions; "one would be chairman of the Draft Board one year, and another one the other," Mr. Brand Jr. explained. "They tried to be fair. They had a lot of people. . . that wanted to get out [of the draft]. [They] couldn't let 'em all out." (3)

William Brand Sr., who had worked for (L. H.) Cottongim Seed in downtown Atlanta, moved his family to Buckhead in the late twenties, when the company opened a store on Roswell Road. Brand eventually bought the Buckhead store and renamed it the Roswell Seed Store, which he operated until about 1939, when he went to work for Fulton County. (4)

"The good ol' boy bunch was Dorough and Bill Brand, they were the unofficial city hall of Buckhead," Pete Rolader explained. (5) Dorough was described by Barrett Howell as "a very powerful man." (6)

"If you would go into central casting to find a fellow to play the mayor of a small town, or the sheriff in a small Georgia community, you'd pick him [Dorough] out," Cecil Alexander mused. "He was rather short, a good ol' boy, you always felt like what he was saying to you wasn't what he was thinking. He was an entrepreneur, a politician, and a maneuverer." (7)

"I used to call him a 'mug worm,'" Irwin G. Baumer said. "It's a bird that sits on the side of a fence. It's an expression for people [who] sometimes are on the one side, and sometimes on the other. We were very close friends and owned [and developed] property together." (8)

"If you wanted to do anything in Buckhead, if you wanted to run for office, for instance, the first thing you'd do was to go to Red and sit down and talk," J. T. Tolbert remarked. (9)

Guy Patterson was delivering the mail in Buckhead during the war when he got his "Greetings" from the United States government. "Delivered my own notice…Mr. Dorough and Bill Brand talked it over and said, 'Let's keep him out [of the army], his wife [and children] need him at home.' They kept putting me back, and that went on for two years, worrying us to death. I'd have been better off if I'd a went on." (10)

"When your number came up you would report out there and get a general physical, and you'd be classified 1A, 1B…Then you'd be sent to the induction center at Fort McPherson," Tom Murray recalled. (11)

"Everyone had to report there for everything pertaining to the draft," Charles Wilson, who spent his war years in the Air Corps, reminisced. "Usually about thirty-five people went into the service every month. I went in in March 1943. We met at the draft board and walked down Peachtree Road to the Buckhead Elks Club [2765 Peachtree Road], just south of Rumson Road, near East Wesley Road. There we were given a good going-away meal. Then they carried us to Fort McPherson on a bus." (12)

***

During evening air-raid drills and black-outs, Buckhead residents kept their curtains closed to prevent light from escaping, in case enemy planes flew over. "My husband was in charge of black-outs in a certain number of blocks," Dorothy Dean (Mrs. Joel Chandler, Jr.) Harris said. "If he saw lights coming from a person's windows, he would knock on their doors," to let them know. (13)

William T. Dreger III remembered the air-raid drills. "It was a frightening experience to a twelve- or thirteen-year-old to hear those air raid sirens go off. Everybody'd turn off the light, we didn't know whether, actually, somebody was going to attack Atlanta, or if it was a drill." (14)

"My uncle [Thomas Cassell] was a warden. He would call us sometimes and say, 'Don't get worried, we're gonna have a black-out,'" Janet Knox (Mrs. Thomas) Moore said. (15)

"We would have air-raid wardens come down the street. I was just eleven when the war started, so I had no fear of having to go off. It was a remote war as far as we were concerned," Marcus Cook III. recalled. (16)

"I volunteered to be a messenger for the air-raid warden on my block," John Ottley III said in a speech. "This guy had a little World War I helmet, white, with Civil Defense insignia on the front. I would meet him on our street. My job was to take any messages he had to the Civil Defense Message Center. I had no idea where that was. Of course, there weren't any messages to be transmitted. Everybody else was in their house with the curtains drawn and the lights off, and he and I were out on the street just making sure that everything was okay." (17)

"I was an air raid warden," Alva Lines recalled. Later he went into the Army Air Force, where he served as a captain in Australia and New Guinea. "I had the Weiuca Road part of that segment. That had to do with going to the houses, telling them what to do, what precautions to take, what type of equipment and supplies to put away. The Red Cross gave us training in resuscitation, first aid…and then we had to go and sell war bonds to all of our neighbors. We had a quota. At one time I had a quota of $50,000 and my next-door neighbor bought the whole thing." (18)

***

The gasoline shortage caused some companies to go out of business. The Colonnade Drive-In on Piedmont Road (across from the present MARTA station) "closed because there was a ban on personal driving during the Second World War," Bill Dreger explained. "You couldn't drive anywhere but to work and back. You couldn't drive to the grocery store, couldn't drive to a drive-in restaurant. It would be a violation of the law." (19)

"Things were being rationed…if your tires wore out, you would have to go to the Ration Board and get permission to have them retreaded," Alva Lines said. (20)

"During World War II gasoline was rationed, and I saved my gasoline, because I had an A card. We walked everywhere or we rode the streetcar," Ellen Newell (Mrs. William Wright) Bryan remembered. She and her Peachtree Road neighbors had walking groups to take their young children to E. Rivers School and to Mrs. Bloodworth's Kindergarten. During the war, her husband, Wright, who was managing editor of *The Atlanta Journal*, served as a stringer for the National Broadcasting Company (NBC) in Europe. On June 6, 1944, he watched the Allied invasion of France from a transport plane, then returned to London to be the first to report D-Day to the world. Later, while covering the war on the ground in Europe, he was shot and captured by the Germans in France in 1944, and held prisoner until 1945. While laying up in a hospital recuperating from a leg wound, he was visited by his Buckhead neighbor, Dr. F. Phinizy Calhoun Jr. (21)

"We carpooled a great deal during the war, we really did pick up people." Louise Richardson (Mrs. Ivan, Jr.) Allen said. "We had a tractor and I think there was a gas pump…Every now and then we'd have to borrow a little gas from the tractor pump." (22)

Lon Bridges was "my life-saver because we had so little gas," Judy Beers (Mrs. Rufus) Darby said. "I'd walk to Buckhead with the kids…And Lon, bless his heart, I'd park the babies [twins Judy and Frank] and the children [Rufus Jr. and Billy] at the filling station with him, and he'd look after 'em for me while I went in the grocery store…And then usually he would take me home in his truck, because he could get a little more gas." (23)

"Our family got a gallon can of gas, and I remember digging a hole in the back yard to hide that gallon can. I was afraid for days that somehow the rationing people would hear about it and seek us out and say, 'We know you've horded some gas in your backyard.' It was strictly for emergencies, in case somebody had to go to the hospital or something like that," John K. Ottley III said. (24)

"I remember food rationing, and Mother waiting in line for meat, and the coupon books, and going to Rhodes Bakery, the lines…You couldn't make cakes…because you were just allowed so much sugar," Janet Knox (Mrs. Thomas) Moore said. (25)

***

The war turned citizens into savers and collectors as they gathered newspapers, string, aluminum cans, and coathangers from neighbors. Tin foil was stripped from gum and cigarette wrappers and rolled into balls. Used toothpaste tubes were collected in barrels. "They said that a barrel would be enough to provide material for welding one fighter plane," Alva Lines explained. "They were in great demand, they were made of lead." (26)

"I can remember going down in the woods behind, about where the A&P is now at Peachtree Battle…looking for aluminum cans to bring to the school for the scrap drive," John K. Ottley III remembered. "They would pile these up, each grade, out on the lawn and the class with the biggest pile got to take a jeep ride down Peachtree Battle." (27)

"Building materials had been allocated for the war, and you could not go to the lumber companies and buy anything," Emily Anderson (Mrs. George) Hightower explained. "You had to prove it was necessary to repair your roof." Shortly after their marriage in 1943, her husband was sent to China for two years, where he flew with Gen. Claire Chennault's Flying Tigers. (28)

War shortages also affected high school ROTC programs. "I recall in 1945 we had wooden rifles because all of the rifles had been shipped off to the army," said Bill Dreger, who took ROTC at North Fulton High School. (29)

There were a few enterprising people working on some of the estates in Buckhead who made extra money selling food during the war. One of these entrepreneurs was Earnest Smith, Gov. John M. Slaton's handyman, who tended to the house and farm. "Ernest would sell the milk," Betty Slaton (Mrs. John) Wallace said. "This was mostly during World War II." (30)

"I know during the Second World War...Frank [Owens, who worked for the John W. Grants] would sell eggs in the neighborhood, and fresh milk, because they had more than they could handle," William Rudolph recalled. "When there was extra vegetables [the Inmans and the Slatons] got some...If there was some left, Frank would go round and sell it to make spending money." (31)

The ladies of Buckhead pitched in to help the war effort. "We would go down and make dressings...and bandages and ship them over to England [before America entered the war]," Dorothy Dean (Mrs. Joel Chandler, Jr.) Harris, who became chairman of the Nurses's Aides, said. They worked in an empty home on West Peachtree Street at the corner of Sixth Street across from the Biltmore Hotel, and because of the gasoline rationing, the women rode the streetcar to work. "Some of the ladies fussed at not having come down in their own automobiles." Some of Mrs. Harris' fellow workers were her sister Carol Spratlin, Margaret Mitchell, Callie and Cornelia Healey, Helen McDuffie, and Mrs. Eugene Black. After the war ended, many of these women continued their public and philanthropic service as "pink ladies" or "grey ladies" in local hospitals. (32)

***

During the war troop convoys traveled through Buckhead, going in two separate directions. In order to get the troops to Bell Bomber Plant in

Marietta, US 41 (Northside Parkway) was widened to four lanes. Other convoys went out Peachtree Road, passing through the business center on their way to and from Camp Gordon, now DeKalb Airport in Chamblee. "We used to stand and watch the troop convoys...hundreds of 'em...That was fascinating to us children," Ken Moss remembered. (33)

Luther Randall Sr.'s daughter, Mrs. (Helen Randall) Shreve, recalled, in an article, that army convoys passed in front of her parent's house on West Paces Ferry Road. "'It was during the summer and very hot. Mother always had pitchers of ice water and iced tea for the soldiers and one of the servants would take them down to the roadside.'" (34) The Luther Randalls built their house in 1941 on thirty acres of West Paces Ferry Road land (Pace Academy) which had once been owned by his great-great-great grandfather Hardy Pace. (35)

Mrs. George Murray Sr. did the bookkeeping at Buckhead Hardware during the war, and would ride in the company truck wearing her fur stole, 'Cause she didn't want anybody to think she *had* to ride in a truck," Tom Murray mused. "A truck is a status symbol nowadays, but it wasn't fifty years ago." He recalled that Buckhead during this period was a happy and congenial community, where children were welcome in the shops. There was no shoplifting, no drugs, and people were well-mannered. (36)

CHAPTER FORTY
1940s
Buckhead During the War

$\mathcal{D}$espite a shortage of building materials, homes continued to be built in Buckhead for a growing population. The Buckhead Theater, Buckhead Pool Hall, and the Buckhead Duck Pin Bowling Alley provided entertainment for the community, and Fred's Fruit Stand became a landmark known for its ice cold watermellon.

The Rufus M. Darbys moved onto Habersham Road north of West Paces Ferry Road in 1942, when "There were only three houses on the street," Judy Beers (Mrs. Rufus) Darby said. She remembered shooting at tin cans in the woods, and that their children picnicked and played in the nearby creek. (1)

Mrs. Darby's parents, Harold William Beers and the former Nancy Akers Carroll, of Carroll County, followed their daughter to Buckhead, and moved to the corner of Habersham and east Pine Valley. Mr. Beers founded Beers Construction Co. in 1920, after he bought out the shares his partner, Charles Loridan, held in the Southern Ferro Concrete Co. (2)

In the early forties, Mr. and Mrs. Thomas Mallard Cassells and their daughter Elizabeth moved to 114 West Paces Ferry, which was located where Slaton Drive now cuts in. "Every time I ride by I feel like I'm riding through my house," Elizabeth Cassells (Mrs. Richard) Rubenoff mused. "I remember the cars and the trucks going by, and when they did, our pictures on the wall…and the china in the kitchen would shake. Mother said, 'I just hate this when the big, heavy cars and truck pass; everything gets out of position.'" (3)

***

In 1943 Joseph Edward Tatum retired from his railroad job and took over the running of the North Side Service Station, following the death of his wife, Nora Irene (Rolader). The business, which was being run by Ivon Rolader at the corner of Northside Drive and Moores Mill Road, began as a small store. It was built around 1900 by Tatum's father-in-law, the Rev. Lorenzo Dow Rolader. At the Rev. Rolader's death, the station was inherited by his daughters, Nora Irene Tatum and Maybelle Pirkirt. (4)

Rev. Rolader "leased this store to my father (Ivon) when he came back from World War I," Pete Rolader said of his great-uncle. "In the early forties my father's uncle's daughters had married, and their husbands wanted that store. So it was taken away from my father and his brothers and given to my uncles." (5)

Mr. Tatum's cash and credit business sold gasoline, milk, soft drinks, and some canned goods. During the construction boom, after the war, building crews bought "crackers, some sardines, cans of pork and beans, Vienna sausages, and they would all sit down underneath his shed," said Maybelle "Snookie" Tatum (Mrs. Daniel) Osburn of her father's station. "You could hardly pull a car in there to get gas from twelve o'clock to two o'clock." During cold weather, the workmen ate inside the station, around the wood and coal heater where Tatum placed an old couch, a table and some chairs around for their convenience. For many years the station also served as Tatum's bank, where he kept a bag of money in a tin can secreted in a hole in the station's cement floor. (6)

The service station was forced to close in the mid-1950s, when the City of Atlanta said the property was not zoned commercial, and threatened to condemn it unless Tatum sold his property. "They wanted it for the waterworks," Mrs. Osburn explained. "There were some pretty well-to-do people that tried to help Daddy keep the store." The City moved their house across the street from where the water tower now sits on Moores Mill Road (at the condos and behind the Miriam Heiskell School property). (7)

***

Fred's Fruit Stand, on Peachtree Road in front of the present Peachtree Battle Shopping Center, was a popular spot from 1940 until 1963. On the back patio, Fred J. Golden's customers could sit at tables and eat ice cold watermelon.

"You'd have your slice of watermelon on usually a Coca-Cola tray and you would spit the seeds to the side," Barrett Howell remembered. (8) "Fred was a crusty old character," Henry Howell added. (9)

Louise "Weezie" (Mrs. John, III) Grant remembered, "Sitting at tables in the back room, you felt like you were in a summer house, in a completely undeveloped part of town." (10)

"During the hot nights of summer, before air-conditioning, my parents (the Louis Fox Srs.) would put me and my brother Louis in the car and drive out to Buckhead (from the Ponce de Leon area). Their destination was cold slices of watermelon at Fred's," Peggy Fox Goldberg said. She remembered the salt shakers that sat on oil-clothed tables. (11)

Fred's Fruit emporium "was just a shack and how it stayed up I don't remember. But it was a very popular place. We'd get chewing gum and fruit," Judson Hawk Jr. said. (12)

***

The Buckhead Theater continued to be the *in* spot for the young set on Saturday afternoons. "Had a bicycle stand to put [bikes] in and lock it up, cause we were always afraid somebody'd steal those bicycles. I think my father had paid seven dollars and a half, and I sure didn't want to lose it," Bill Dreger said. (13)

"A big date was to take your girl to the Buckhead movie and then down to Wender & Roberts and Hitchcock and Simmons, and sit out there and drink cherry Coke and eat cheese crackers," Pete Rolader said. (14)

"We would go to the Buckhead Theater on Saturday afternoon. Sometimes Mr. Frost, who was the manager, would kick us out for being bad, and then we'd go over to Jacobs' and get a Coca-Cola," Barrett Howell mused. "When we got a little older, we'd venture into the pool hall (now Laura Ashley's), only to watch at first." Sometimes the boys lost their movie money to better pool players. (15)

"The Buckhead Pool Hall…was a terrible place, according to my mother," Bill Dreger mused. "Anyone who set foot in the Buckhead Pool Hall was damned." (16)

Bowling at the Buckhead Duck Pin Bowling Alley (presently the Buckhead Commons shopping center) on Peachtree Road was another popular activity. "The Rolader boys were well known," Pete Rolader mused. "I remember one day my uncle came by and said, 'Boys…Mr. Sutton up at the bowling alley says you guys were in there Saturday and bowled, and one or two walked out and didn't pay anybody. I paid your bill, now pay me.'" (17)

***

During World War II, while the Andrew Calhouns were in Europe, some Buckhead teens broke into Trygveson/The Pink Palace, their house on West Paces Ferry Road, and trashed it. "Somebody discovered it was so easy to go in there, so every night after the midnight movie, they'd go there and have parties," Mary Ann (Mrs. Lon, Jr.) Bridges recalled. "They vandalized the kitchen first, then they went upstairs to the bedrooms. They just used the house for fun. They hushed it up very quickly." (18)

"They (the Calhouns) came back and found obscenities scrawled along the walls. [The vandals] partied and tore up the place," Jack Spalding remembered. (19)

Maybelle "Snookie" Osburn said the kids threw rotten eggs and catsup on the walls of the Calhoun house. (20)

"It was just a wild episode. It was during World War II, and my father was the assistant district attorney and very much in charge of the prosecution of the offenders," Reuben Garland Jr. explained. "The detectives eventually rounded up all the high school students involved…There was a whole series of houses…[the newspapers] referred to them as 'The Buckhead Vandals.'" (21)

CHAPTER FORTY-ONE
1945
Buckhead Life Following the War

"Things speeded up and it never has slowed back down."
- Ken Moss

"*P*ost-war days found Buckhead with a population of 75,000, an upper-drawer but haphazardly fabricated community. Although it was the second largest city in Georgia, it had no mayor or police force...And though its residents had the highest per-capita income south of Philadelphia, Buckhead offered mainly 'fish and groceries,'" newspaperman Hugh Park wrote in 1967. (1)

"The real changes started after the war, with a tremendous influx of business people from the east and mid-west, as companies expanded branch offices and regional offices in Atlanta," T. Sinclair "Tory" Jacobs explained. "People complained about the streets being torn up, and I remember (Mayor William B. Hartsfield) saying, 'The day that you don't see construction on the streets will be a sad day, it'll mean that we are in a depression.'" (2)

***

Home and apartment construction went into full production as materials, once needed for the war effort, were again available to the public, creating a building boom all over the country. Large property owners in Buckhead began selling off lots, as more people wanted to move into the community.

"The only way you could get an apartment in Atlanta was to know the person who was building them. It helped a bit if you had been in the army," Emily Anderson (Mrs. George) Hightower said. The Hightowers were fortunate to get an apartment at 3630 Peachtree through a contact of her pediatrician father, Dr. W. W. Anderson. (3)

The John Ottley Jr. family moved to Rivers Road, where young John

III and Dudley walked or rode their bikes to E. Rivers School. The imaginative children shot snakes and bottles in the woods on Northside Drive near King Road, slid on ice cut from their frozen fish pond, and placed in the garage, and threw spitballs at the audience at the Garden Hills Theater. (4)

Mr. Ottley recalled that home delivery from grocery stores and pharmacies was popular during the 1940s. Hawk's Drugstore had a delivery man who "would deliver on his Harley motorcycle...he had an aviator helmet, with flaps flying. He'd bring the goggles down just for effect and come roaring up the driveway," Mr. Ottley said in a speech. "At the time there was no leash law, and all dogs were loose...they would converge on our driveway like a pack of wolves...[the delivery man] knew they were coming, so he would give it an extra twist on the throttle so it would make a loud exhaust noise." (5)

Reuben Garland Jr., whose family lived on Peachtree Road north of Peachtree Dunwoody, "had chickens and a goat — a milk goat — because my father was allergic to cow's milk and beef. I had a saddle horse for several years." He participated in the horse shows at John Ottley's, where there was a large stable with around forty stalls, training areas, and special riding rings. (6) The Garland home "has a big granite wall around the lot. Mr. Garland had defended someone, as I recall, for murder, and he got him out of the electric chair and he served a period of time in prison," William T. Dreger III said. "When he got out, he owed Mr. Garland a lot of money, so [Garland] used him as an indentured servant to build that wall. It took him a year or so, stayed out there every day building that wall before he released the debt." (7)

***

The death knell was sounded for the black Bagley Park community in the mid-1940s. "One of the Fulton County commissioners decided he didn't want them there...his house backed up to it," Tom Murray said. "He got together with the county commissioners and had the whole area condemned, so they could turn it into a park. They came by and bought houses from the landlords, and the landlords got together and said that only for eternity could it be used for a park. They wouldn't let them condemn it just to get rid of the people, and then sell it to a private party twenty years later so they could develop it into homes. It will always be a public park." (8)

Between 1945 and 1952 Fulton County bought the twelve acres of Bagley Park and spent fifteen thousand dollars turning the land into a park, which retained the name of Bagley. It was renamed Frankie Allen Park in

1980. (9) "Frankie Allen Park was named after a police officer who was killed in the line of duty," Bill Dreger explained. "He did a lot of work with Little League." (10)

***

Among the new businesses that opened in Buckhead after the war was Peachtree Federal Savings and Loan, at the corner of Peachtree Road and Buckhead Avenue (once the site of the Buckhead Men's Shop). Alex McLennan was president. (11) In 1946 the Piedmont Supper Club opened at the corner of Piedmont and Lindburgh roads, and Rusty's drive-in began operation at 2225 Peachtree Road. (12) The Piedmont Drive-in opened on the site of the present Lindburgh MARTA Station in 1947, the same year that angle parking along Peachtree Road from Mathieson Drive south to Palisades was discontinued. (13)

The Margaret Bryan Dance School moved above the present Laura Ashley store at Roswell and West Paces Ferry roads in 1947, replacing the Sarah Wagstaff Rogers School of Dancing, and became a social landmark in Buckhead during the 1940s and 1950s.

"There were two sets of stairs to Margaret Bryan's Dance School, one on West Paces and one on Peachtree [now Roswell]," Henry Howell explained. "when your mother dropped you off...you went up the stairs on West Paces. Those of us who didn't particularly know how to dance and weren't real interested went down the stairs on Peachtree and out to explore Buckhead. And when the time came to be picked up, we'd reverse that and go up the Peachtree stairs and go out and meet our parents on West Paces and tell them how much we loved the dancing." (14)

"Of course she (Margaret Bryan) would find lots of the boys in the pool hall below," Barrett Howell said. (15)

In 1948 WQXI Radio opened Buckhead's first radio station on Mathieson Drive behind Peachtree Road. (16) Broadview Shopping Center, now Lindburgh Plaza, was built the following year on Piedmont Road at Lindburgh Drive, for $113,000. (17)

***

Murder in Buckhead became a front page item when Margaret Alston (Mrs. Paul) Refoule was found murdered on May 14, 1947, on the bank of Peachtree Creek, behind her home on Howell Mill Road. Miss Alston had met young artist Paul Refoule while attending the Sorbonne in Paris in the mid-1930s, and the two were married in 1937 and lived in Paris. When

World War II broke out, Refoule enlisted in the French Army; he was captured by the Germans and imprisoned in Poland. After escaping from the prison camp in December of 1944, he was reunited with his wife and son Jon in Orleans, France. (18)

The Refoule family moved to Atlanta in the summer of 1945 and bought and renovated an old woolen mill that sat on Howell Mill Road at Peachtree Battle Avenue. In their home, which overlooked Peachtree Creek, Refoule opened a private studio while also teaching at Oglethorpe University and the High Museum. (19)

On the day of the murder, nine-year-old Jon came home from school to find a locked front door and muddy footprints near the unlocked door on the back porch. Refoule came home an hour later. Around eight o'clock, he became concerned that his wife had not returned home, and summoned the police. Tracking dogs discovered Mrs. Refoule's body in the creek "lying face up, her arm twisted behind her back, her feet tied together with shoelaces." She had been strangled to death, and her wedding ring, watch, a camera and two diamond rings were missing. (20)

At first the police thought Mrs. Refoule had been killed by a burglar. But the investigation turned towards the husband when it was discovered that he had had an affair with one of his High Museum art students and had "told her he was unhappy with his marriage." Some Oglethorpe University students supplied him with an alibi when they said he was in the classroom building the afternoon of the murder. (21)

Refoule lost his jobs and went on the offensive. In July of 1947, he petitioned the U.S. District Court to prevent the Fulton County police from "further illegal detention or questioning," and sued Chief Neil Ellis and other police officers for physical brutality and harassment. The police were enjoined from further questioning Refoule, unless he was arrested for his wife's murder. Though he demanded a trial for "judgment of acquittal which I am entitled under the law," he died soon after in February of 1948 after undergoing surgery for lung cancer. (22) Today the case still remains a mystery.

***

A new public school was established in Buckhead to educate the growing youth population, and one old school was burned down during a disastrous attempt to exterminate wasps.

Morris Brandon Elementary School was built in 1947 on Howell Mill Road, on the former site of Key's Dairy. The school's namesake and benefactor (1862-1940) was the son of Minerva Elizabeth (Morris) and Lt. Col.

N. Brandon. (23)

Col. Brandon lost his plantation in Dover, Tennessee, during the Civil War and moved to Atlanta in 1886 to practice law. "During the Reconstruction Era times were hard, and my grandfather instilled into his son, Morris, who in turn passed it along to his own children, the basic philosophy that in times of national financial strain, the only thing which couldn't be taken away from an individual was his mentality, and that the best way to provide against such eventuality was to provide for his own, and that of his descendants, the best possible education," Inman Brandon wrote in a letter in 1977. "So that when the opportunity arose it seemed only fitting to donate property to Fulton County on which to establish an elementary school bearing Morris Brandon's name." (24)

One Saturday in September of 1948, E. Rivers School was destroyed by fire. The culprit was a blow torch-wielding janitor trying to get rid of wasp's nests in the building. The Temple and the Second Ponce de Leon Baptist Church opened their facilities to the school during the construction of a new modern school, which was opened in January of 1950. (25)

CHAPTER FORTY-TWO
1952
Annexation

"Trying to do it, failing, trying to do it and pass."
- Barrett Howell

*M*ayor William B. Hartsfield, concerned that so many Atlanta residents were moving north of the city, offered his first plan to annex and incorporate the Buckhead community on April 1, 1938. This plan proved unsuccessful. In 1947 the mayor renewed his annexation effort, and included the community of Cascade Heights, and again the referendum failed. (1)

"Buckhead was always very jealous of its independent status; it did not want to be part of Atlanta," Joseph K. Heyman said. "Then there was an attempt to call for one government to consolidate the governments of Fulton County and Atlanta. And that also proved to be unsuccessful." (2)

"As a compromise, the Legislature, in 1949, set up a local Government Commission of Fulton County, which had representatives from both Fulton County and DeKalb County, because they weren't going to do anything with Atlanta unless they got DeKalb's permission. Part of Atlanta is in DeKalb," Mr. Heyman explained. Joseph K. Heyman and Philip Hammer went to work for the Local Government Commission and wrote the Plan of Improvement. (3)

"The Plan...was a three-part deal," Mr. Heyman continued. "One, greatly extend the City limits of Atlanta...two, make sure that the County was out of the business of delivering any sort of City services...three, provide eventually for automatic extension of the Atlanta city limits on very easy terms...[such as] when a new land lot outside of the then-drawn lines reached a certain density, either in terms of number of families living there or in terms of certain values on the tax digest. Beyond that, they could be moved into the city upon petition either of the local residents or from petition of the city if they met these standards." (4)

The Plan of Improvement for Atlanta and Fulton County was decided at the ballot box on January 1, 1952. The Plan was adopted, and many outlying areas, including Buckhead, were brought into the city, tripling its size from 35 square miles to 118. Atlanta was to provide municipal services, such as "police and fire protection, garbage collection, building, plumbing and electrical inspections, and parks for the new city area." The County was responsible for "the courts, health, welfare, agriculture." (5) The Supreme Court later ruled the plan unconstitutional. (6)

"Hartsfield had tried several times to sway us to vote to come into Atlanta," Tom Murray said. "We went to a meeting at North Fulton in '46, and he made a point. He said, 'Most of you don't want to come into Atlanta, because you say you don't like the mayor. You can't get rid of me until you come in and vote me out.'" (7)

"As far as we were concerned, we saw it had to be," Dorothy Dean (Mrs. Joel Chandler, Jr.) Harris said. "There was a lot of protection that we would get from going into the city that we wouldn't have if we stayed out...We knew we couldn't develop without it." (8)

"Most of my friends thought it was a good idea," Florence "Poncie" Bryan (Mrs. William Bonneau) Ansley said. (9)

"We were always for it," Laura Maddox (Mrs. Edward D.) Smith said. "Ed felt that if you were going to work in the city and live in the city, you ought to support the city and be in the city." (10)

"I was always in favor of it," Ivan Allen Jr. said. "A lot of people didn't want to be in the city, there was gonna be high taxes." (11)

The Herbert Elsas were not only for annexation, but were for enlarging the new boundaries. "It had nothing to do with diluting the black vote...blacks were not encouraged to vote...I felt it was better to center the services needed for a government in one entity." (12)

"My family was very, very, very much for it," Barrett Howell commented. "My father was running a newspaper [*The Atlanta Constitution*] at the time, and the newspaper was very much for it. And they failed the first time...The second time it just squeaked by." (13)

Of course there were opponents to the proposition. Two of the leaders of this effort were Red Dorough and Henry Alexander. They had a ceremony where they displayed coffins and philosophically buried Mayor Hartsfield. During the mock funeral, "Three caskets marked 'Hartsfield', '*The Atlanta Journal*' and '*The Atlanta Constitution*' were borne down Peachtree to solemn strains of Sibelius' 'Finlandia'." (14) "Mayor Hartsfield had his own private bathroom at City Hall and he had that picture over the toilet," Cecil Alexander related. (15)

William Brand Jr. said that some of the people in Buckhead "talked about incorporating and becoming a city, but they never did. Daddy had a good bit of political influence with different representatives...Him and Red had enough political pull that the city couldn't extend the city limits until 1952...till they let the people vote on the Plan of Improvement. It was really an annexation, but the people in Buckhead didn't realize it...They didn't understand what the Plan of Improvement was, they thought they were gonna improve government." (16)

Some of the residents of Buckhead wondered why police were in the community on January 1, 1952. When they asked for an explanation, they were told, "'Oh, you voted to come into the city,'" Lon Bridges Jr. said. (17)

"That's when the politicians sold everybody in Buckhead down the drain," Ken Moss said. "Up until that time they hadn't told everybody what it really was. It was kept completely quiet. Everybody agreed Atlanta needed improving, but what they did sure didn't improve it. They [Atlanta] took everything the county had, all the equipment, all the fire stations, all the police equipment, everything, and they had first class equipment. Sent junky stuff out to Buckhead. They didn't realize that the Plan of Improvement was taking Buckhead into the city. Like I said, the local politicians sold 'em down the river. Red Dorough was very much against it, but on the last go-round Red didn't say a damn word about it." (18)

"One of the things that made the north side grow is Fulton County was big on paving roads," William Brand Jr. said. "The city had raised sand that they were wasting tax payer's money paving subdivision streets. Actually, that's why Buckhead grew where other places really didn't". (19)

"The 1950s is when Buckhead started feeling proud of itself," Roy Milling reflected. "We tried to stay out of the city, and the city limits at that time came out to about Collier Road. We brought it to a standstill one time, but the second time around it went all the way. The powers that be in Buckhead thought we could beat them downtown and then form a city [like College Park]." (20)

CHAPTER FORTY-THREE
1950s
A New Buckhead Emerges

*B*uckhead in the early fifties "was pretty quiet...laid back and un-sophisticated in its commercial core. It was a comfortable place to live," said Samuel Alan Massell Jr., president of the Buckhead Coalition, "unofficial mayor" of Buckhead, former mayor of the City of Atlanta, and a resident of Buckhead since 1952. "It was the direction that Atlanta was taking, and it was where the action was, and I wanted to be a part of it." (1)

After Buckhead's annexation into Atlanta proper, it changed from the once quiet and simple community into a bustling mini-city, with an influx of new residents and a surge of new businesses. Within a few years five new schools were established, a country club was formed, a black neighborhood vanished, and the shopping mall of all shopping malls was built.

***

The increase in population in Buckhead meant more school-age children, and this put a strain on the public school system. The first to feel the effects was the community's one-and-only high school, North Fulton.

Because of increased student enrollment, North Fulton High School began bursting its seams, and to alleviate the overcrowding of its student population, a new school was created. Northside High School was built, and opened in 1950 on Northside Drive. The dividing line for student enrollment was Peachtree Road; students living on the west side of Peachtree went to Northside, and those living on the east side remained at North Fulton.

There was also a boom in private schools in Buckhead during the fifties, which offered students an alternative to public education.

The first was The Heiskell School, which was created by a woman with a need to educate and socialize her child, who was recovering from polio. The Heiskell School began in 1950, when Miriam Heiskell, a certified teacher, organized a play group of fifteen children in her home. (2)

The program continued to grow, and in 1963, Mrs. Heiskell's husband, James H. Heiskell, built a school building at the corner of Northside Drive and Moores Mill Road for classes from kindergarten to the seventh grade, which offered a Christian-oriented program, along with a basic education curriculum. In 1974 Mount Vernon Christian Academy was formed in conjunction with The Heiskell School to educate the high school students. (3)

Trinity Presbyterian Church rose to the educational challenge of the Buckhead community by establishing two nursery school classes at the church on Howell Mill Road in 1951. The program was a success, and additional grade levels were created until the school offered a program for pre-school through the seventh grade. During the period of school desegregation in the sixties, Trinity was the first private school in Atlanta to open its doors to black students. In 1979 the school moved into the old Birney Elementary School building on Northside Parkway. (4)

Before the 1950s there were two private girls' schools in Atlanta, North Avenue Presbyterian School (NAPS), which was founded in 1909, and Washington Seminary, founded in 1878. Because there were no private boys' schools in Atlanta, some community leaders felt a need to establish a private co-ed school that would offer a solid educational background for its students. Consequently, North Avenue Presbyterian School "incorporated the school and changed the name to The Westminster Schools" in 1951, with a boys' program, and they purchased one hundred and seventy-five acres of the Fritz Orr Camp property. Classes were held in their Ponce de Leon Avenue building until Westminster moved onto their new Buckhead campus in 1953. That same year, Washington Seminary merged with Westminster. (5)

After Fritz Orr sold most of the camp property to The Westminster School, he purchased Merrie-Wood Camp in Cashiers, North Carolina. His Buckhead camp, however, continued to operate for awhile under the leadership of Josh Powell and D. L. "Buddy" Fowlkes. (6)

The fourth private school established in Buckhead was Pace Academy, which was chartered on June 30, 1958, under the leadership of Jane Tuggle and T. Benjamin Massey. That same year the school purchased John Ogden's home at 966 West Paces Ferry Road, which today is called Kirkpatrick Hall, in honor of George G. Kirkpatrick, the school's third headmaster. In 1977 the Luther Randall home and property, next door to Pace, was purchased for additional classroom space. The school's campus conforms well to the residential ambiance of West Paces Ferry Road. (7)

***

Some of the affluent Buckhead residents desired to have a private club in close proximity to their homes, for family recreation and social events. In 1955 they met at the home of Pat and James "Hoss" Williams and established the Cherokee Town and Country Club. Within the year, the organization had grown to six hundred members. The following year the Club leased Craigellachie, the home and property of John W. Grant, for their Town Club, with an option to buy for two hundred thousand dollars. Property was also purchased in Dunwoody for the Country Club golf course. (8) Today, the Cherokee Town and Country Club is a place where the social and business elite of Buckhead, as well as Atlanta, meet.

***

As commercialism in Buckhead spread, and residents of Johnson Town and Piney Grove moved to other areas, several more black neighborhoods in the community went into a decline. Developers purchased the property, and by the fall of 1982 Johnson Town was no more. (9)

Columbus Johnson, grandson and namesake of *the* Johnson of Johnson Town, feels there was a deliberate plan to do away with that neighborhood. "They began to manipulate the property over there, burned up houses and eliminating people, eliminating houses so they wouldn't have nowhere to live. There were five houses on our property and they burned them down, every one of them." (10)

***

The building of Lenox Square in 1959, on the site of the John K. Ottley property, had a great impact on the city of Atlanta and Buckhead, and dealt a terrible blow to the small retail businesses in the community.

Edward E. Noble, of the Noble Foundation, and president of Lenox Square, Inc., was the creator of the first shopping mall in America. His foundation in Ardmore, Oklahoma, did an extensive survey of possible sites for his new shopping concept and chose the Buckhead area because "the foundation's study showed the property...is in the heart of the fast growing [sic] section in the Atlanta trade area." The report further stated that from 1950 until 1957 "some 68,000 new dwelling units have been added, which brings the 1957 customer potential to 338,000 families." (11)

The City of Atlanta Board of Aldermen gave their approval to the new concept in 1956, and Noble purchased the Ottley property (on Peachtree

Road), and adjoining land for a total of seventy-two acres. (12)

After fourteen months of construction, the $15 million mall opened for business on August 3, 1959. The shopping center was anchored by Rich's and Davison's, in their first foray into the suburbs, and featured other stores that "ranged from bakers to brokers, from barbers to bankers, from bags to boots," said John D. Smith, vice-president and general manager of Lenox Square, Inc. (13)

America's premier mall attracted shoppers from the greater metropolitan Atlanta area, drawn by the free parking for six thousand cars, accessibility of a multitude of various shops in one area, and a pleasant atmosphere. For his vision of the future in retail, Noble was named the Atlanta Sales Executive Club's "Sales Executive of the Year" in 1960. (14)

With the opening of Lenox Square, businesses in the central business district suffered. Those that chose not to move to the mall suffered from a lack of customers and, consequently, many went out of business.

"Developers have been trying to kill off Buckhead for 25 years," Jim Fisher of Fisher's Men's Shop said in a newspaper article. "In 1959 when the mall opened, they [Lenox] wanted to be completely separate from Buckhead." (15)

"Lenox wanted everybody [the businesses] in Buckhead to go out there, but their one demand was that you had to close up your Buckhead location. They wanted to choke Buckhead off," Tom Murray explained. "In the long run, I don't really know how Buckhead succeeded over the years, only thing it offered was location." (16) "Before Lenox opened, all the ladies would meet downtown, have lunch at Rich's or Davison's or the Frances Virginia Tea Room, and they'd browse around for five or six hours, shop and come home. And when Lenox opened, they began to go there," Jane (Mrs. George, Jr.) Murray said. (17)

"When the Ottleys sold the land where Lenox is today, a total new concept of shopping [began]," Barrett Howell said. "We were no longer a little rural community; we became similar to what we are today." (18)

CHAPTER FORTY-FOUR
The End of the Story ... or Is It?

*B*uckhead's progress is a microcosm of the progress of Atlanta, reflecting its changes and growth over the years.

The Indians who lived along Buckhead's river and creeks are gone. The old mills, ferries, pottery factories, and dairies are no more, and only road signs and tombstones recall the names of the early settlers and businessmen, who came and left their mark on the Buckhead community and Atlanta.

Those who remember Buckhead before it became a "city" of commerce and an entertainment mecca, remember peaceful times, with little traffic and crime, and a warm and friendly community. Buckhead today is overcrowded with traffic gridlocks. Homes and businesses that once had no fear of crime are now armed with burglar alarms, and Peachtree Road now mirrors New York's Fifth Avenue.

Despite the negatives of progress, Buckhead is the community with the proper address, and is certainly "a place for all time."

FOOTNOTES

Preface

1. *The Buckhead Guide Book*, 1995, Published by Buckhead Coalition, Inc.; Sam Massell, Editor, printed by Stein Printing Co, Inc., Atlanta, 1995.

Chapter 1

1. Betty Parham and Gerrie Ferris, "Q & A On The News," *The Atlanta Constitution*, July 12, 1993, p. A-2.
2. David W. Chase and Susan K. Barnard, *An Archaeological Investigation of the Historic Peachtree Fort Area Atlanta, Georgia 1993*, p. 9.
3. David W. Chase and Susan K. Barnard, *An Archaeological Investigation of the Historic Peachtree Fort Area Atlanta, Georgia 1994,* p. 7.
4. Ibid, p. 4.
5. Lawrence W. Meier, "The Profile Papers: A Preliminary Report of Research at 9 CO1, Standing Peach Tree Site, Cobb County, Georgia, SPEGH Newsletter, Number 6, May 1973, p. 2.

Chapter 2

1. Letter to Susan K. Barnard from Marion R. Hemperley; Georgia State Department of Archives and History; November 13, 1986.
2. Walter G. Cooper, *Official History Of Fulton County;* The History Commission, Ivan Allen, Chairman, 1934, p. 22.
3. Franklin M. Garrett, *Atlanta and Environs*, Volume I; University of Georgia Press; Athens, 1954; p. 8.
4. Virlyn Moore Jr. interview.
5. Grace M. Schwartzman and Susan K. Barnard, "A Trail of Broken Promises: Georgians and Muscogee/Creek Treaties, 1796-1826," *The Georgia Historical Quarterly*, Volume LXXV, Number 4, Winter 1991, p. 698.
6. Ibid.
7. Ibid, p. 700.

Chapter 3

1. Grace M. Schwartzman and Susan K. Barnard, "A Trail of Broken Promises: Georgians and Muscogee/Creek Treaties, 1796-1826," *The Georgia Historical Quarterly*, Volume LXXV, Number 4, Winter 1991, p. 701-03.

2. The Forts Committee, Department of Archives and History, "Georgia Forts, The Fort at Standing Peachtree," *Georgia Magazine*, November 4, December 16, 1966, January 1967, p. 21.

3. Letter to Gen. A. Jackson from Gen. Pinckney, Southern Army commander, January 26, 1814; "Georgia Forts," p. 22.

4. James C. Flanigan, *History of Gwinnett County Georgia, 1818-1968*, Volume II; Longino & Porter, Inc., Hapeville, Georgia, 1959, p. 7 [Footnote: Gwinnett was named for Button Gwinnett, a member of the Georgia House of Assembly, who, as a delegate to the 2nd Continental Congress in Philadelphia, signed the Declaration of Independence in 1776 and later helped draft the Georgia Constitution.]

5. James C. Flanigan, *History of Gwinnett County Georgia, 1818-1943*, Volume I; Longino & Porter, Inc., Hapeville, Georgia, pp. 8, 18.

6. Franklin M. Garrett, *Atlanta and Environs*, Volume I; University of Georgia Press, Athens, 1954; p. 15.

7. Schwartzman and Barnard, "A Trail," p. 703.

8. George R. Gilmer, *Sketches of the First Settlers of Upper Georgia*; Genealogical Publishing Company, Baltimore, 1970; p. 196.

9. E. Katherine Anderson, "James McC. Montgomery of Standing Peachtree"; *The Atlanta Historical Bulletin*, No. 3, December 1937, p. 21.

10. Schwartzman and Barnard, "A Trail," p. 703.

11. Gilmer, pp. 198.

12. Schwartzman and Barnard, "A Trail," p. 704.

13. Anderson, "James McC Montgomery," pp. 22-23.

14. Schwartzman and Barnard, "A Trail," p. 704

Chapter 4

1. Franklin M. Garrett, *Atlanta and Environs*, Volume I; University of Georgia Press, Athens, 1954; p. 20. *Pioneer History of Forsyth County, Georgia,* Compiled and edited by Don L. Shadburn County Historian, Forsyth County Heritage Services, Volume I, 1981; W. H. Wolfe Associate, Roswell, Georgia 30077; p. 2.

2. Garrett, *Atlanta and Environs,* pp. 20, 24, 361.

3. Ibid, pp. 363-366.

4. Ibid, p. 13.

5. Virlyn Moore Jr. interview.

6. "The Old Montgomery House at the Standing Peachtree," WAGA TV, December 10, 1965.

7. E. Katherine Anderson, "James McC. Montgomery of Standing Peachtree," *The Atlanta Historical Bulletin*, Number 3, December 1937, pp. 13-20.

8. Moore interview.

9. Garrett, *Atlanta and Environs*, p. 17.

10. Walter G. Cooper, *Official History of Fulton County*; The History Commission, Ivan Allen, Chairman, 1978; p. 24.

11. Anderson, "James McC. Montgomery," pp. 13-20.

12. Moore interview.

13. Alan Patureau, "Familiar names hide violence, DeFoor of DeFoors Ferry Road was axed to death in his house," *The Atlanta Journal and Constitution*, June 23, 1985, p. 4-H. Moore interview.

14. Eugene Cofield interview.

15. Moore interview.

16. Ibid.

17. Ibid.

18. Anderson, "James McC. Montgomery," p. 15.

19. Moore interview.

Chapter 5

1. Franklin M. Garrett, *Atlanta and Environs*, Volume I; University of Georgia Press, Athens, 1954; p. 35.

2. Ibid, p. 34.

3. Merrell Collier interview. Garrett, *Atlanta and Environs*, Ibid, pp. 58, 35.

4. Collier interview. Garrett, *Atlanta and Environs*, Ibid, pp. 34-35.

5. Garrett, *Atlanta and Environs*, p. 564.

6. Franklin M. Garrett interview.

7. Garrett, *Atlanta and Environs*, p. 237.

8. Ibid, p. 363.

9. Ibid, p. 376.

10. Ruth C. Vanneman interview. Garrett, *Atlanta and Environs*, p. 108.

11. Luther Randall Jr. interview.

12. Vanneman interview. Garrett, *Atlanta and Environs*, pp. 108, 170.

13. Margaret Chapman (Mrs. Leon) Townsend interview.

14. "Sardis Methodist Church, Special Homecoming Service, Sunday,

October 9, 1949"; J. R. Roseberry, "143 Years on the Same Site, Sardis Methodist State's 3rd Oldest," newspaper, date and page unknown; Atlanta History Center Library/Archives, Sardis Methodist Church subject file.

15. Letter to Miss Bess Fouche, Clerk Superior Court, Henry County, McDonough, Georgia, from Edgar A. Padgett, Pastor, March 23, 1956. Sardis Methodist Church files.

16. Ibid.

17. Townsend interview.

18. Agnes Fahy, "State's Third Oldest Church at Buckhead", *The Atlanta Journal*, May 23, 1926, p. 11.

19. Ibid.

20. Sara Hammett (Mrs. Binion) Jordan interview.

21. Sardis Cemetery Records, June 1991.

22. Sara H. Jordan interview.

23. Grace M. Schwartzman and Susan K. Barnard, "A Trail of Broken Promises: Georgians and Muscogee/Creek Treaties, 1796-1826," *The Georgia Historical Quarterly*, Vol. LXXV, Winter 1991, Number 4, p. 718.

24. Henry Thompson Malone, *Cherokees Of The Old South: A People in Transition*; The University of Georgia Press, Athens, 1956; p. 182.

25. Ibid, p. 183.

Chapter 6

1. "Railway, Historical Development," *Encyclopedia Britannica*, Vol. 18, Encyclopedia Britannica, Inc.; William Benton, Publisher, 1970, USA; p. 1106. Virlyn Moore Jr. interview. Franklin M. Garrett, *Atlanta and Environs*, Volume I; University of Georgia Press, Athens, 1954; p. 78.

2. Moore interview.

3. "Railroad, Historical Development," p. 1106.

4. Moore interview.

5. Franklin M. Garrett, *Atlanta and Environs*, p. 100.

6. Ibid, pp. 122-23.

7. Ibid, p. 145.

8. Ibid, p. 150

Chapter 7

1. Franklin M. Garrett, *Atlanta and Environs*, Volume I;University of Georgia Press, Athens, 1954; p. 160.

2. Sara Hammett (Mrs. Binion) Jordan interview.

3. Ibid.

4. Wilbur Kurtz Manuscript Collection 130; Atlanta History Center Library/Archives.

5. Jordan interview.

6. Hugh Park, "Buckhead's Seen Tough Days," *The Atlanta Journal*, March 14, 1967, page unknown.

7. Frances Gibson Satterfield, "Buckhead-And How It Was Born: The Mystery of a Community Pivot, Told By Old Residents," *North Side News*, date and page unknown; Atlanta History Center Library/Archives, Buckhead subject file.

8. Garrett, *Atlanta and Environs*, p. 160.

9. Jordan interview.

10. Garrett, *Atlanta and Environs,* pp. 141, 160.

11. Ibid.

12. Ibid, pp. 141, 143.

13. Bill Bell, "Pioneers Benjamin & Sarah Plaster," *Peachtree Hills Views*, November 1988, p. 3.

14. Garrett, *Atlanta and Environs*, p. 143.

15. Ibid.

16. Franklin M. Garrett, "1838 Buckhead - When Buckhead Took Its Name 150 Years Ago, It Was Nothing More Than A Crossroads Leading To Fort Peachtree, Roswell And Decatur," *Inside Buckhead*, Special 150th Anniversery Collector's Edition, Summer, 1988, p. 7.

17. Luther Randall Jr. interview.

18. Garrett, *Atlanta and Environs*, pp. 108, 170, 236.

19. Ruth Carter Vanneman interview.

20. Garrett, *Atlanta and Environs*, p. 191.

21. Virlyn Moore Jr. interview.

22. Randall interview.

23. Garrett, *Atlanta and Environs*, p. 246.

24. Ibid, p. 246.

25. Ibid, p. 42.

26. Moore interview.

Chapter 8

1. Franklin M. Garrett, *Atlanta and Environs*, Volume I; University of Georgia Press, Athens, 1954; p. 185.

2. Ibid, p. 189.

3. Ibid, p. 225.

4. Ibid.

5. Ibid, p. 224.

Chapter 9

1. Franklin M. Garrett, "1838 Buckhead-When Buckhead Took Its Name 150 Years Ago, It Was Nothing More Than A Crossroads Leading To Fort Peachtree, Roswell and Decatur," *InsideBuckhead, Special 150th Anniversary Collector's Edition,* Summer, 1988, p. 7.

2. Ibid, p. 6.

3. Henry Howell interview.

4. Barrett Howell interview; Garrett, *Atlanta and Environs,* Volume I; University of Georgia Press, Athens, 1954; p. 343.

5. Barrett Howell interview. Garrett, *Atlanta and Environs*, p. 334.

6. Barrett Howell and Henry Howell interviews. Garrett, *Atlanta and Environs*, pp. 344, 595.

7. Barrett Howell interview.

8. Henry Howell interview.

9. Ibid.

10. Eugene Cofield interview.

11. Garrett, *Atlanta and Environs*, p. 495.

12. Virlyn Moore Jr. interview.

13. Ibid.

14. *The Family History Book, A Genealogical Record*, compiled by Robert Alvin Walker, no page number; Atlanta History Center Library/Archives, Geneaology, Walker family subject file.

15. Moore interview.

16. Ibid.

17. Ibid.

18. Ibid.

19. Ibid.

20. Ibid.

21. Franklin M. Garrett interview.

22. Garrett, "Buckhead, When Buckhead Took Its Name 150 Years Ago," p. 7.

23. Sara Hammett (Mrs. Binion) Jordan interview.

24. Ibid.

25. William Hammack, "149-Year Old Church Splits To Grow, Sardis Methodist Started in a little log cabin and has been expanding ever since", *The Atlanta Journal and Constitution Magazine*, April 30, 1961, p. 48.

26. Sardis Cemetery Records.

27. Garrett, *Atlanta and Environs,* p. 415.

28. Ibid.

Chapter 10

1. Franklin M. Garrett, *Atlanta and Environs*, Volume I; University of Georgia Press, Athens, 1954; pp. 410-11.

2. Ibid, pp. 411-412.

3. Walter G. Cooper, *Official History of Fulton County*; The History Commission, Ivan Allen, Chairman, 1934; p. 92.

4. Ibid, p. 93.

5. Ibid, p. 102.

6. Garrett, *Atlanta and Environs*, p. 496.

7. Ibid, pp. 526-27.

Chapter 11

1. William E. Erquitt interview.

2. Franklin M. Garrett, *Atlanta and Environs,* Volume I; University of Georgia Press, Athens, 1954; p. 564.

3. Ibid.

4. Ibid, p. 567.

5. Erquitt interview.

6. William R. Scaife, and William E. Erquitt, *The Chattahoochee River Line an American Maginot;* published by William R. Scaife, and William E. Erquitt, Atlanta, 1992; p. 2.

7. Ibid.

8. Ibid, pp. 3, 5.

9. Ibid, p. 14.

10. Erquitt interview.

11. J. Britt McCarley, "'Atlanta Is Ours and Fairly Won': A Driving Tour of the Atlanta Area's Principal Civil War Battlefields," *The Atlanta Historical Journal*, Volume XXVIII, Number 3, Fall 1984, p. 15.

12. Luther Randall Jr. interview.

13. Ibid.

14. Garrett, *Atlanta and Environs,* p. 607.

15. Erquitt interview.

16. Ibid.

17. William R. Scaife, *Campaign for Atlanta*; published by William R. Scaife, Atlanta, 1985; p. 53.

18. Erquitt interview.

19. Ibid.

20. Ren Davis, "Fading Echoes: Three Walking Tours Of Atlanta's Civil War Battlefields," *The Atlanta Journal and Constitution*, August 5,

1989, p. 4.

21. Scaife, *Campaign for Atlanta,* pp. 53, 54.

22. Erquitt interview.

23. Ibid.

24. Davis, "Fading Echoes," p. 5.

25. Erquitt interview.

26. Davis, "Fading Echoes," p. 5.

27. Garrett, *Atlanta and Environs,* p. 634.

28. Merrill Collier interview.

29. Alan Patureau, "Familiar names hide violence, DeFoor of DeFoors Ferry Road was axed to death in his home," *The Atlanta Journal and Constitution*, June 23, 1985, p. 4H.

30. Sara Hammett (Mrs. Binion) Jordan interview.

31. Georgia Department of Archives and History, Form no. CWRS-4, 1966. Sharon Matthews' personal Irby files.

32. Sharon Matthews' personal Irby files.

33. Virlyn Moore Moore Jr. interview.

34. Patureau, "Familiar Names." Moore interview.

35. Garrett, *Atlanta and Environs,* p. 379.

36. Franklin M. Garrett, "1838 Buckhead - When Buckhead Took Its Name 150 Years Ago, It Was Nothing More Than A Crossroads Leading To Fort Peachtree, Roswell and Decatur," *Inside Buckhead, Special 150th Anniversary Collector's Edition*, Summer, 1988, p. 8.

37. Erquitt interview.

Chapter 12

1. Virlyn Moore Jr. interview.

2. Ibid.

3. Barrett Howell interview.

4. Moore interview.

5. Barrett Howell interview.

6. Ibid.

7. Henry Howell interview.

8. Margaret Cheshire (Mrs. Hilton) Dickerson interview.

9. Dickerson interview. Leita Thompson, "House Where Time Stands Still," *The Atlanta Journal*, July 24, 1932, p. 10.

10. Dickerson interview.

11. Ibid.

12. Ibid.

13. Frank Daniel, "Historic Home Site Facing Sale Here," *The Atlanta*

Journal, March 22, 1961, page unknown.

. Thompson, "House Where Time Stands Still," p. 10.

. Dickerson interview.

. Thompson, "House Where Time Stands Still," p. 10.

. Dickerson interview.

. Frances Gibson Satterfield, "Chief Mathieson Recalls Buckhead Memories of 1900," *The North Side News,* p. 2, date unknown. Atlanta History Center Library/Archives, Buckhead subject file.

. Betty Hodges, "Irby's Tavern, Hunter's Pride, Genesis of 'Buck's Head,'" *Buckhead Atlanta*, August 23-September 6, 1976, Vol. I., No. 5, p. 5. Buckhead Library/Archives, Buckhead subject file.

. Satterfield, "Chief Mathieson Recalls," p. 2.

. The "Gold in Fulton County," *Daily New Era,* December 15, 1866. Franklin M. Garrett, *Atlanta and Environs,* Volume I; University of Georgia Press, Athens, 1954; p. 728.

. Garrett, *Atlanta and Environs*, p. 728. Luther Randall Jr. interview.

. Sara Hammett (Mrs. Binion) Jordan interview.

. Ibid.

. Ibid.

. Anne Irby (Mrs. J. M., Jr.) Comer interview.

. Jordan interview.

. Ibid.

. Agnes Fahy, "State's Third Oldest Church at Buckhead," account of Mrs. Poss, p. 1.

. Ibid, p. 2.

. Garrett, *Atlanta and Environs,* pp. 775, 777.

. Moore interview.

Chapter 13

. Margaret Cheshire (Mrs. Hilton) Dickerson interview.

. Ibid.

. Ibid

. Ibid.

. Elizabeth C. Few, "Interdenominational Theological Center, a Research Paper, The History of New Hope African Methodist Episcopal Church: 1869-1988," p. 3.

. Elizabeth (Mrs. Moses) Few interview.

. Sharon J. Salter, "Black church in Buckhead holding sing-along service," *The Atlanta Journal and Constitution*, Intown Extra, February 24, 1983, page unknown.

8. Few interview.

9. Barbara L. Smith, "Response: Many People Remember Old Harmony Grove Church," *Northside Neighbor*, April 26, 1978, p. 7.

10. Few interview.

11. Few, "Interdenominational," pp. 4, 5.

12. Ibid.

13. Ibid, p. 5.

14. Few interview.

15. Few, "Interdenominational," p. 5.

16. Sarah Huff, *"My 80 Years in Atlanta,"* Atlanta: Privately Printed, 1937; p. 2.

17. Mary Daniel interview.

18. Ibid.

19. Few, "Interdenominational," p. 7.

20. Franklin M. Garrett, "1838 Buckhead-When Buckhead Took Its Name 150 Years Ago, It Was Nothing More Than A Crossroads Leading To Fort Peachtree, Roswell And Decatur," *Inside Buckhead*, Summer, 1988, p. 8.

21. J. R. Roseberry, "143 Years On Same Site, Sardis Methodist State's 3rd oldest," newspaper, date and page unknown. Atlanta History Center Library/Archives, Sardis Methodist Church subject file.

22. Agnes Fahy, "State's Third Oldest Church at Buckhead," *The Atlanta Journal*, April 23, 1926, p. 11.

23. Franklin M. Garrett, *Atlanta and Environs*; Volume I, University of Georgia Press, Athens, 1954; p. 791.

24. Henry Howell and Barrett Howell interview.

25. Virlyn Moore Jr. interview.

26. Frances Gibson Satterfield, *A Church Surrounded, Paces Ferry Methodist Church,* October, 1965, p. 2.

27. "Paces Ferry Methodist Church, age 93, invites all to its homecoming," *The North Side News*, September 10, 1970. Franklin M. Garrett interview.

28. Franklin M. Garrett, *Garrett Cemetery Records, Volume I*; Pleasant Hill Methodist Churchyard, recorded by Franklin M. Garrett, 1931; p.208. Atlanta History Center Library/Archives. Garrett interview.

29. Ibid.

30. Garrett, *Atlanta and Environs*, p. 160.

31. Sara Hammett (Mrs. Binion) Jordan interview.

32. Ibid.

33. "Irby's great-grandaughter wonders if he really buried gold in Buckhead," *The North Side News*, July 11, 1968.

34. Jordan interview.

35. Ibid.

36. *The Family History Book, A Genealogical Record*, compiled by Robert Alvin Walker, page on Martin DeFoor. Atlanta History Center Library/Archives, Genealogy subject file. Virlyn Moore Jr. interview.

Chapter 14

1. "High Lights In History of Fulton County School System"; Reprint, Newsletter, *Fulton County Economic Clubs*, May, 1933. Fact sheet on the Fulton County School System, Fulton County Schools Teaching Museum North. Walter G. Cooper, *Official History of Fulton County*, The History Commission, Ivan AllenChairman, 1934; p. 459.

2. Ibid. April 3, 1888, Fulton County Board of Education Minute Book, p. 326, A-18; Fulton County Board of Education minutes, April 7, 1886, Minute Book, p. A-13.

3. Ibid. June 17, 1886, Minute Book, A-16, p. 305.

4. Frances Gibson Satterfield, "Buckhead - And How It Was Born," *The North Side News*, date and page unknown; Atlanta History Center Library/Archives, Buckhead subject file. Annye Mae Cobb interview.

5. Frances Gibson Satterfield, *"A Church Surrounded, Paces Ferry Methodist Church,"* October, 1965, p. 6.

6. Cobb interview.

7. Matt Perkins, "The Buckhead Story," *The North Side News*, July 26, 1973, p. 10.

8. Satterfield, *"A Church Surrounded,"* p. 8.

9. Ibid, p. 12.

10. Margaret Chapman (Mrs. Leon) Townsend interview.

11. Ibid.

12. Hugh Parks, "Hard-Working Spinster, "Around Town, *The Atlanta Journal*, date and page unknown.

13. Marcell Cobb (Mrs. Lon) Simpson interview.

14. Parks, "Hard-Working Spinster." Townsend interview.

15. Edith Adams (Mrs. George) Minhinnett interview.

Chapter 15

1. John A. Burrison, *Brothers in Clay: The Story of Georgia Folk Pottery*; University of Georgia Press, 1983; p. 191.

2. Weyman Brown interview.

3. John Burrison, *Brothers in Clay*, p. 195.

4. Ruth Cox Adams interview. Franklin M. Garrett, *Atlanta and Environs* Volume I; University of Georgia Press, 1954; p. 118.

5. Adams interview.

6. Ibid.

7. Ibid.

8. Donald W. "Pete" Rolader interview.

9. William R. Bowen and Linda F. Carnes, "Historical and Archaeological Investigations of an Atlanta Folk Pottery: The Rolader Site," *The Atlanta Historical Journal*, Volume XXVIII, Number 4, Winter 1984-85, pp. 19-37.

10. Rolader interview.

11. Ibid.

12. William T. Dreger III interview.

13. Ibid.

14. Ibid.

15. Atlanta Museum brochure, pp. 2-3; The Atlanta History Center Library/Archives, Rufus M. Rose House subject file.

16. Catherine Fox, "Folklorist John Burrison Serves Up A Tradition, Pot Luck"; *The Atlanta Constitution*, date unknown, p. 6-B.

Chapter 16

1. Franklin M. Garrett, *Atlanta and Environs*, Volume II; University of Georgia Press, Athens, 1954, p. 220.

2. Ibid, p. 241.

3. Ibid, pp. 260-61.

4. Ibid, p. 262.

5. Virlyn Moore Jr. interview.

6. Ellen Newell (Mrs. William Wright) Bryan interview.

7. Maybelle Rolader Pirkert, "Center Congregational Church, Atlanta, Georgia, An Historical Sketch."

8. Ibid.

9. Maybelle "Snookie" Tatum (Mrs. Daniel) Osburn interview.

10. Fulton County Board of Education minutes, November, 1899, Minute Book, p. A-7. Fulton County Schools Teaching Museum North.

11. "The History Of The Piney Grove Missionary Baptist Church," p. 1.

12. Warranty Title Deed, State of Georgia, Fulton County, Book 139, p. 152.

13. Actor Cordell, "Local cemetery may be put on National Register," *The Atlanta Journal and Constitution*, Intown EXTRA, August 2, 1990, p. 4.

14. John W. Pattillo, "Peachtree Park A Brief History," 1985; The

Atlanta History Center Library/Archives, Peachtree Park subject file.

Chapter 17

1. Franklin M. Garrett, "1838 Buckhead - When Buckhead Took Its Name 150 Years Ago, It Was Nothing More Than a Crossroads Leading to Fort Peachtree, Roswell and Decatur," *Inside Buckhead,* Special 150th Anniversary Collector's Edition, Summer, 1988, p. 8.

2. *The Atlanta Journal and Constitution,* March 14, 1967, title and page unknown; Atlanta History Center Library/Archives, Buckhead subject file.

3. Frances Gibson Satterfield, "Buckhead - And How It Was Born, The Mystery of a Community Pivot, Told by Old Residents"; date and page unknown; Atlanta History Center Library/Archives, Buckhead subject file.

4. Ibid.

5. Ibid.

6. Ibid.

7. Sara Hammett (Mrs. Binion) Jordan interview.

8. Ibid.

9. Ibid.

10. Ibid.

11. Agnes Dorsey Roberts interview.

12. Annye Mae Cobb interview.

13. Ruby Chapman interview.

14. Lois Coogle, "The Power Family" (as told by Ruby Power Chapman), *Sandy Springs Past Tense,* 1971; Decor Master Co., Atlanta, p. 53.

15. Chapman interview.

16. Edith Adams (Mrs. George) Minhinnett interview.

17. Linton Broom, "News of Northside: Tavern Name Stuck Buckhead Section Developing Fast," *The North Side Neighbor,* date and page unknown.

18. Matt G. Perkins, "The Buckhead Story," *The North Side News,* September 13, 1973, page unknown.

19. Ibid.

20. Minhinnett interview.

Chapter 18

1. *The Book of Georgia, A Work for Press References*; edited by Clark Howell, Georgia Biographical Association, 1920; Atlanta, p. 2. Jack J. Spalding interview.

3. Ibid.

4. Franklin M. Garrett, *Atlanta and Environs*, Volume II; The University of Georgia Press, Athens, 1954, p. 525.

5. Spalding interview.

6. Ibid.

7. Franklin M. Garrett, "1838 Buckhead-When Buckhead Took Its Name 150 Years Ago, It Was Nothing More Than a Crossroads Leading to Fort Peachtree, Roswell and Decatur," *Inside Buckhead,* Summer, 1988, p. 8. Kenneth Coleman and Charles   Stephen Gurr, *Dictionary of Georgia Biography*, Volume Two; The University of Georgia Press, Athens, 1984; pp. 676-7.

8. Laura Maddox (Mrs. Edward D.) Smith interview.

9. Garrett, *Atlanta and Environs*, p. 460.

10. Smith interview.

11. Linton Broom, "News of Northside: Tavern Name Stuck Buckhead Section Developing Fast," *The North Side Neighbor*, date and page unknown; Atlanta History Center Library/Archives, Buckhead subject file.

12. William Rudolph interview.

13. Ibid.

14. John W. Grant III's genealogy chart.

15. John W. Grant III interview.

16. Garrett, *Atlanta and Environs*, pp. 275-277.

17. Betty Slaton (Mrs. John) Wallace interview.

18. Rudolph interview.

19. Wallace interview. Rudolph interview.

20. William Dreger III interview.

21. Lil (Mrs. Thomas) Salter interview.

22. Garrett, *Atlanta and Environs*, p. 563.

23. Ibid.

24. *The Book of Georgia, A Work*, p. 140. Richard Funderburk, "Cathedral Plans New Life for Landmark," *The Brookhaven Buzz*, January 1995, Volume 5, No. 1, p. 16.

25. Ibid.

26. Ibid.

27. "A Brief History of Peachtree Presbyterian Church," September 2, 1991; Peachtree Presbyterian Church Archives.

Chapter 19

1. Susan Jones Medlock, "This Home Was A Once Schoolhouse," *The Atlanta Journal and Constitution Magazine*, November 8, 1953, p . 2 9 . Fulton County, Georgia 1911 map, Atlanta History Center Library/Archives,

Kauffman Maps.

2. Stanley P. Meyerson interview.

3. "The Chatter Box"; Atlanta, GA., May 26, 1932, Volume V., No. 2. Atlanta History Center Library/Archives, Public Schools subject file.

4. Joseph K. Heyman interview.

5. "R. L. Hope School…What Is its Future? Hope Landmark Stands As Tribute To Its Namesake," *The North Side News*, November 15, 1973, p. 3.

6. Rhunette H. Morse and Marshall Turner, "Buckhead-New Hope School Fourth Reunion, Friends Forever," August 21, 1993. Courtesy of Elizabeth Few.

7. Mary Daniel interview.

8. Helen Few interview.

9. Ibid.

Chapter 20

1. *A Community History of the Johnsontown Neighborhood*; Prepared for Division of Planning and Marketing Department of Planning and Public Affairs, Metropolitan Atlanta Rapid Transit Authority by The History Group, Inc., May 1981, p. 17, Atlanta History Center Library/Archives, Johnsontown subject file.

2. Ibid, p. 19.

3. Ibid.

4. Columbus Johnson interview.

5. *A Community History of the Johnsontown*, p. 20.

6. Columbus Johnson interview.

7. *A Community History of the Johnsontown*, p. 8.

8. Columbus Johnson interview.

9. Ibid, p. 25.

10. Parthenia Jetter interview.

11. Ibid.

12. Janie Johnson interview.

13. Lenard Walker Jr. interview.

14. Jetter interview.

15. John K. Ottley III interview.

16. Janie Johnson interview.

Chapter 21

1. Author unknown, "Buckhead Will Not Be Bought for "Model Town,"

The Atlanta Journal, April 7, 1911, p. 1.

2. Guy Patterson interview.

3. *A History of the Second-Ponce de Leon Baptist Church Atlanta, Georgia, Centennial Year 1854-1954*; Darby Printing Company, 1954; p. 36.

4. Ibid, p. 37.

5. S. E. Dellinger, "Lengthening Shadows of the Second Baptist Church Atlanta, Georgia," S. E. Dellinger, Director Library Services, 1978; p. 91.

6. "Sixty Peachtree Hills Avenue," *Peachtree Hills Views*, May, 1989. Alan Patureau, "Peachtree Hills, Taking a Close Look at an Easy-to-overlook Community," *The Atlanta Journal and Constitution,* Sunday Homefinders, November 11, 1990, p. 7.

7. Franklin M. Garrett, *Atlanta and Environs*, Volume II; University of Georgia Press, Athens, 1954; pp. 575, 460.

8. Garrett, *Atlanta and Environs*, p. 575. Author unknown, "Buckhead Will Not Be Bought."

9. Laura Maddox (Mrs. Edward D. Addison) Smith interview.

10. Ibid.

11. Martha Tate, "Governors' Mansion grounds owe a debt to former owners," *The Atlanta Journal and Constutition*, May 27, 1990, p. R1.

12. Smith interview.

13. Ibid.

14. Kenneth H. Thomas Jr. (prepared by), "Georgia Department of Natural Resources *Announcement of Listing in the National Register of Historic Places*, August 3, 1988"; The Atlanta History Center Library/Archives, Villa Lamar House subject file.

15. Reuben A. Garland Jr. interview.

16. Franklin M. Garrett interview. Thomas Jr., *"Announcement of Listing."*

17. Garland interview.

18. S. Russell Bridges Jr., Excerpts from "The History of Pace Academy," p. 3, from an address made to Pace High School students on April 2, 1974. Atlanta History Center Library/Archives, Pace Academy subject file.

19. Julie Greer, "Neel Reid—490 West Paces Ferry," *Buckhead-Atlanta*, August 1977, p. 9. Atlanta History Center Library/Archives, Reuben Arnold subject file.

20. Compiled by Florence Bryan (Mrs. Bonneau) Ansley, *The Block*, p. 14.

21. Ibid, p. 15.

22. *Ibid*, p. 18.

23. John K. Ottley III interview.

24. Joseph K. Heyman interview.

25. Ottley interview.

26. Ibid.

27. Ibid.

28. Heyman interview.

29. Ibid.

30. Ibid.

31. Frances Gibson Satterfield, "Chief Mathieson Recalls Buckhead Memories of 1900," *The North Side News*, p. 2, no date. The Atlanta History Center Library/Archives, Buckhead subject file.

32. Sara Hammett (Mrs. Binion) Jordan interview.

33. Sam Dorsey interview.

34. Ibid.

35. Henry Howell interview.

Chapter 22

1. Ron Martz, "Leo Frank pardon may heal 70-year wound," *The Atlanta Constitution*, April 26, 1983, p. 1-B.

2. Franklin M. Garrett, *Atlanta and Environs*, Volume II; University of Georgia Press, Athens, 1954, p. 621.

3. Ibid, p. 623.

4. Ibid, p. 624.

5. Ibid, p. 626.

6. Martz, "Leo Frank pardon," p. 1-B.

7. Garrett, *Atlanta and Environs*, p. 628.

8. Priscilla Painton, "Alonzo Mann dies, urged Leo Frank pardon," *The Atlanta Constitution*, March 19, 1985. Allen Rabinowitz, "Alonzo Mann dies, Witness hoped to live to see Leo Frank cleared," *The Southern Israelite*, March 22, 1985, p. 1.

9. Gary Pomerantz, "In His Own Words, Leo Frank: Leaflets written in his cell by the man convicted of Mary Phagan's murder protested his innocence. A year later, a mob lynched him," *The Atlanta Journal and Constitution*, November 12, 1995, p.H2.

10. Ellen Newell (Mrs. William Wright) Bryan interview.

11. Cecil Alexander interview.

12. Ibid.

13. Betty Slaton (Mrs. John) Wallace interview.

14. Joseph K. Heyman interview.

15. Slaton interview.

16. Ibid.

17. Ibid.
18. Bryan interview.
19. William Rudolph interview.
20. Ibid.
21. Martz, p. 1-B.

Other sources:

1. Vida Goldgar, "Historic day in Georgia Paroles board grants pardon to Leo Frank," *The Southern Israelite*, March 14, 1986, p. 1.

2. Charles and Louise Samuels, *Night Fell on Georgia*; Dell Publishing Company, Inc., New York, 1956.

Chapter 23

1. T. Sinclair (Tory) Jacobs interview.
2. Ibid.
3. Franklin M. Garrett, *Atlanta and Environs*, Volume II; University of Georgia Press, Athens, 1954; p. 75.
4. Ibid, pp. 121-22.
5. Jacobs interview.
6. Ibid.
7. Margaret Cheshire (Mrs. Hilton) Dickerson interview.
8. Garrett, *Atlanta and Environs*, p. 75.
9. Jacobs interview.
10. Piromis H. Bell, "Joseph Jacobs," *Galen Pharmaceutical Society, The Galenite Yearbook, 1930*, no page number. Atlanta History Center Library/Archives, Dr. Joseph Jacobs personality file.
11. Jacobs interview.
12. Mary Brennan, "In Celebration of a Great School For a Great neighborhood: E. Rivers Elementary School," *Peachtree Hills Views*, August 1990, p. 5.
13. Yolanda Gwin, "Craigellachie, Once Private Home Is Now Private Club," *The Atlanta Journal and Constitution*, May 20, 1973, p. 5-G. Atlanta History Center Library-Archives, John W. Grant Home subject file.
14. William Rudolph interview.
15. Gwin, "Craigellachie". Rudolph interview.
16. Rudolph interview.
17. Ibid.
18. Ibid.
19. Ibid.
20. Grant interview.

21. Rudolph interview.

22. Dr. F. Phinizy Calhoun Jr. interview.

23. Yolanda Gwin, *Atlanta Journal* Society Editor, "Exceptional Facilities for Insuring Your Antiques and Other Fine Art Objects, 'Rossdhu' 2906 Andrews Drive, N.W. House History," The Tom McLain Agency, p. 1; Atlanta History Center Library/Archives, Dr. Phinizy Calhoun subject file.

24. Calhoun interview.

25. Ibid.

26. Ibid.

27. Ibid.

28. Ibid.

29. Ruth Cox Adams interview.

30. Ibid.

31. Franklin M. Garrett interview.

32. Joseph K. Heyman interview.

33. Ibid.

34. Laura Maddox (Mrs. Edward D.) Smith interview.

35. Lillie Pace (Mrs. Paul) Scoville interview.

36. Ibid.

37. Ibid.

38. Ibid.

39. Yolande Gwin, "Handsome Estate to Open April 20," *The Atlanta Journal and Constitution*, March 17, 1974, page number unknown; Atlanta History Center Library/Archives, Dillard-Manley-Hopkins subject file.

40. Author unknown, "Old Harmony Grove Church Cemetery Last of Old Buckhead's Land Marks Standing in Area's Finest Section," date and newspaper unknown; Atlanta History Center Library/Archives, Harmony Grove Church subject file.

41. Elizabeth DuBose (Mrs. Vernon) Skiles interview.

42. "Beverly DuBose, Historian, Dies, Prominent Insurance Official Also Noted As Collector of Items on Confederacy," *The Atlanta Journal*, Obituary, April 1, 1953; Atlanta History Center Library/Archives, Beverly Means DuBose Sr. personality file.

Chapter 24

1. Franklin M. Garrett, *Atlanta and Environs*, Volume II; The University of Georgia Press, Athens, 1954; p. 669.

2. Jack Fairey and Samuel Taylor, "The Fallacy of the Atlanta Origin of the K. K. K.," *Quizzical Quest of Atlanta*; 1945, p. 65; Atlanta History

Center Library/Archives, Ku Klux Klan subject file.

3. Ibid.

4. Ibid, p. 66.

5. Ibid.

6. Ibid.

7. "Historical Review," *Peachtree Hills Views*, September 1989, Volume 2, No. 5, p. 3.

8. Fairly and Taylor, p. 67.

9. "Historical Review," p. 3.

10. "Buckhead Building With Dubious History," *The Brookhaven Buzz*, Volume 3, No. 5, May 1993, p. 1. Historic Preservation, IS Cotton Exchange/Fulton County file.

11. Ibid, p. 7.

12. "Historical Review, p. 3.

13. "Forrest Announces Plans for University of America; Big Non-Sectional Institution to be Ready by Fall, Proposed Klan College To Occupy Historic Spot," *The Atlanta Constitution*, February 5, 1922, p. 7.

14. *The Cathedral of Christ the King, the First Fifty Years*; Published by the Cathedral of Christ the King, no date, p. 21.

15. "Forrest Announces Plans for University of America," p. 7.

16. Garrett, *Atlanta and Environs*, p. 670.

17. Ken Moss interview.

18. Ibid.

19. Guy Patterson interview.

20. Ellie Patterson interview.

21. Guy Patterson interview.

22. Ibid.

23. Leon Townsend interview.

24. Ruth Cox Adams interview.

25. Jack J. Spalding interview.

26. Ibid.

27. Ibid.

28. Dr. F. Phinizy Calhoun Jr. interview.

29. J. T. Tolbert interview.

30. Laura Maddox (Mrs. Edward Addison) Smith interview.

31. Florence Bryan (Mrs. William Bonneau) Ansley interview.

32. Betty Slaton (Mrs. John) Wallace interview.

33. John K. Ottley III interview.

34. Barrett Howell interview.

35. Henry Howell interview.

36. Columbus Johnson interview.

37. Parthenia Jetter interview.

38. Janie Johnson interview.

39. T. Sinclair (Tory) Jacobs interview.

40. William Brand Jr. interview.

41. Marcus Cook III interview.

42. William T. Dreger III interview.

Chapter 25

1. Mrs. Hilton Stanaland interview.

2. Margaret Chapman (Mrs. Leon) Townsend interview.

3. Sunny David, "Mooney's Lake," *Garden Hills Views*, July/August 1993, p. 3.

4. William T. Dreger III interview.

5. David, "Mooney's Lake," p. 3.

6. Helen McDuffie interview. Obituary of Fred Loring Seely, *The Atlanta Journal and Constitution*, March 15, 1942, p. 5B.

7. McDuffie interview.

8. Ibid.

9. George Hightower interview. Harold D. Hirsch, "The Hightower House—2652," compiled by Florence Bryan (Mrs. Bonneau) Ansley, *The Block*, 1982, p. 18.

10. George Hightower interview.

11. Ansley, *The Block*, pp. 5, 14.

12. Jack J. Spalding interview.

13. Ibid.

14. James Grady, *Architecture of Neel Reid in Georgia*; University of Georgia, Athens, 1973; p. 112.

15. Ibid, p. 123.

16. Kathy Trocheck, "Doors open to Villa Juanita," *The Atlanta Journal and Constitution*, May 11, 1986, p. L2.

17. Ibid.

18. Deborah Royston, "Legendary landmark estate for sale in Tuxedo Park," *The Atlanta Journal and Constitution*, August 25, 1991.

19. Franklin M. Garrett, *Atlanta and Environs*, Volume II; University of Georgia Press, Athens, 1954; p. 563.

20. *1921 Atlanta City Directory*.

21. John W. Pattillo, "Peachtree Park: A Brief History," 1985; Atlanta History Center Library/Archives, Peachtree Park subject file.

22. Bill Bell, "Buckhead Baseball and Macedonia Park," *Peachtree Hills Views*; January/February 1993, p. 3.

23. Ibid.

24. Ibid.

25. Thomas M. Murray interview.

26. Ibid.

27. Barrett Howell interview.

28. Charlene W. Shucker, "Buckhead: Merchants say future is bright," *The Atlanta Journal and Constitution*, Intown Extra, July 1982, p. 4E. Edith Adams (Mrs. George, Jr.) Minhinnett interview.

29. Thomas M. Murray interview.

30. Ibid.

31. Ibid.

32. Ibid.

33. Jane (Mrs. George, Jr.) Murray interview.

34. Thomas M. Murray interview.

35. McDuffie interview.

36. J. T. Tolbert interview.

37. Spalding interview.

38. Laura Maddox (Mrs. Edward D.) Smith interview.

39. Wilbur Kurtz Notebook Number 10, p. 288; Atlanta History Center Library/Archives, Manuscript Collection Number 130.

Chapter 26

1. Ann Cobb interview.

2. Sue Webb Stephens interview.

3. Ibid.

4. Edith Adams (Mrs. George) Minhinnett interview.

5. Ibid.

6. Cobb interview.

Chapter 27

1. Kennneth H. Thomas Jr., "United States Department of the Interior National Park Service, National Register of Historic Places," June 25, 1976, p. 2. Atlanta History Center Library/Archives, Garden Hills subject file.

2. "Your Dreams of Home Will Come True in Beautiful Garden Hills Atlanta's Development Suberb!", Garden Hills brochure put out by P. C. McDuffie Co, 63 N. Broad St. Atlanta History Center Library/Archives, Garden Hills subject file.

3. Letter to Robert W. Barnwell, Atlanta, Georgia, from Will D. Muse, Secretary and Treasurer of The Piedmont Company, 14-18 West

Peachtree Street, August 25, 1925; Atlanta History Center Library/Archives, Garden Hills subject file.

4. Ibid. p. 1.

5. Thomas, "United States Department of the Interior."

6. Florence "Poncie" Bryan (Mrs. William Bonneau) Ansley interview.

7. Ibid.

8. Ibid.

9. Ibid.

10. Ibid.

11. Mildred Rand (Mrs. Alva) Lines interview. Susannah Wilson, "Show House, Leighton, Spills, Thrills and Lots of Living In a Warm Family Setting," *"Decorators' Show House,"* Junior Committee of the Atlanta Symphony Associates, Volume XXIV, April 9-May 1, 1994; Wiesner Publishing, 1994; pp. DS-15, 16.

12. Mildred Rand (Mrs. Alva) Lines interview.

13. Nick Jones, "A Time of Uncertainty, Nick Jones examines the Atlanta Symphony's troubled early years, from 1946 to 1952"; Atlanta Symphony Orchestra archives.

14. Alva Lines interview.

15. Sam Dorsey interview.

16. Julie Greer, "Neel Reid, 541 West Paces Ferry Road, N.W.," *Buckhead Atlanta*, late March 1977, p. 9. "1979 Decorators' Show House," *Score: Women's Association Atlanta Symphony Orchestra*, April 1979, p. 1. Both found at the Atlanta History Center Library/Archives, Rhodes House subject file.

17. "Gracious Living in the Heart of Buckhead," *The Decorators' Show House*, May 1-May 23, 1993, Volume XXIII; Junior League Committee of the Atlanta Syphony Orchestra Associates, p. 7.

18. Dorothy Dean (Mrs. Joel Chandler, Jr.) Harris interview.

19. Louise Richardson (Mrs. Ivan, Jr.) Allen interview. Clark Howell, Editor-in-Chief, *The Book of Georgia, A Work for Press Reference*; Georgia Biographical Association, Atlanta, 1920. Molly Sinclair, "The City's First Lady, Mrs. Ivan Allen shuns the limelight, but leads busy civic life," *The Atlanta Journal and Constitution Magazine*, October 19, 1969, p. 20. The Atlanta History Center Library/Archives, Ivan Allen Jr. personality file. George Erwin, "Pioneer Family Richardsons Put Faith in Home Land," *Atlanta Journal and Constitution* September 16, 1962, page unknown; Atlanta History Center Library/Archives, Hugh Inman Richardson personality file.

20. Franklin M. Garrett, *Atlanta and Environs*, Volume I; University of Georgia Press, Athens, 1954, p. 807, II, p. 343.

21. Louise Richardson (Mrs. Ivan, Jr.) Allen interview.

22. Ibid.

23. Franklin M. Garrett interview.

24. Ivan E. Allen Jr. interview.

25. Biographical Questionnaire; "Ivan Allen Sr. Dies; 70 Years a Leader," *The Atlanta Constitution*, October 17, 1968, p. 1, 14. Atlanta History Center Library/Archives, Ivan Allen Sr. personality file.

26. Katherine Barnwell, "The Ivan Allen Jr. Story Close Look At Atlanta's Next Mayor," *The Atlanta Journal and Constitution Magazine*, December 31, 1961, p. 13.

27. Bo Emerson, "Louise Allen, Wife of one of Atlanta's most illustrious mayors is a quietly effective force in the city of her birth," *The Atlanta Journal and Constitution*, April 18, 1993, p. M1.

28. Biographical material, Atlanta History Center Library/Archives, Louise R. Allen personality file.

29. Judy Beers (Mrs. Rufus M.) Darby interview.

30. "The Main Event," *The Atlanta Journal and Constitution*, Leisure, January 23, 1993, p. 7.

31. Louise Richardson (Mrs. Ivan Jr.) Allen interview.

32. Ken Willis and Bob Rohrer, "Lowe pays $319,000 for Candler Estate," *The Atlanta Constitution*, July 25, 1975, page unknown; Atlanta History Center Library/Archives, Candler-Low Home subject file.

Chapter 28

1. "Placque Honors Thompsons, Pioneer Buckhead Bankers," *The North Side News*, October 4, 1973, p. 13. Thomas M. Murray interview.

2. Virlyn Moore Jr. interview.

3. Nancy Kamper (Mrs. Henry J.) Miller interview.

4. *"Recipes from a Parish on Peachtree"*; Published by The Women of St. Luke's Episcioal Church, 435 Peachtree Street, N.E., Atlanta, 1974; Williams Printing Company, Atlanta, p. 62. 5. Miller interview. *"Who's Who In America, Fifth Anniversary 1898-1948,"* Vol. 25; The A. N. Marquis Company, Chicago, 1948; p. 1306.

6. Miller interview.

7. Ibid. "F. E. Kamper Dies; Retired OPS Official," *The Atlanta Constitution*, July 15, 1960, Obituary page.

8. Ellie Patterson interview.

9. Dr. Judson L. Hawk Jr. interview.

10. Ibid.

11. William M. Wender Jr. interview.

12. Ibid.

13. Ibid.

14. Ibid.

15. Ibid.

16. Dorothy Dean (Mrs. Joel Chandler, Jr.) Harris interview.

17. Laura Maddox (Mrs. Edward Addison) Smith interview.

18. Louise "Weezie" (Mrs. John W., III) Grant interview.

19. Cecil Alexander interview.

20. Mary Tesler (Mrs. Ike) Kadis interview.

21. Ibid. Rose (Mrs. Herman) Mechlowitz interview.

22. Donald W. "Pete" Rolader interview.

23. Donald Rooney interview.

24. Rolader interview.

25. Ken Moss interview.

26. Rolader interview. Maybelle Tatum Osborne interview.

27. Rolader interview.

28. Lois Coogle, *Tassels of Remembrance, Peachtree Road United Methodist Church, 1953-1989*; Peachtree Road United Methodist Church, 1989, p. 3.

29. Ibid.

30. Ibid.

31. "A Brief History of Peachtree Presbyterian Church", September 2, 1991; "Peachtree Road Presbyterian Church," *Christian Observer*, Peachtree Presbyterian Church archives.

32. "Highlights of Covenant History," a fact sheet. David Turner, "Covenant Presbyterian Church," Atlanta History Center Library/Archives, Covenant Presbyterian Church subject file.

33. Lisa Golem, "Sardis Church: 'I think theologically it says something about a people, that a church has been able to last this length of time in one place," newspaper, page and date unknown; Sardis Methodist Church archives.

34. Guy Patterson interview.

35. Franklin M. Garrett, *Atlanta and Environs*, Volume II; University of Georgia Press, Athens, 1954, p. 833.

36. "Haynes Manor, Out Where The Hills Begin," date and page unknown; Atlanta History Center Library/Archives, Haynes Manor subject file.

Chapter 29

1. Joseph K. Heyman interview.

2. George Hightower interview.

3. Virlyn Moore Jr. interview.

4. Ibid.

5. New Hope Church history written by Rhunette H. Morse and Marshall Turner, given to me by Elizabeth Few.

6. Helen McDuffie interview.

7. Ivan Allen Jr. interview.

8. Louise Richardson (Mrs. Ivan, Jr.) Allen interview.

9. McDuffie interview.

10. Hightower interview.

11. Thomas M. Murray interview.

12. Ellie Patterson interview.

13. Roy Milling interview.

14. Ibid.

15. Laura Maddox (Mrs. Edward D.) Smith interview.

16. Ibid.

17. Ibid.

18. Hightower interview.

19. Ivan Allen Jr. interview.

20. Hightower interview. Bob McCollough, "Sample of Interesting Events, While We Were Living In 'Peachtree Block,'" a personal account. Courtesy of Robert Hightower.

21. Hightower interview.

22. Jack J. Spalding interview.

23. J. T. Tolbert interview.

24. Miss Harriet (Hattie) Grant interview.

25. Milling interview.

26. McDuffie, Milling and Murray interviews.

27. Spalding interview.

28. Dr. F. Phinizy Calhoun Jr. interview.

29. Mary Ann (Mrs. Lon, Jr.) Bridges interview.

30. Spalding interview.

Chapter 30

1. "Student Confesses in Two Atlanta Killings," *The Atlanta Journal,* October 28, 1928, p. 1.

2. Ibid, p. 10.

3. Franklin M. Garrett, *Atlanta and Environs*, Volume II; University of Georgia Press, Athens, 1954; pp. 844-845.

4. Ibid, p. 845.

5. Jack J. Spalding interview.

6. Lillie Pace (Mrs. Paul) Scoville interview.

7. Ivan Allen Jr. interview.
8. Ibid.

Chapter 31

1. Polly Orr Bates interview. Franklin M. Garrett, *Atlanta and Environs*, Volume II; University of Georgia Press, Athens, 1954; pp. 854-55.
2. Ibid.
3. Ibid.
4. Henry Howell interview.
5. Bates interview.
6. John W. Grant III interview.
7. Bates interview.
8. Barrett Howell interview.
9. Bates interview.

Chapter 32

1. Franklin M. Garrett, *Atlanta and Environs*, Volume II; University of Georgia Press, Athens, 1954; p. 897.
2. Hugh Park, *Around Town*, "Buckhead's Seen Tough Days," *The Atlanta Journal*, March 14, 1967.
3. Ibid.
4. Garrett, *Atlanta and Environs*, p. 896.
5. Donald W. "Pete" Rolader interview.
6. Ken Moss interview.
7. Guy Patterson interview.
8. Ruth Cox Adams interview.
9. Sam Dorsey interview.
10. Ellie Patterson interview.
11. Jack J. Spalding interview.
12. Bruce F. Woodruff Jr. interview.
13. Sue Webb Stephens interview.
14. Dr. F. Phinizy Calhoun Jr. interview.
15. Thomas M. Murray interview.
16. Jane (Mrs. George, Jr.) Murray interview.
17. Roy Milling interview.
18. Barrett Howell interview.
19. Milling interview.
20. Ibid.
21. Marcus Cook III interview.

22. Lillie Pace (Mrs. Paul) Scoville interview.
23. Ibid.
24. Jane (Mrs. George, Jr.) Murray interview.

Chapter 33

1. Franklin M. Garrett, *Atlanta and Environs*, Volume II; University of Georgia Press, Athens, 1954; p. 866.
2. Guy Patterson interview.
3. Bruce F. Woodruff Jr. interview. Garrett Cemetery Records, Microfilm Number 14, Frame number 524; Atlanta History Center Library/Archives.
4. Woodruff interview.
5. Ibid.
6. Ibid.
7. Ellen Newell (Mrs. William Wright) Bryan interview.
8. Barrett Howell interview.
9. Henry Howell interview.
10. Mark Harclerode II, "Roxy Theater Nomination History Preservation and Conservation," December 3, 1991. IS/Roxy Theater/Fulton County, Historic Preservation.
11. John K. Ottley III interview.
12. Milton Few interview.
13. William Brand Jr. interview.
14. T. Sinclair "Tory" Jacobs interview.
15. Betty Slaton (Mrs. John) Wallace interview.
16. Ken Moss interview.
17. Ibid.
18. Ibid.
19. Ibid.
20. Ibid.
21. Susan K. Barnard, "Hail & Farewell North Fulton High School, Part I," *Peachtree Hills Views*, March/April 1992, p. 6.
22. Rose Tesler (Mrs. Herman) Mechlowitz interview.
23. Thomas M. Murray interview.
24. Dorothy (Mrs. Joel Chandler, Jr.) Harris interview.
25. Murray interview.
26. S. E. Dellinger, Director Library Services, *Lengthening Shadows of the Second Baptist Church, Atlanta, Georgia*; S. E. Dillinger, 1970, p. 89. Church archives.
27. Sara Hammett (Mrs. Binion) Jordan interview.
28. Dellinger, *Lengthening*, p. 90

29. *A History of the Second-Ponce de Leon Baptist Church Atlanta, Georgia, Centennial Year 1854-1954*; Darby Printing Company, Atlanta, 1954; p. 5.

30. Author unknown, "As to the Cathedral of St. Philip Moving to Buckhead"; information sheet, courtesy of Richard P. Perry.

31. Mrs. Allan V. Gray, "Brief Summary of the History of Old St. Philip and of the 'Move'"; Atlanta History Center Library/ Archives, The Cathedral of St. Philip subject file.

32. Author unknown, "As to the Cathedral of St. Philip."

33. Ibid. Richard Funderburke, "Cathedral Plans New Life for Land-mark," *The Brookhaven Buzz*, January 1995, p. 16.

34. "As to the Cathedral of St. Philip."

35. Elizabeth Cassells (Mrs. Richard) Rubenoff and Janet Knox (Mrs. Thomas) Moore interview.

36. Jacobs interview.

37. Ibid.

38. Moore interview.

39. William R. Mitchell Jr., "Fine Atlanta Homes Presented by Harry Norman," *The Atlanta Journal and Constitution*, October 2, 1983, p. 12-F. H. M. Cauley, "International center wants spotlight," *The Atlanta Journal and Constitution*, November 17, 1994, p. JE3.

40. William Rudolph interview.

41. Franklin M. Garrett interview.

42. "Pace Academy" fact sheet. Pace Academy library.

43. Author unknown, *A Georgian Mansion in Atlanta;* The Rooker Company, date unknown; Atlanta History Center Library/Archives, Howell home subject file.

44. Dr. Judson Hawk Jr. interview.

45. "Knollwood", *House History, The Junior Committee of the Women's Association Atlanta Symphony Orchestra, 1977 Decorators' Show House.* Yolande Gwin, "William H. Kiser Residence, Show House Is City Land-mark," *The Atlanta Journal and Constitution*, March 6, 1977, p. 10-G.

46. Garrett, *Atlanta and Environs*, p. 911. Ottley interview.

47. Ottley interview.

48. Garrett, *Atlanta and Environs*, p. 911.

49. Ibid, p. 912.

50. Ottley interview.

Chapter 34

1. The History Group, Inc., "The History Group, Inc. A Community History of the Planning and Marketing, Department of Planning and Public

Affairs Metropolitan Atlanta Rapid Transit Authority"; May 1981, p. 30; Atlanta History Center Library/Archives, Johnsontown subject file.

2. Elizabeth Campbell (Mrs. Moses) Few interview.

3. Milton Few interview.

4. Ibid.

5. Berneda Johnson Haney interview.

6. Ibid.

7. Donald W. "Pete" Rolader interview.

8. William Brand Jr. interview.

9. Jack J. Spalding interview.

10. Columbus Johnson interview.

Chapter 35

1. Guy Patterson interview.

2. Marcus Cook III interview.

3. Patterson interview.

4. Marcelle Cobb (Mrs. Lon) Simpson interview.

5. Margaret Chapman (Mrs. Leon) Townsend interview.

6. Patterson interview.

7. Leo Aikman, "Chastain Bowl Grows No Grass," *The Atlanta Constitution*, June 24, 1954, page number unknown.

8. Simpson interview.

Chapter 36

1. Author unknown, "Mrs. Grant and Mrs. Manley Direct Peachtree Rd. Beautification Project," *The Atlanta Journal*, 1936, page unknown; Peachtree Garden Club Scrapbook 1923-1947; Atlanta History Center Library/Archives.

2. Jack J. Spalding interview.

3. Betty Slaton (Mrs. John) Wallace interview.

4. Ibid.

5. Aline Cocke (Mrs. Eugene) Cofield interview.

6. Ibid.

7. Charles Wilson interview.

8. Ibid.

9. Lon Bridges Jr. interview.

10. "Salute To Philip Trammell Shutze," brochure. Atlanta History Center Library/Archives, Thornton-Jones home subject file.

11. Andrew Sparks, "You Can See These Beautiful Atlanta Homes Next

Week End," *The Atlanta Journal and Constitution*, March, 28, 1954, p. 25.

12. Marcus Cook III interview.

13. Ibid.

14. Ibid.

15. Franklin M. Garrett, *Atlanta and Environs*, Volume II; The University of Georgia Press, Athens, 1954; p. 936.

16. Cofield interview.

17. Barrett Howell interview.

18. "Atlanta House Beginning for Hearsts," *The Atlanta Journal*, July 12, 1978, p. 19-A.

19. Cecil Alexander interview.

20. Ibid.

21. Ibid.

22. "House History," *Decorators' Show House, Sponsored by The Junior Committee of the Woman's Association Atlanta Symphony Orchestra, 1971*; Atlanta History Center Library/Archives, Henry A. Alexander home subject file.

23. Alexander interview.

24. Frances Yudelson (Mrs. Harry) Kuniansky interview.

25. William T. Dreger III speech to the Kawannis Club.

26. Ellen Newell (Mrs. William Wright) Bryan interview.

27. Ibid.

28. Ibid.

29. John W. Grant III interview.

30. Ibid.

31. "Ring, Ring, Ring....Goes the trolley, Part II," *Peachtree Hills News*, April 1991, p. 4.

32. Mrs. Hilton Stanaland interview.

33. Barrett Howell interview.

34. Ken Moss interview.

35. Donald W. "Pete" Rolader interview.

36. Grant interview.

37. John K. Ottley III interview.

38. Dreger interview.

39. Ottley interview.

Chapter 37

1. Thomas M. Murray interview.

2. Bruce F. Woodruff Jr. interview.

3. Florence and Sam Inman interview.

4. Ellen Hillyer (Mrs. William Wright) Bryan interview.

5. Roy Milling interview.

6. Vernon B. Kellett, *History of The Lovett School*, May 1962, p. 4;The Lovett School.

7. Ibid, p. 3.

8. Ibid, p. 4.

9. Ibid, pp. 4-8, 9, 13.

10. Edith (Mrs. Herbert) Elsas interview.

11. Sheldon M. Bellury, "Dream Became Reality for Atlanta Speech School Founder," *Buckhead, Atlanta*, Vol. I, No. 9, October 19 - November 1, 1976, pp. 1, 4; The Atlanta History Center Library/Archives, Atlanta Speech School subject file. *Atlanta Speech School, 1938*, pp. 1, 2. "Atlanta Speech School Fact Sheet"; Atlanta Speech School.

12. Elizabeth Campbell (Mrs. Moses) Few, *"Interdenominational Theological Center, a Research Paper, The History of New Hope African Methodist Episcopal Church: 1869-1988"*; submitted to Faculty Foundations for Ministry December 6, 1988. Courtesy of Elizabeth Campbell (Mrs. Moses) Few. Elizabeth Campbell (Mrs. Moses) Few interview.

13. Milton Few and Helen Few interview.

14. "Establishing the Parish, The Cathedral of Christ the King," p.23; Atlanta History Center Library/Archives, Cathedral of Christ the King subject file.

15. Ibid.

16. Franklin M. Garrett, *Atlanta and Environs*, Volume II; University of Georgia Press, Athens, 1954; pp. 966-68.

17. William Brand Jr. interview.

18. Mrs. Lillie Pace (Mrs. Paul) Scoville interview.

19. William T. Dreger III interview.

20. Stanaland interview.

21. Donald W. "Pete" Rolader interview.

Chapter 38

1. William T. Dreger III interview.

2. Edith and Herbert Elsas interview.

3. Herbert Elsas interview.

4. Ibid.

5. Mary Ann (Mrs. Lon, Jr.) Bridges interview.

6. Thomas M. Murray interview.

7. Bridges interview.

8. Murray interview.

9. Weyman Brown interview.

Chapter 39

1. Matt G. Perkins, "The Buckhead Story," *The North Side News*, September 6, 1973, p. 1.
2. William Brand Jr. interview.
3. Ibid.
4. Ibid.
5. Donald W. "Pete" Rolader interview.
6. Barrett Howell interview.
7. Cecil Alexander interview.
8. Irwin G. Baumer interview.
9. J. T. Tolbert interview.
10. Guy Patterson interview.
11. Thomas M. Murray interview.
12. Charles Wilson interview.
13. Dorothy Dean (Mrs. Joel Chandler, Jr.) Harris interview.
14. William T. Dreger III's speech at the Kiwannis Club.
15. Janet Knox (Mrs. Thomas) Moore interview.
16. Marcus Cook III interview.
17. John K. Ottley III speech at the Kiwanis Club.
18. Alva Lines interview.
19. Dreger interview.
20 Lines interview.
21. Ellen Newell (Mrs. William Wright) Bryan interview. Franklin M. Garrett, *Atlanta and Environs, Family and Personal History*, Volume III; Lewis Historical Publishing Company, Inc., New York, 1954; p.158.
22. Louise Richardson (Mrs. Ivan, Jr.) Allen interview.
23. Judy Beer (Mrs. Rufus) Darby interview.
24. Ottley interview.
25. Moore interview.
26. Lines interview.
27. Ottley speech.
28. Emily Anderson (Mrs. George) Hightower interview.
29. Dreger interview.
30. Betty Slaton (Mrs. John) Wallace interview.
31. William Rudolph interview.
32. Harris interview.
33. Ken Moss interview.
34. Yolande Gwin, "Pace Academy Campus, Randall Home Is Saved,"

The Atlanta Journal and Constitution, December 26, 1976, p. 12-G.
  35. Luther Randall Jr. interview.
  36. Murray interview.

Chapter 40

1. Judy Beers (Mrs. Rufus M.) Darby interview.
2. Ibid.
3. Elizabeth Cassells (Mrs. Richard) Rubenoff interview.
4. Maybelle "Snookie" Tatum (Mrs. Daniel) Osburn interview.
5. Donald W. "Pete" Rolader interview.
6. Osburn interview.
7. Ibid.
8. Barrett Howell interview.
9. Henry Howell interview.
10. Louise (Mrs. John W., II) Grant interview.
11. Peggy Fox Goldberg interview.
12. Judson Hawk Jr. interview.
13. William T. Dreger III interview.
14. Rolader interview.
15. Barrett Howell interview.
16. Dreger's speech to the Kiwanis Club.
17. Rolader interview.
18. Mary Ann (Mrs. Lon, Jr.) Bridges interview.
19. Jack J. Spalding interview.
20. Osburn interview.
21. Reuben Garland Jr. interview.

Chapter 41

1. Hugh Park, "Buckhead's Seen Tough Days," *The Atlanta Journal*, March 14, 1967, page unknown.
2. T. Sinclair "Tory" Jacobs interview.
3. Emily Anderson (Mrs. George) Hightower interview.
4. John K. Ottley III interview.
5. John K. Ottley III speech to the Kawanis Club.
6. Reuben Garland Jr. interview.
7. William T. Dreger III interview.
8. Thomas M. Murray interview.
9. Bill Bell, "Buckhead Baseball and Macedonia Park," pp. 3, 10; *Peachtree Hills Views*, January/February 1993.

10. Dreger interview.

11. Murray interview.

12. Author unknown, "North Side News tells tale of story of progress"; *The North Side News*, December 7, 1967, page number unknown. Atlanta History Center Library/Archives, Buckhead subject file.

13. Ibid.

14. Henry Howell interview.

15. Barrett Howell interview.

16. "North Side News tells tale."

17. Ibid.

18. Harold H. Martin, *Atlanta and Environs, A Chronical of Its People and Events, Years of Change and Challenge, 1930-1976*, Volume III; Atlanta, The University of Georgia Press, Athens, 1987, p 135.

19. Ibid, p. 135.

20. Ibid, pp. 135-6.

21. Ibid, p. 136.

22. Ibid, pp. 136-7.

23. Letter from Inman Brandon May 17, 1977 to Mr. Walter Bell. Courtesy of Nancy Pritchett, art teacher at Morris Brandon Elementary School.

24. Ibid.

25. Mary Brennan, "In Celebration of a Great School for a Great Neighborhood: E. Rivers Elementary School," *Peachtree Hills Views*, August 1990, p. 5.

Chapter 42

1. Franklin M. Garrett, *Atlanta and Environs*, Volume II; University of Georgia Press, Athens, 1954; pp. 959, 1004.

2. Joseph K. Heyman interview.

3. Ibid.

4. Ibid.

5. Garrett, *Atlanta and Environs*, pp. 106, 1008.

6. Heyman interview.

7. Thomas M. Murray interview.

8. Dorothy Dean (Mrs. Joel Chandler, Jr.) Harris interview.

9. Florence "Poncie" Bryan (Mrs. William Bonneau) Ansley interview.

10. Laura Maddox (Mrs. Edward D.) Smith interview.

11. Ivan Allen Jr. interview.

12. Herbert and Edith Elsas interview.

13. Barrett Howell interview.

14. Hugh Park, *Around Town*, "Buckhead's Seen Tough Days," *The Atlanta Journal*, March 14, 1967.

15. Cecil Alexander interview.

16. William Brand Jr. interview.

17. Ken Moss interview.

18. Lon Bridges Jr. interview.

19. Brand interview.

20. Roy Milling interview.

Chapter 43

1. Samuel Alan Massell Jr. interview.

2. "Brief History of the Heiskell School". Information sheet, courtesy of The Miriam Heiskell School.

3. Ibid.

4. "Historical Overview of Trinity School". Information sheet, courtesy of Trinity School.

5. "The Formative Years," information sheet on Westminster Schools; Atlanta History Center Library/Archives, Westminster Schools subject file.

6. Polly Orr Bates interview.

7. Excerpts from "The History of Pace Academy," from an address made to Pace High School Students on April 2, 1974, p. 3. Pace Academy fact sheet. Both found at Atlanta History Center Library/Archives, Pace Academy subject file. Yolande Gwin, "Pace Academy Campus, Randall Home Is Saved," *The Atlanta Journal and Constitution*, December 26, 1976, p. 12-G.

8. "History of Cherokee Town and Country Club," September 1, 1993; Cherokee Town and Country Club, p. 5. Courtesy of James Bryant, president of the Cherokee Town and Country Club.

9. Letter from Richard Stanger, Manager, Urban Design, Marta, 2200 Peachtree Summit, 401 West Peachtree Street, N.E., Atlanta, Ga. 30365 to Mr. Paul Hartwig, Head, Preservation Services, Richard B. Russell Federal Building, 75 Spring Street, Atlanta, Ga, 30303, October 7, 1982. *Johnsontown: A Black Settlement on Atlanta's White Northside*, Historic Preservation file ID Sites/Fulton County/Johnsontown.

10. Columbus Johnson interview.

11. George Erwin, "32 Million Center For Shopping Here, Rich's Food Fair, Kresge First Tenants In Lenox Square; Space for 6,000 Autos," *The Atlanta Constitution*, May, 12, 1957, pp. 4, 5;

12. Harold H. Martin, *Atlanta and Environs, A Chronicle of Its People and Events, Years of Change and Challenge, 1940-1976*, Volume

III; University of Georgia Press, Athens, 1987, pp. 247, 307.

13. Ibid.

14. "Lenox' Noble Named Year's No. 1 Salesman," *The Atlanta Constitition*, February, 13, 1960, page number unknown; Atlanta History Center Library/Archives, Lenox Square subject file. 15. Charlene Shucker, "Buckhead merchants say future is bright," *The Atlanta Journal*, Intown Extra, July 22, 1982, p. 4E.

16. Thomas M. Murray interview.

17. Jane (Mrs. George, Jr.) Murray interview.

18. Barrett Howell interview.

INDEX

Blind Willie, p. 139
Bloodworth, Mary Hardwick (Mrs. Herbert Raines), pp. 149, 150
Bloodworth's Kindergarten, Mrs., pp. 149, 150
Bonner, William, p. 115
Bowen, Pryor, pp. 156, 157
Boy Scout Troop 5, 45, p. 135
Boynton, Mrs. Jesse, p. 163
Brambles, The (Dr. Joseph Jacobs' home), pp. 96, 97
Brand, William, pp. 147, 173, 181, 182, 198, 199
Brand, William, Jr., pp. 108, 147, 150, 160, 173, 176, 181, 198, 199
Brandon, Inman, p. 195
Brandon, Morris, pp. 194, 195
Brandon, Col. N. and Minerva Elizabeth (nee Morris), p. 194, 195
Bridges, Lon, Jr., p. 199
Bridges, Lon, Sr., pp. 166, 173, 184
Bridges, Mary Ann (Mrs. Lon), pp. 139, 178, 189, 190
Bridges Service Station, pp. 152, 166, 173
Broadview Plaza (Lindbergh Square), pp. 111, 193
Brown, Bowling, p. 59
Brown, Edward C., p. 59
Brown, Horace V., p. 59
Brown, J. Epps, pp. 113, 121
Brown, Millard, p. 59
Brown, Ulysses Adolphus "Dolphus", pp. 59, 179
Brown, Weyman, p. 179
Brown, William, pp. 52, 53
Brown's Pottery, p. 59
Broyles, Norris, p. 174
Brumbelow, George (Blacksmith Shop), p. 69
Bruner, Dr. J. Weston, p. 83
Bryan, Ellen Newell (Mrs. William Wright), pp. 64, 93, 94, 150, 169, 183, 184
Bryan, Margaret, p. 193
Bryan, Judge Shepherd and Florence Cobb, pp. 121, 122
Bryan, William Wright, pp. 169, 184
Bryan's, Margaret Dance Studio (Buckhead), p. 193
Buckhead Baptist Church, pp. 83, 135, 153
Buckhead Billiard Parlor/Pool Hall, p. 181
Buckhead Draft Board, pp. 181, 182
Buckhead Duck Pin Bowling Alley, pp. 149, 187, 189
Buckhead Elk's Club, pp. 116, 182
Buckhead 50 Club, pp. 116, 153

Hammett, George W. and Edna Corrine (nee Ivey), p. 68
Hammett, Joseph L., p. 88
Haney, Berneda Johnson, p. 160
Hanleiter, W. R., p. 26
Happy Hill, p. 78
Harmony Grove Cemetery, pp. 50, 101
Harmony Grove Church, pp. 50, 101
Harris, Dorothy Dean (Mrs. Joel Chandler, Jr.), pp. 123, 129, 152, 182, 185, 198
Harris, Joel Chandler, Jr., p. 123
Harris, Joel Chandler, Sr., pp. 52, 123
Harris, Nathaniel E., p. 93
Harrison, Pres. Benjamin, pp. 40, 63, 133
Harsh, George, pp. 141, 142
Hart's Restaurant, p. 155
Hartsfield, Mayor William B., pp. 191, 197, 198
Hawk and Stephens Drugstore, pp. 128, 149, 192
Hawk, Judson L., pp. 128, 129, 156
Hawk, Dr. Judson L., Jr., pp. 128, 156, 189
Haynes, Eugene V., p. 133
Haynes Manor, pp. 88, 133
Healey, Callie, p. 185
Healey, Cornelia, p. 185
Hearst, Patty, p. 168
Hearst, Randolph A. and Catherine (nee Campbell), p. 168
Hearst, William Randolph, p. 168
Heiskell, James H. Heiskell, p. 202
Heiskell, Miriam (Mrs. James H.), pp. 201, 202
Heiskell School, The, pp. 188, 201, 202
Henry County (naming) p. 11
Henry, Patrick, p. 11
Hewit, Dan, p. 65
Heyman, Arthur, pp. 77, 87, 88
Heyman, Dora, pp. 77
Heyman, Herman, pp. 78, 88
Heyman, Joseph K., pp. 77, 87, 93, 100, 135, 197, 198
Heyman, Minna Simon (Mrs. Arthur), p. 87
Hicks, George, p. 40
Hicks, James Early, p. 40
Hicks, Rial Bailey, pp. 17, 29-31, 40, 46, 53, 67, 68
Hicks, Sara Jane Irby (Mrs. Rial Bailey), pp. 17, 30, 40, 68

Howell, Isaac, p. 27
Howell, John, p. 27
Howell, Joseph, Jr. and Margaret Eleanor (nee Garmon), p. 27
Howell, Julia (Mrs. Evan P.), p. 43
Howell, Martha Ann Winn (Mrs. Clark) (judge's first wife), p. 28
Howell, Mary D. Hook (Mrs. Clark) (judge's third wife), p. 28, 51, 60
Howell Mill Road (naming), p. 28
Howell's Ferry, p. 27
Howell's Mill, pp. 28, 43
Howell's Mill Post Office, p. 59
Huff, Sarah, p. 51
Humphries, Judge John D., p. 157
Humphries, Perry, p. 67
Humphries' Wagon Yard and Blacksmith Shop, p. 67

Inman, Abednego, p. 124
Inman, Mr. and Mrs. Edward, p. 126
Inman, Hugh Theodore, p. 124
Inman, Meshach, p. 124
Inman, Samuel, Jr. and Florence, p. 173
Inman, Mrs. and Mrs. Samuel, p. 83
Inman, Shadrach, p. 124
Inman & Sons, S. W., p. 24
Irby, Agnes, p. 21
Irby Alley, pp. 78, 105, 150, 151
Irby, Fulton, p. 54
Irby, George, pp. 31, 40
Irby, Henry, pp. 17, 21, 22, 33, 46, 53, 54, 114
Irby, Neppie, p. 150
Irby, Sardis Walraven (Mrs. Henry), pp. 21, 54
Irby's Tavern, pp. 21, 30, 46, 67, 115
Irbyville, p. 22
Irbyville Post Office, p. 22
Ivey Road/Ivy Road (naming), p. 53
Ivey, Alice Hicks (Mrs. Russell), p. 53
Ivey, Hardy, p. 53
Ivey, Mary Ophelia Hicks (Mrs. Seaborn L.), pp. 17, 30, 53, 68, 102
Ivey, Russell, p. 56
Ivey, Seaborn L., pp. 21, 56, 68, 153
Ivey, Thomas B. and Sarah (nee Adcock), p. 53

Richardson, Lee and Louise (nee French), p. 124
Richardson, Leonard, p. 126
Richardson Realty Co., p. 124
Riley, J. L., p. 138
Riley, James, p. 114
Riley, Katherine Murphy (Mrs. Julian), p. 114
Rivers, Gov. Ed, p. 142
Rivers, Eretus "E.", pp. 75, 97, 149
Roan, Judge Leonard S., p. 91
Roberts, Agnes Dorsey, p. 68
Roberts, Marvin, p. 129
Robertson, Sam, p. 65
Robinson, Roly, Jr. and Louise (nee Calhoun), p. 113
Rogers School of Dancing, Sarah Wagstaff, p. 193
Rolader, Anne Gunter (Mrs. William J.), p. 30
Rolader, Arrie Cofield (Mrs. William Washington), p. 60
Rolader, Clark, p. 130
Rolader Dairy, p. 119
Rolader, Donald W. "Pete", pp. 60, 130, 131, 145, 160, 170, 176, 181,
    188, 189
Rolader Gas Station and General Store, pp. 65, 131
Rolader, Homer, p. 130
Rolader, Horace V., p. 59
Rolader, Ivon, pp. 119, 130, 131, 145, 187
Rolader, Dr. Ivon, Jr. "Ike", p. 131
Rolader, Lorenzo Dow "L. D.", pp. 65, 131, 188
Rolader, Mary Elizabeth Haley (Mrs. Lorenzo Dow), p. 65
Rolader Pottery, pp. 59, 60
Rolader Spring Water Co., pp. 130, 131, 135, 136
Rolader, Rev. William Joseph "W. J.", pp. 17, 30, 53, 60
Rolader, William Washington "W. W.", pp. 59-61
Rolleston, Mrs. Morton, p. 152
Rose, Rufus M., pp. 60, 61
Rossdhu/Shadow Hill (Dr. F. Phinizy Calhoun Sr. home), p. 98
Rosser, Luther Z., Sr., p. 91
Rosserville, p. 65
Roswell, William R., p. 24
Roswell Seed Store, p. 181
Roxboro Post Office, p. 65
Rubenoff, Elizabeth Cassells (Mrs. Richard), p. 187
Rudolph, William, pp. 74, 94, 97, 98, 155, 185

Rushton, Mrs. W. W., p. 155
Rushton, Wright, p. 155
Rusty's Drive-in, p. 193

S